Postwar Interior Design: 1945–1960

Postwar Interior Design: 1945–1960

Cherie Fehrman
Kenneth Fehrman

VNR VAN NOSTRAND REINHOLD COMPANY
New York

Library of Congress Catalog Card Number 85-31461

ISBN 0-442-22617-9

Printed in the United States of America

Designed by Caliber Design

Van Nostrand Reinhold Company Inc.
115 Fifth Avenue
New York, New York 10003

Van Nostrand Reinhold Company Limited
Molly Millars Lane
Wokingham, Berkshire RG11 2PY, England

Van Nostrand Reinhold
480 La Trobe Street
Melbourne, Victoria 3000, Australia

Macmillan of Canada
Division of Canada Publishing Corporation
164 Commander Boulevard
Agincourt, Ontario M1S 3C7, Canada

16 15 14 13 12 11 10 9 8 7 6 5 4 3 2 1

Library of Congress Cataloging-in-Publication Data

Fehrman, Cherie, 1945–
Postwar interior design, 1945–1960.

Bibliography: p.
Includes index.
1. Interior decoration—History—20th century.
2. Organic design. 3. Architect-designed furniture.
I. Fehrman, Kenneth. II. Title.
NK1986.073F4 1986 729′.09′04 85-31461
ISBN 0-442-22617-9

Contents

Introduction ix

Part 1 Major Influences on Postwar Interior Design 1

Summary of Designers from the Interwar Years/11

Part 2 The Designers and Manufacturers 15

Charles Eames/17
Eero Saarinen/23
George Nelson/28
Harry Bertoia/34
Hans and Florence Knoll/37
Gilbert Rohde/42
Isamu Noguchi/46
Arne Jacobsen/52
Børge Mogensen/57
Hans J. Wegner/61
Russel Wright/65
The Italians/71

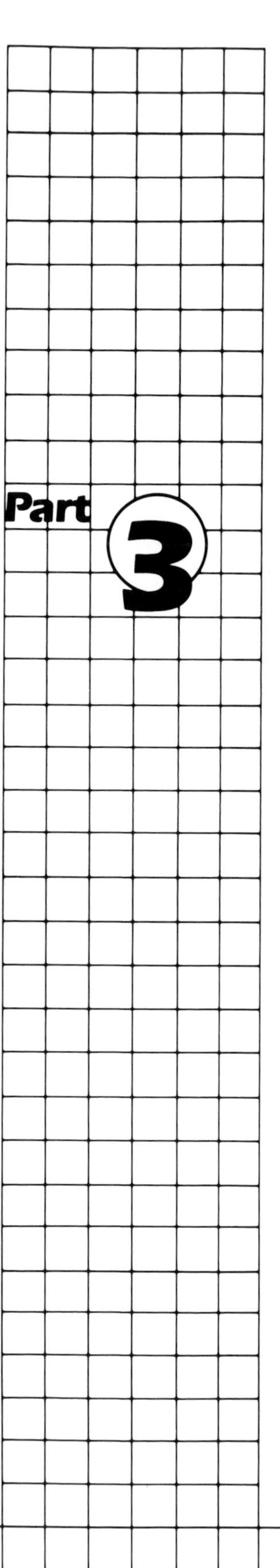

Supplemental Designers 76

Lis Ahlmann; Anni Albers; Franco Albini; Winslow Anderson; Olof Bäckström; Hans Theo Baumann; Sigvard Bernadotte; Max Bill; Artur Braun; Achille, Livio, and Piergiacomo Castiglioni; Fedo Cheti; Gino Colombini; Lucienne and Robin Day; Freda Diamond; Paul Frankl; Alexander Girard; Hans Gugelot; Eszter Haraszty; Finn Juhl; Katavalos/Littell/Kelley; Poul Kjaerholm; Ebsen Klint; Ray Komai; Jack Lenor Larsen; Raymond Loewy; Enid Marx; Paul McCobb; Grethe Meyer; Orla Mølgaard-Nielsen; Verner Panton; Ernest Race; Edward Wormley

Part 3 Materials and Methods of Construction 85

Construction Materials and Methods/87

Wood/87
Metal/89
Plastic/90
Engineering/91

Designers and Their Designs/93

Charles Eames/93
Eero Saarinen/100
George Nelson/102
Harry Bertoia/104
Florence Knoll/104
Gilbert Rohde/105
Isamu Noguchi/105
Arne Jacobsen/106
Børge Mogensen/108
Hans J. Wegner/109
Russel Wright/109
The Italians/111
Conclusion/111

The Furniture and Designs 113

Appendix A: Resources 187

Appendix B: Supplemental Charts 189

Notes 192

Bibliography 194

Index 195

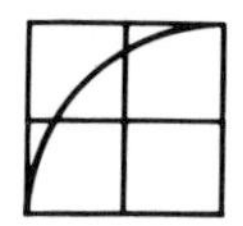

Acknowledgments

We are forever in the debt of those who have given so freely of their time and expertise in helping with the preparation of *Postwar Interior Design: 1945–1960*. First, to David Sachs and Dorothy Spencer of Van Nostrand Reinhold, who believed in the project enough to tackle it. To Linda Folland, archivist at Herman Miller, who placed a vast body of research materials at our disposal and helped immeasurably in the production of the Herman Miller sections. To Ralph Cutler, Mark McDonald, and Mark Isaacsen of Fifty/50 Midcentury Decorative Arts in New York and to David Pinson of Boomerang Gallery in Chicago for their help in providing photographs. And to Earl Speas and Hitoshi Shigeta for their continued support.

Further thanks to Flemming Eskildsen of Royal Copenhagen A/S; I. A. Cordula Kranefeld of Tecta-Mobel; Beatrice Villa of Ecart International; Armando Garcia-Perez of Jack Lenor Larsen; Marketta Kahma of Iittala Glassworks; Dr. Storek and Peter Frank of Rosenthal Aktiengessellschaft; Nancy J. Reedy and Anna Ramsey of Atelier International; Monica Cavaletto of Images/Kaleidos; Glenda Galt of The Brooklyn Museum; Kurt Jørgensen of Le Klint; Heidi Hatfield of Knoll International; Bård Henriksen of Fritz Hansens Eft A-S; Hanne Kjaerholm; George Nelson; Hans J. Wegner; and Grethe Meyer.

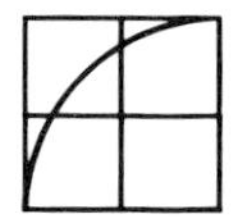

Introduction

If one term can represent a movement in design, then surely the phrase "organic design" is the essence of the postwar movement. Organic design was an attempt at harmony on a grand scale, a humanistic approach that considered people as its focal point and endeavored to combine all the elements of design into one unified whole derived from concepts laid down by nature. Eliot Noyes, the Director of the Department of Industrial Design at New York's Museum of Modern Art during the Organic Design in Home Furnishings Exhibit of 1940, outlined the purpose and goal of organic design in the exhibit catalog:

> A design may be called organic when there is an harmonious organization of the parts within the whole, according to the structure, material, and purpose. Within this definition there can be no vain ornamentation or superfluity, but the part of beauty is none the less great—in ideal choice of material, in visual refinement, and in the rational elegance of things intended for use.[1]

The Organic Design in Home Furnishings Exhibit introduced Charles Eames's and Eero Saarinen's prize-winning designs to the public at large, giving stature to concepts born at America's version of the Bauhaus, the Cranbrook Academy of Art. Cranbrook, under the direction of Eliel Saarinen, employed a similar approach to that of the Bauhaus: the Cranbrook Academy of Art was a working place for creative people; a place where artists working in various media were encouraged to interact with each other. Eliel Saarinen's philosophy can be summarized by his statement, "Creative art cannot be taught by others. Each one has to be his own teacher. But connection with the other artists and discussions with them provide sources for inspiration."

At Cranbrook, as at the Bauhaus, designers and artists were encouraged to consider their work as a totality, relating it not only to its intended function but to the environment as a whole. Organic design can be likened to a tree with rambling, far-reaching roots sucking nourishment from many creative sources. The Bauhaus, the international style, the Vienna School, the Scandinavians, and the Japanese are all represented within the tangled mat of its roots, yet organic design is unique; not a copy, but a synthesis—a hybrid species that, while bearing a resemblance to its forebears, is complete and whole unto itself.

We think the postwar period is one of the most exciting in design history, not only because it is responsible for the introduction of completely new furniture forms and materials but because of its dedication to achieving perfection. The designers of the postwar period took the technology of war and turned it into something positive. They proved that the wheels of progress need not run over us but can be made to carry us to new destinations. They achieved this with their minds and spirits and with hours of endless trial and error in the search for that perfect combination of structure, material, and purpose that would culminate in a successful organic design.

Organic designers were totally committed, with a passion almost forgotten in this day of instant gratification. When Eero Saarinen's architectural firm entered the competition for the design of the Smithsonian art gallery, they made 100 studies of each element that went into the building, then 100 studies of the combinations of each element, then 100 studies of the combinations of combinations. This degree of dedication runs throughout the organic design movement. Like Saarinen, Eames made hundreds, possibly thousands, of experiments in his search for the ideal molded plywood form, in his attempt to achieve unification of materials and construction.

The purpose of the Organic Design competition was to encourage good designers in the task of creating a better environment. Realizing that modern techniques were being used only to duplicate weary old styles that were often neither beautiful nor practical, the Museum of Modern Art undertook the task of "fostering a collaboration between designer, manufacturer, and merchant, to fill this strange gap in the conveniences for modern existence."

The winning designs were manufactured and made available through Bloomingdale's department store at prices that ranged from $2.75 a yard for Marli Ehrman's fabric, to $75.00 for the "Revolutionary Body-Molding Desk Chair" by Saarinen and Eames.

Unfortunately, the best designs of an era are not always those that become publicly accepted. Mass-production costs are always a factor to be considered, and it is sad but true that it is easier and cheaper to turn a quick profit on endless runs of ceramic pink flamingos and panther TV lamps than to produce some of the fine designs of the postwar period. The aim of *Postwar Interior Design* is to present the best designs of the postwar era. In the spirit of organic design, we have chosen to discuss them in a holistic fashion—not just by exhibiting furniture designs alone but by attempting wherever possible to present the designs in an environmental context. For this reason, we have included accessories, textiles, and lighting, as well as architecture and the furnishings themselves.

Many of the furniture designers of this period were trained as architects. We think it is important to consider their work as a whole, relating their furniture designs to their architecture, since very often both are derived from the same basic design philosophy. While it would not be practical to cover every designer who contributed to this period, we have tried to include those whose work is of significance either in the use of new materials and construction techniques or in the use of traditional materials in new ways. In so doing, we salute the innovations of the postwar period, without which we might be living very different lives today.

In an industry where mediocrity often masquerades as "good taste," it is a privilege and a pleasure to chronicle the work of such visionary designers, who persevered in their beliefs to create the innovative explosion of postwar interior design.

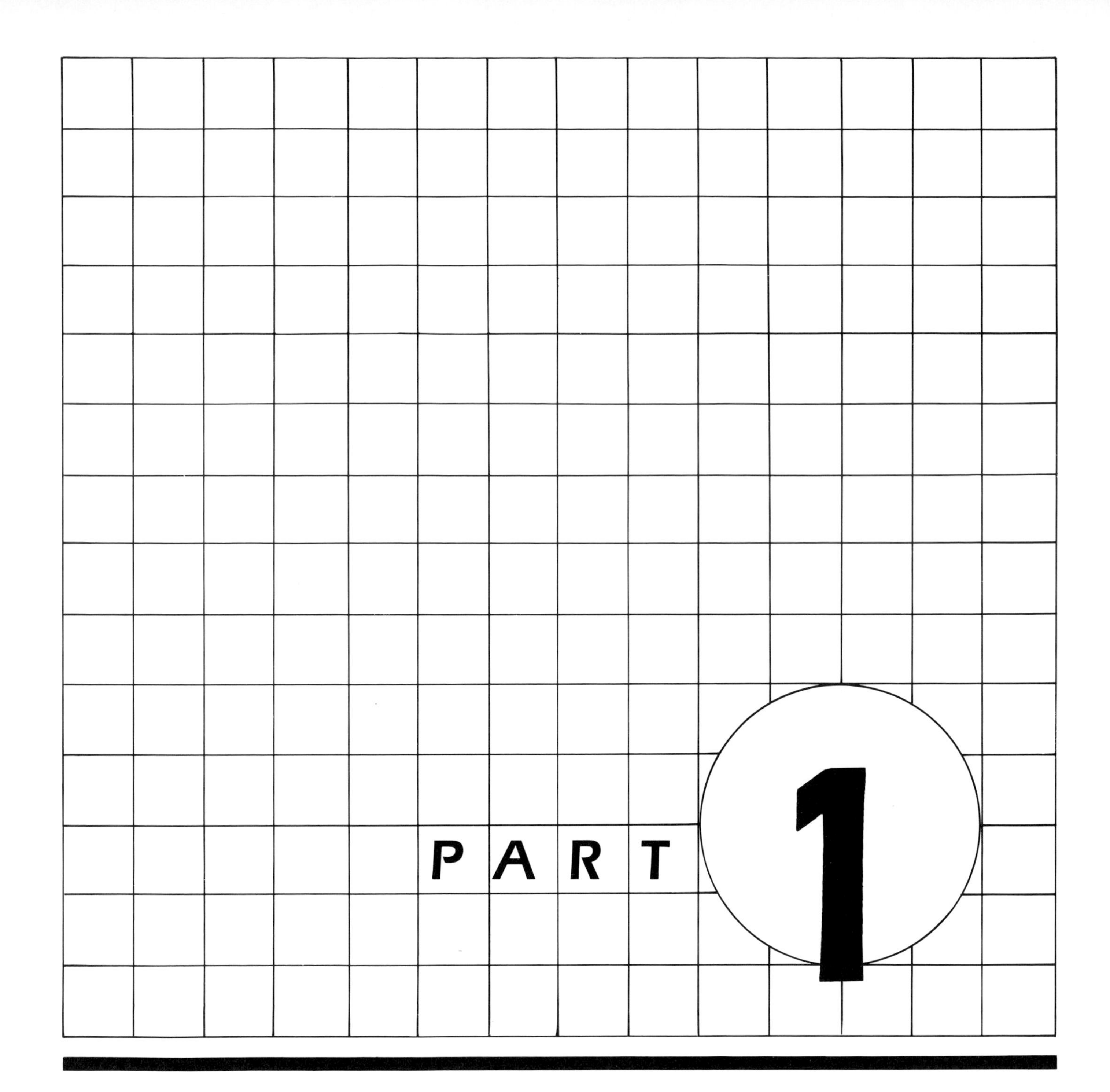

Major Influences on Postwar Interior Design

Interior design is sometimes considered a frivolous pursuit, not quite given the respectability of architecture, yet it affects our lives—all our lives—every day. It affects how we sit, eat, sleep, read, play, and study—even how we think. It can cause us to be irritable, with strained eyes and aching backs, or blissfully aware of the sumptuous comfort into which we sink our bodies. In modern industrial society, the individual has forfeited much of his participation in the creation of his physical environment. The designer has now become the agent bridging the gap between the craftsperson and the consumer and thus exercises a major influence on the environment.

Design, like any aspect of life, cannot exist in a vacuum. It relies heavily on what has gone before and influences what will follow. This thread, this connection that links one era to the next, is clearly evidenced in the period of postwar interior design, yet there is no clearly defined time line. As with any creative work in any era, progression and regression often occurred simultaneously, producing amorphous results from which it may be impossible to pinpoint an absolute inventor of a concept or design.

The postwar era was a focal point at which many diverse and seemingly unrelated paths converged to create new forms for living, new ways of looking at our physical surroundings. The technologies of war, repression and subsequent liberation, a democratic purge of ornamentation, the struggle to achieve something never before accomplished—all had a major effect on the postwar period of design.

One might even partially credit the two world wars with the development of modern furniture. War changes everything: its destruction forces rebuilding; its technology provides new materials and methods that, while originally used in the machinery of war, can be adapted to more domestic uses. The economic upheaval following World War I opened doors for the conceptualization and design of furnishings scarcely dreamt of previously.

The Bauhaus was a major influence in the period between the wars. Located in Weimar from 1919 to 1925 and in Dessau from 1925 to 1932, it was influenced as much by the Dutch De Stijl movement as by Russian constructivism and the Japanese tradition. The goal of the Bauhaus was to integrate all the visual arts into society. The Bauhaus designers invented a new conception of interior space that focused on man. The steel of wartime now found its way into the tubular metal furniture of Breuer and Mies van der Rohe—designs that were to become hallmarks of the 1920s.

The Bauhaus influence soon spread beyond Germany, moving to England in the 1930s. The British steel tube manufacturer Accles & Pollock was looking for ways to expand into related areas of business. Representatives from Accles & Pollock saw examples of Bauhaus furniture in the then-new Strand Palace Hotel in London and hit upon the idea of producing steel-tube furniture. PEL (Practical Equipment Limited), an offshoot of the Accles & Pollock group, was first registered as a company in 1931, and its first catalogs were presented in 1932. PEL furniture was sold through the British Marshall and Snelgrove's stores and was used extensively in the Lyon's Corner House restaurants and the BBC's Broadcasting House, but it never achieved popularity with consumers.

With its groundbreaking and radical approach to design, the Bauhaus was not without its detractors and came under repeated attack from conservatives. The fact that it survived and gained respect and stature can be attributed to the skill and diplomacy of its director, Walter Gropius (1883–1969). One of Gropius's greatest talents was certainly his ability to relate to and communicate with the diversity of artistic temperaments that formed the Bauhaus movement. Gropius's (and the Bauhaus's) main goal was to merge art and crafts. As such, the ideal artist/craftsperson would have as thorough a knowledge and experience of materials as of design theory. From this, it was believed, would emerge a wholeness of design, a totality impossible when art and crafts remained separate. With this goal constantly in mind, the Bauhaus curriculum was divided into two main segments: the teaching of construction and materials and the teaching of form and design. This concept was to have far-reaching effects on the designers of the postwar years, who experimented with designing forms based on the inherent properties of construction materials.

In 1925 Gropius wrote:

> A thing is determined by its essence. In order to design it so that it functions properly—whether it is a vase, a chair, or a house—its essence must first be studied; for it shall have to serve its purpose absolutely, in other words, fulfill its practical functions, be durable, cheap, and "beautiful." This research into the essence of objects, taking into full account all modern manufacturing methods, constructions, and materials, will result in forms that in their divergence from tradition will often seem unusual and surprising. . . . The Bauhaus will attempt . . . to train a new, hitherto unknown type of employee for industry and trade who has mastered both techniques and form in equal measure.[1]

In the same year, Gropius eloquently encapsulated the Bauhaus philosophy and direction:

> The ability to give an object beautiful form is based on a mastery of all economic, technical, and formal conditions of which its organism is a result.
>
> The Bauhaus school holds the view that the contrast between industry and the craftsmen's trades is characterized less by the difference in the tools used than by the *division* of labor in the former and the *unity* of labor in the latter. The craftsmen's trades and industry are, however, continuously moving towards each other. The craftsmen's trades of the past have changed. They will be absorbed by a new unity of labor and they will conduct the *experimental work for industrial production*. Speculative experiments in laboratory workshops will create the models for the final production in the factories.
>
> The final models developed in the Bauhaus workshops will be mass produced in other factories with which the workshops have a working relationship.[2]

Mies van der Rohe's conception of open interior space pointed the way for an entire generation of architects. By the 1930s the modern movement was strongly felt in both Europe and the United States, although the United States during this period continued to cling to European tradition by adding Gothic or Renaissance gingerbread to its architecture and by shying away from the totally clean lines of European modernism. Outside of Hollywood musicals, where interior sets often rivaled the sumptuousness of an Eileen Gray art deco design, most furniture sold in the United States continued to be that of eclectic styles of questionable aesthetic value.

Perhaps the most famous of all Bauhaus furniture designs is Mies van der Rohe's steel and leather chair created for the German pavilion at the Barcelona Exhibition of 1929. With its sweeping curves of chromium steel, it became a kind of symbol of the whole modern movement. It is still in production today as the Barcelona chair (Plate 3).

An original aspect of the metal furniture designed by Mies van der Rohe and Breuer is the employment of the cantilever principle in order to combine strength and lightness. Mies designed an elegant cantilever chair in 1926, shortly followed by a more practical and better proportioned design by Breuer.

Marcel Breuer entered the Bauhaus as a student in 1920. His initial attempts at expressionist- and De Stijl-influenced design were soon superseded by an interest in the standardization of furniture making and architecture. By 1924 Breuer had been made head of the furniture department at the Bauhaus, at a time when political pressure forced the school to move to Dessau. The need to furnish the new school gave him a chance to put his knowledge and skill into operation, and experiments such as the chairs for the new auditorium and the stools for the cafeteria, constructed from seamless steel tubing, were to become prophetic images of later prototypes.

Breuer stated: "Metal furniture is part of a modern room. It is styleless, for it is expected not to express any particular styling beyond its purpose and the construction necessary theretofore."[3]

With reference to his own designs he said:

> I purposely chose metal for this furniture in order to achieve the characteristics of modern space elements. . . . The heavy, imposing stuffing of a comfortable chair has been replaced by a tightly fitted fabric and some light, springy pipe brackets. The steel used, and particularly the aluminum, are remarkably light, though they withstand severe static strain (tractive stress of the material). The light shape increases the flexibility. All types are constructed from the same standardized elementary parts which may be taken apart or exchanged at any time. This metal furniture is intended to be nothing but a necessary apparatus for contemporary life.[4]

Breuer's Wassily chair (Plate 8), first shown to the public in 1927 in the lobby of the Weissenhof housing development, was constructed of tubular steel. It was foldable and was covered with extra-strong fabric of woven cotton threads strengthened by paraffin. The first tubular steel chairs of both Breuer and Mies van der Rohe used this fabric, which was invented by Grete Reichardt at the Bauhaus in Dessau.

In 1925 Breuer stated:

> The appearance of objects depends upon the different functions they have. Since they satisfy our demands individually and do not clash with each other, they produce collectively our style. They are unified as a whole through the fulfillment of their individual tasks. Thus the question of our style is not one of conviction, but of quality. A chair, for example, should not be horizontal-vertical, nor expressionist, nor constructivist, nor purely practical, nor compatible with the table. It should be a good chair, then it will be compatible with a good table.[5]

In 1948, his convictions were still as strong:

> I don't feel a very strong impulse to set "human" (in the best sense of the word) against "formal." If "human" is considered identical with redwood all over the place, or if it is considered identical with imperfection and imprecision, I am against it; also, if it is considered identical with hiding

architecture with plants, nature or romantic nonsense.

If "international style" is considered identical with mechanical and impersonal rigor, down with international style. Anyway, the term is an unfortunate one—just as unfortunate as "functionalism."

"Human" it seems to me should mean more than just an amiable tolerance of imperfection; it should mean precision of thought and quality in planning, and include the consequences for materials, details and construction.

God knows, I am all for informal living and for architecture which supports and serves as background for it, but we won't sidestep the instinct toward perfection, a most human instinct. The most contradictory elements of our nature should serve happiness simultaneously, in the same work, and in the most definite way. The drive toward experiment is there, together with and in contrast to the warm joy of security at the fireplace. The crystallic quality of an unbroken white flat slab is there, together with and in contrast to the warm joy of natural wood or natural stone. The perfection of construction and detail is there, together with and in contrast to simplicity, generosity of form and use. There is the courage of design, together with and in contrast to modest responsibility towards one's client. There is the sensation of man-made space, geometry, and architecture, together with and in contrast to the organic forms of nature and of man. *Sol y sombra*, as the Spanish say; sun *and* shadow; not sun *or* shadow.[6]

As is often the case with scientific or artistic developments, many ideas were "in the air" in the 1920s, with simultaneous discoveries frequently occurring. Mies van der Rohe, Breuer, and the Bauhaus were certainly not the only ones working to develop steel-tube furniture, which was rapidly becoming the modern counterpart to the bentwood chair. Mart Stam, also affiliated with the Bauhaus but not yet a member, was working along similar lines. In fact, Stam described the prototype of a steel-tube chair without back legs in an exhibition in Stuttgart in 1926, several months before Mies van der Rohe unveiled his MR chair at the Werkbund Exhibition.

Steel tubing seemed an inspirational solution to satisfying the "form follows function" dictum while retaining beauty. It also fulfilled all the requirements for mass production, making it an ideal choice for which to seek industrial support.

At its finest, the Bauhaus's interior design workshop had the closest working relationship with industry of any department in the school. Its designers were trained not only in aesthetics but in the humanities and social sciences, then went from their apprenticeships in the school's experimental workshop to jobs in industry, with industry in turn publicizing the products they designed through Bauhaus advertising campaigns. There were numerous exhibitions that lent themselves well to promotion of Bauhaus designs: the Werkbund Exhibition in Stuttgart (1927), the International Exhibition in Paris (1930), and the Bauhaus Exhibition in New York (1931).

In 1932 the Bauhaus moved to Berlin; only one year later the existing National Socialist government forced it to close, causing many of its teachers and students to flee Germany, thus spreading Bauhaus concepts to art and architecture schools in Europe and the United States.

The Vienna School was led by Adolf Loos, Otto Wagner, and the Wiener Werkstätte. It was controversial and full of ebullient ideas that ended abruptly at the outbreak of World War I when Wagner died (1918), Loos went to Paris, and the Werkstätte faltered due to the economic crisis of the interwar years. Furniture was simple, well proportioned, and in complete harmony with its environment, similar to that of the Biedermeier period of the early 1800s.

There are many parallels between the furniture of the Vienna School and that of early Scandinavian forms: highly skilled craftsmanship, a lightness of form, and attention to detail. Josef Frank, a prominent Viennese architect, even emigrated to Sweden where he worked with the Svenska Tenn Company, putting his Viennese design experience to work for the Scandinavian market.

The Austrian architect and designer Adolf Loos (1870–1933) is considered by many to have been the prime theoretician of purity in approaching furniture design and interior space planning. During the span of years from 1893 to 1896, he studied at the Chicago School where, like Frank Lloyd Wright, he came under the influence of Louis Sullivan and his insights into the relation between form and function. When he returned to Vienna, Loos began an attack on ornamentation in architecture, stripping away what he considered to be the extraneous decoration of art nouveau design, replacing it instead with an absence, a void, leaving only pure form expressing its true function. This he considered the essence of beauty. He stated: "Ornament is squandered work and hence squandered health. And it has always been so. Today, however, it also means squandered material, and both mean squandered capital."[7]

Loos concentrated on apartments, furnishing a total of about fifty, while designing very few houses. His interiors reflect his craftsmanlike use of materials in the woods and marble chosen, yet they were sparsely furnished. It was not until 1922, with the Rufer house, that he had an opportunity to put his spatial planning theories—solving a floor plan in space—into effect. Individual rooms were not only of different sizes but located on different levels, producing a cubic structure. This unconventional, even revolutionary, approach not only affected the form of the furnishings but also the lives of the people who inhabited the space.

The Dutch De Stijl movement appeared on the scene about 1917, when a group of painters, architects, and writers in the city of Leiden came together with a common goal of the "radical renewal of art." The De Stijl movement ("the style," in Dutch), took its name from the art review magazine *De Stijl*, begun by Mondrian and van Doesburg. The first issue appeared in October 1917. De Stijl's architecture was invariably based on the cube form but allied with the concept that buildings were an integral part of the environment for which they were conceived—a tradition common in Japan. An attempt was made to integrate interior and exterior space. De Stijl architects used the primary colors red, blue, and yellow plus the neutrals white, black, and gray, drawing heavily from the paintings of Piet Mondrian, who was a founding member of the De Stijl movement.

Théo van Doesburg (1883–1931), also a founding member of the group, elucidated the De Stijl philosophy in an article written in 1929:

> Instead of repeating what had already been found, we wanted to take architecture and painting to heights scarcely imaginable before and to integrate them with one another as closely as possible. The house was taken apart, divided up into its plastic elements. The static axis of the old construction was destroyed; the house became an object that can be circled around from all sides. This analytic method led to new construction possibilities and to a new floor plan. The house was freed from the ground, and the roof became a roof terrace, a story opened up to the outside. At that time these problems were completely new, and nobody tackled them so seriously as the young Dutch architects and painters.[8]

Gerrit Thomas Rietveld (1888–1964) was perhaps one of the best known proponents of the De Stijl movement in furniture design. Like the architecture of the De Stijl movement, his furniture shares many features of Japanese spatial concepts. Rietveld wrote of his Red and Blue chair:

> We have attempted . . . to make every part very simple, in other words to choose a primary shape that conforms to the kind of function and the material used, and in a form that is best suited to produce harmony. The construction serves to join the single parts to one another without distorting them in the least, and in such a manner that no one part overlaps the next to any great extent or is subordinate to the next. In this way the whole stands free in space. Form has resulted from material.[9]

How closely this statement relates to the ideologies of Frank Lloyd Wright, Charles Eames, and Eero Saarinen, who later adopted similar principles. Yet each, in his own way, made his own unique statement and contribution to design.

Most of the De Stijl designs could easily be reproduced by machine, some of Rietveld's later pieces being made in limited series. His "crate furniture" of 1934, for instance, was sold in kit form—if not the original then certainly a pioneer form of knockdown furniture. De Stijl designs had a direct influence on the Bauhaus, and it is doubtful that Marcel Breuer would have produced his designs had it not been for the pioneering efforts of Rietveld, although the Bauhaus designers were more concerned with the problems of function than were the De Stijl designers. The latter reduced elements of composition to geometric forms and the asymmetrical balance of supporting and supported parts. In a nutshell, De Stijl was more concerned with form and appearance than with function, while the Bauhaus attempted a unification of form, function, and appearance.

The work of Loos, De Stijl, and the Bauhaus gave rise to a new form in the late '20s and early '30s—the international style. In their 1932 book, *The International Style: Architecture Since 1922*, Henry-Russell Hitchcock and Philip Johnson wrote:

> The unconscious and halting architectural developments of the nineteenth century, the confused and contradictory experimentation of the beginning of the twentieth, have been succeeded by a directed evolution. There is now a single body of discipline, fixed enough to integrate contemporary style as a reality and yet elastic enough to permit individual interpretation and to encourage general growth.
>
> . . . There is, first, a new conception of architecture as volume rather than as mass. Secondly, regularity rather than axial symmetry serves as the chief means of ordering design. These two principles, with a third proscribing arbitrary applied decoration, mark the productions of the international style.[10]

Walter Gropius, Marcel Breuer, Ludwig Mies van der Rohe, Alvar Aalto, and Le Corbusier all came under the umbrella of the international style. Le Corbusier (1887–1965) concentrated on architecture rather than the design of furniture. Although he relied on Thonet chairs, wicker furniture, and even iron garden furniture to occupy his houses, the few pieces of furniture he did design have become classics. Le Corbusier chose to have his occupants live "in space rather than among furniture." His chaise longue of 1928 (Plate 18), which went into series production in the 1950s, provided a solution that not only suited the human anatomy but also his sense of aesthetics.

Le Corbusier's conceptions of space owed much to Adolf Loos. His architecture typically relied on the body of the house being a cube raised off the ground, with access to the rooms provided by ramps. The roof garden unified the house with the natural environment, although the austere white mass contrasted sharply with the surrounding landscape. In all of Le Corbusier's structures, one feels that the furniture was placed as a random afterthought rather than being an integral part of the interior space, the overall feeling being one of passing through—a transiency of human existence that mirrors the existential philosophy of the "transiency of man" so often found in the Japanese tradition.

Another designer who had a great impact on the postwar movement was Eileen Gray (1879–1976). Gray was born in Ireland but spent most of her adult life working in France. Her early years in design were spent in learning and perfecting lacquering techniques. Gray's early work (up to 1923) was luxurious and opulent, in keeping with the art deco style, but during the later 1920s and '30s she became one of the leading exponents of the revolutionary new theories of design and construction that came to be known as modernism. During this period, Gray held the first exhibitions of her furniture designs and worked closely with some of the outstanding figures of the modern movement, including Le Corbusier and Oud. Gray exhibited chrome, steel-tube, and glass furniture as early as 1925—the same year as Mies van der Rohe and Marcel Breuer and well in advance of Le Corbusier.

Gray was one of the few women architects of her day. Encouraged by Le Corbusier and Oud, she designed two houses in the Alpes Maritimes, one at Castellar (1923–24) and one at Roquebrune (1927–29). Both houses are considered to be among the purest examples of domestic architecture and interior design of the period.

Some of Gray's furniture is still in production, and her adjustable table (Plate 27) is in the collection of the Museum of Modern Art in New York.

Eileen Gray was one of the few designers to work in both the art deco and modern styles. While the art deco movement did not directly affect postwar design, its impact on interior design in general makes it worthy of note. Art deco was born in France and took its name from an exhibition held in Paris in 1925, *L'Exposition Internationale des Arts Décoratifs et Industriels Modernes*. This exhibit presented to the world a totally new style and launched some of the art deco movement's finest furniture designers, such as Emile-Jacques Ruhlmann, whose work equaled the technical standards set by the finest of his eighteenth-century predecessors. Art deco was noted for its use of luxurious, opulent materials: exotic woods, ivory, shagreen, and mother-of-pearl inlay were commonplace.

The most typical art deco interiors of the first half of the 1920s combined the rich colorings popularized by the Russian ballet with furniture styles adapted from Directoire and Empire models. In most cases, however, the seats of art deco chairs and sofas were lowered, with subsequent readjustment of proportions. Because of the new lower seats, lower tables were required, and art deco can be credited with the development of the coffee table, or cocktail table, as it was then called.

Occasionally, art deco designers dabbled in new materials such as chrome but, for the most part, metals and experimental materials were left to the modernists. In its purest form, art deco furniture was quite expensive because of the use of costly materials and careful crafting techniques. The economic problems that heralded World War II were primarily responsible for destroying the art deco movement, although pale versions of art deco furniture trickled down to the general public in the form of confused amalgams of design that did no credit to the original concepts of restating the old ideals of fine craftsmanship. By the outbreak of World War II, the modernist approach of experimenting with strictly functional forms made from readily available materials had replaced the opulence of art deco.

American designer Frank Lloyd Wright (1869–1959) is today recognized as one of the greatest pioneers of modern architecture because of his ideas on the function of form and material. He was one of the first to try linking architecture and furnishings to compose a harmonious whole. Wright's flaw, however, was in trying to make his furniture architectural while neglecting to consider the humans who were to use it. Wright himself said, "Somehow I always had black and blue spots my whole life long from all too close contact with my own furniture."

Wright drew his ideas from many different sources. Early memories of his grandfather's farm impressed on him a deep respect for nature that influenced him to use natural materials in his designs. As a young man, he apprenticed with the greatest American architect of the day, Louis Sullivan (1856–

1924), who proposed that ornament is a luxury, not a necessity. Following in Sullivan's footsteps, Wright developed a style that promoted the use of natural materials that spoke for themselves, rather than being cluttered with extraneous ornamentation.

Japanese design also had a great influence on Wright. He was first exposed to Japanese architecture at close range at the Japanese exhibit at the Chicago World Exhibition in 1893, where he was impressed by the replica of a typical Japanese building used to house a collection of paintings and woodblock prints. In 1905 he visited Japan for the first time and had the idea of adapting the open Japanese floor plan to American suburban residential architecture. The simplicity and openness of Japanese architecture in combination with the Japanese proclivity to let nature inside, as well as the British tradition of making the hearth the center of the home, came together in Wright's design for the "Prairie Houses" (1900–1910), which were his first important contribution to modern architecture.

The rapid technological development that affected furniture production during the 1930s became even more rapid in the post–World War II period of the '40s and '50s. The war years affected the furniture industry drastically in Europe, while little effect was felt in the United States. Materials in Europe were in short supply, and what was available was earmarked for defense, not furniture. In 1942 the British government issued an ultimatum that the only furniture to be manufactured in Britain was Utility. Hundreds of small firms throughout the country, all with different production methods, were to come together under the control of a small central committee to manufacture a single line of furniture. The committee consisted of representatives from finance, from the lay public, and from the church, forming a near perfect cross section of the national taste. After the usual round of committee debates, a Utility Panel was formed, consisting of six designers, with architect Gordon Russell as chairman. The Utility Panel was charged with the task of researching furniture design both for wartime use and for the future. (It should be noted that finding designers for the Utility Panel was no easy task, for most had been called into wartime service.)

The Utility Panel researched furniture design in two main directions: temporary furniture to cope with the devastation that would result if bombing should intensify; and long-term planning for peacetime, when supplies of plywood, cellulose, and steel would once again be available. The result was a line of plain, solid furniture constructed primarily of native oak. Its forms were stark and lacking in grace, the workmanship often shoddy, and yet some historians see Utility Furniture as a great democratic purge that freed the public from the excesses of the art deco period. In any event, the presentation of Utility Furniture on a widespread public scale (continuing until 1951) did much to break down any remaining resistance to modernism in furniture design.

With new furniture forms becoming more readily acceptable, modern design divided itself into three main traditions—American, Scandinavian, and Italian—each being a product of its environment. American designers were in close alliance with ergonomics and technology, producing pure forms and amalgamations of man's mind and the machine. Charles Eames and Eero Saarinen were two outstanding examples of the American school. Scandinavian designers such as Arne Jacobsen kept pace with the times, and Jacobsen's Swan chair (Plate 118), produced in 1959, was as advanced in technology and materials as anything produced in the United States. Italy was perhaps an unlikely candidate for strong design leadership in the furniture industry because of Fascist censorship during the war years, but luckily the Fascist control in Italy had not been as strong or as thorough as that of the Nazis in Germany. The war stimulated Italian technological advances. Some Italian postwar designs were directly derived from campaign furniture provided for the Italian armies—the folding canvas chair on a butterfly framework is one example.

Perhaps the most important component of the Italian style, however, was the Italian reaction to liberation. A naturally free-spirited people, they embraced liberation with such a sense of elation that it seemed to free their daring spirit, allowing it to take the form of brilliant imagination. They attacked design problems with equal liberation, approaching functional problems without preconceived ideas, instead relying heavily on their sense of style, and producing form, color, and luxury rarely duplicated.

Credit for pioneering innovative attitudes toward furniture forms must also go to the Scandinavian designers of the 1930s, among them Carl Malmsten of Sweden, Kaare Klint of Denmark, and Alvar Aalto of Finland.

Scandinavian furniture does not rely on trends but rather on form and function, allying it strongly with the philosophies of Sullivan, Wright, and Gropius and the Bauhaus. However, Scandinavian design is firmly rooted in the Vienna School, whose designers rejected the revolutionary aspects of Bauhaus design for that of a more carefree and stable culture.

While sharing a common framework, each of the four Scandinavian countries—Finland, Denmark, Norway, and Sweden—retained its individuality in the use of native woods and materials. There is an inherent reasonableness in Scandinavian form. It is neither shockingly revolutionary nor pretentious. Rather, it has the quiet harmony of design synonymous with that of Japan. It perhaps lacks some of the spirituality of Japanese design, but there is a great security in its reliability and in its refreshing simplicity. In keeping with the Scandinavian philosophy of unpretentious well-being, Scandinavian furniture brings to mind the basic ideals of Biedermeier furniture, which was also designed by and for a solid middle-class market.

Sweden contributed its own style to the Scandinavian design scene under the influence of Carl Malmsten (1888–1972), who has been referred to as the father of modern Swedish furniture. Malmsten said that his teachers were two: nature and the traditional Swedish furniture he was exposed to in museum collections. To a lesser degree, he was influenced by the British Arts and Crafts Movement, and as such subscribed to the tenet that utility must be combined with beauty no matter what fashion or trends dictate. In a sense, he modeled himself after William Morris, becoming teacher, philosopher, and artist.

Malmsten is noted for attempting to adapt old forms to twentieth-century needs, but he never quite came to terms with the twentieth century. He was invited to participate in an exhibition at the Stockholm Workshops in 1930, yet he refused because he objected to the very modern glass and steel buildings in which the exhibition was to be held. His objection was primarily based on his fear that the buildings might be too great an influence on younger designers. One of the designers so influenced was Bruno Mathsson, who designed chairs based on detailed anatomical studies. They were first produced in 1933 and are still in production.

In developing these chairs, Mathsson was concerned with the relationship between chair seat, backrest, and floor, thus evolving a method for dividing the chair into separate segments consisting of seat and back as one unit, with the legs being considered a separate unit with separate functions. While produced in varying forms, Mathsson's chairs all had a solid wood frame covered with tightly stretched webbing on a lower frame of laminated wood.

The foundations of modern Danish furniture design were laid by Kaare Klint (1888–1954). Klint followed the traditional ideologies of most of the Scandinavians, adapting a number of conventional forms to modern furniture design. His prime criteria were simplicity of form and adherence to function, again paralleling the "form follows function" philosophy of Sullivan, et al. Klint called his furniture "tools for living," echoing Le Corbusier's "a house is a machine for living in" philosophy.

Danish design paid considerable attention to the bentwood process, so much so that stagnation seemed inevitable due to lack of new ideas. Then, in 1950, the firm of Fritz Hansen began producing the work of innovative younger designers such as Arne Jacobsen, Hans Wegner, and Finn Juhl, thereby revitalizing the industry.

One of the most famous designers of laminated wood furniture was the Finnish architect Alvar Aalto (1898–1976). Aalto borrowed ideas originally pioneered by Thonet's bentwood process and developed them within the context of the established principles of modern design. His furniture was light, practical, and inexpensive, finding its way into many bathrooms, nurseries, and kitchens of the 1930s home.

Aalto was a disciple of the Vienna School. While a student in Helsinki he heard lectures on the Wiener Werkstätte and Joseph Hoffmann, later commenting on how important they were to his development and work. One of Aalto's focal points was the belief that the human body should only come into contact with organic materials. To this end, he opened an experimental workshop, with the cooperation of a local woodworking firm, to develop a process for molding wood to his specifications. His primary idea was to utilize the natural moisture in wood, capitalizing on its inherent pliability, rather than depending solely on steaming, as the Thonet process had done. His first experimental chairs had plywood seats supported by metal tubing. On later models, the metal tubing was replaced by wood.

A man of dedicated purpose, Aalto also realized the importance of allowing room for creativity in the design process. He stated:

> In order to reach practical goals and lasting aesthetic forms in connection with architecture, you cannot always begin from a rational and technical standpoint—perhaps even never. Man's imagination must be given free rein. That's the way it usually was with my experiments in wood. Purely playful forms, with no purpose at all, did not lead to useful forms in some cases until ten years later.[11]

Between 1935 and 1939 Aalto designed chairs and standardized furniture, such as bookcases, usually of flexible laminated wood attached to wooden frames. His stool of 1954 (Plate 36), manufactured by Artek, is perhaps his masterpiece, a culmination of his years of experimentation. Constructed of bent, solid wood with fanned bends that blend beautifully into the wood of the seat, no screws are used to hold it together, proving that bent solid wood can be transformed by the process of sawing into laminated wood. The effect is near perfection of design, a whole considerably greater than the sum of its parts.

Until the 1950s, Scandinavian furniture, like Viennese furniture of the 1920s and 1930s, resulted from a close union and cooperation among designers, craftsmen, and small- to medium-sized furniture companies willing to take a risk with new and sometimes revolutionary designs. The relative lack of industrialization in the Scandinavian countries afforded the luxury of extensive hand finishing on industrial products. This contributed to their distinctive appearance and quality, which helped to rocket them to prominence after World War II.

On a subconscious level, the consumer may have been responding to a fatigue with the cold hard steel and glass technology that had come to symbolize the war machine. This also may have contributed to the way in which the public embraced the natural materials produced by the collaboration between Scandinavian designers and craftsmen. Technology had become symbolic of destruction, while nature afforded a hope for the future.

While the Scandinavian designers focused on natural materials, the Italian and American designers of the postwar period turned their attention to making new materials and new technologies work for them. The development of inexpensive and reliable plywoods and laminated boards was one of the chief technical advances of the decade before World War II. The other, taken from experiments made in the automobile industry, was foam-rubber upholstery. These advances had great significance for the future. Plywood and other kinds of wood products not only offered an alternative to frame and panel construction, they also made it possible to put a large part of furniture production on a fully industrialized basis. Another important development was the way in which architects began to think of rooms as capsules in which the building structure, furniture, and function were completely integrated. All of these elements merged in the postwar period. It is to this era of postwar interior design, its designers, and manufacturers, that we will now turn our attention.

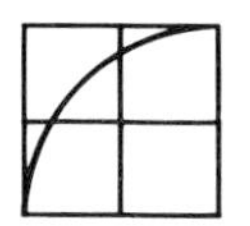

Summary of Designers from the Interwar Years

ALVAR AALTO

1898 Born in Kuortane, Ostro-Bothnia, Finland
1916 Began studies at the Helsinki Institute of Technology
1923 Established architectural offices in Jyväskylä; began experimenting with molded wood
1927 Introduced the wooden stacking chair for the auditorium of Jyväskylä Civic Guard building
1927–35 Designed Viipuri Library
1929 Began experimenting with molding plywood
1928–33 Paimio Sanatorium (1929-introduced the Paimio armchair)
1930 Introduced the "Aalto leg" on his furniture
1933 Relocated offices to Helsinki
1933–35 Introduced the Viipuri furniture collection
1935 Began producing furniture through Artek
1936 Introduced the Aalto serving cart
1937 Designed the Finnish Pavilion at Paris World's Fair
1939 Designed the Finnish Pavilion at New York World's Fair
1938–39 Designed Villa Mairea in Noormarkku, Finland
1940–41 Accepted professorship at Massachusetts Institute of Technology (MIT)
1941 Returned to Helsinki for duration of WW II
1946 Resumed professorship at MIT
1947–49 Designed Baker House Dormitory at MIT
1949 Returned to Finland
1954 Introduced the fan-leg stool
1976 Died

MARCEL BREUER

1902 Born in Hungary
1920–24 Studied at the Bauhaus in Weimar
1925–28 Taught at the Bauhaus in Dessau
1925 Introduced the Wassily chair
1928 Left the Bauhaus and opened office in Berlin
1929 Introduced the Barcelona chair
1930 Over thirty designs offered through Gebrüder Thonet catalog, including Bauhaus designs, the Cesca chair, the Breuer lounge chair, and tubular steel tea carts, dining tables, and folding chairs
1934–37 Emigrated to England and worked as an architect
1935 Returned to using plywood and produced the Breuer plywood lounge chair, stacking plywood chairs, armchairs, and nesting tables for Isokon Furniture of England
1937–46 Moved to the U.S.; professor of architecture at Harvard University, Massachusetts
1938–44 Worked with Walter Gropius in Massachusetts architectural firm
1946–81 Moved offices to New York
1981 Died

THÉO VAN DOESBURG

1883 Born in Holland
1915 Met painter Piet Mondrian
1917 With Mondrian, produced the first issue of *De Stijl* magazine, which became the forum for the exchange of ideas on which the De Stijl movement was based
1923 Did studies for a house (with Cor van Eesteren) that presented the construction and spatial principles on which the De Stijl theory of architecture was based
1927 Designed Aubette cafe and cinema in Strasbourg
1931 Died

EILEEN GRAY

1879 Born, August 9, at Enniscorthy, County Wexford, Ireland
1898 Began studies at Slade School, London; began studying lacquering techniques as an apprentice at the shop of D. Charles, 92 Dean Street, London
1902 Moved to Paris; attended classes at the Academie Colarossi and Academie Julien
1907 Began working with Japanese master lacquerer Sugawara
1913 Exhibited lacquer work in Salon de la Societé des Artistes Decorateurs

1914 Produced four-panel screen depicting nude youths in red and blue-black lacquer
1919 Designed interior for Madame Mathieu Levy (also known as actress Suzanne Talbot) at Rue de Lota apartment
1920 Continued lacquer work and received publicity in *Vogue* and *Harper's Bazaar*
1922 Opened gallery *Jean Desert* to sell her designs; promoted her carpet designs as well as lacquer and furniture
1923–24 Designed architecture and interior of house at Castellar
1925 Introduced her steel-tube and glass furniture
1927–29 Designed architecture and interior of house at Roquebrune
1927 Designed the Transat chair
1930 Closed gallery, *Jean Desert*
1930–31 Designed apartment for Jean Badovici in Paris, putting into practice her design concepts of storage and sensitive use of textures including metal, mirrors, textiles, and furs
1932–40 Continued with architectural studies and construction as well as interior design
1946–49 Did last major project of a cultural center in France, then went into near total retirement
1976 Died

WALTER GROPIUS

1883 Born in Berlin
1903–7 Studied architecture in Berlin and Munich
1910 Opened own architectural office in Berlin
1919 Became director of the art college in Weimar; founded the Bauhaus
1925 Bauhaus transferred to Dessau
1928 Left the Bauhaus for private works in Berlin
1934 Emigrated to England; became architect in London
1937 Became professor at the Graduate School of Design, Harvard University
1938–54 Opened and ran an architectural office in Massachusetts with Marcel Breuer
1969 Died in Boston, Massachusetts

KAARE KLINT

1888 Born in Denmark
1924 Became professor of furniture design at the Kunstakademi (Copenhagen Art Academy, School of Architecture), where he conducted systematic studies of the theoretical principles, physiological correctness, and function of furniture
1928 Worked as furniture designer for the furniture-making firm of Rudolph Rasmussen
1933 Designed deck chair of canework and wood, which was manufactured by Rasmussen; designed sideboard based on detailed studies of the space requirements for tableware and utensils resulting in double the storage space of similar cabinets (sideboard was manufactured by Rasmussen); designed collapsible safari chair of solid wood frame with canvas or leather sling seat (manufactured by Rasmussen)
1936 Designed chair of wood slat construction with a string seat (manufactured by Fritz Hansens Eft)
1954 Died

LE CORBUSIER (BORN CHARLES EDOUARD JEANNERET)

1887 Born at La Chaux-de-Fonds, Switzerland
1905 Received commission to design Villa Fallet, La Chaux-de-Fonds
1908–10 Worked as draftsman in Paris
1910 Studied architecture in Germany under Peter Behrens; influenced by Walter Gropius and Ludwig Mies van der Rohe
1920–25 Began writing for *L'Esprit Nouveau* under the pseudonym of Le Corbusier, the family name of his maternal grandmother
1927 Began collaboration with Charlotte Perriand, an interior and furniture designer
1929 First public showing of the chaise longue at Salon d'Automne
1928–29 Introduction of the Basculant armchair, the Grand Confort Petit chair, the Grand Confort Grand chair, and the Table en Tube d'avion section ovoide at Villa Church, Ville d'Avary, Paris (publicly shown at Salon d'Automne)
1931–33 Designed Swiss dormitory at Cité Universitaire, Paris
1948–52 Unité de Habitation, Marseille
1947–54 Chapelle de Notre-Dame-du-Haut, Ronchamp
1951–57 Government buildings in Chandigarh, India

1957–60 Cistercian monastery of La Tourette, Éveux, France
1965 Designed Heidi Weber house, Zurich
1965 Died

ADOLF LOOS

1870 Born in Brno, Czechoslovakia
1893–96 Came to U.S. and absorbed ideals of the Chicago School, then returned to Vienna
1908 Published his influential article, "Ornament und Verbrechen" (Ornament and Crime), which appeared in the Berlin review *Der Sturm*. (In the article, Loos outlined his belief that ornament represents a cultural degeneracy and that modern civilized society is best represented by undecorated form. The publication of this philosophy was to have a great influence on the modern movement)
1909 "Ornament and Crime" reprinted in Le Corbusier's journal, *L'Esprit Nouveau*
1910 Designed Loos house
1922 Designed Rufer house
1930 Designed Muller house in Prague
1938 Died

LUDWIG MIES VAN DER ROHE

1886 Born in Aachen, Germany
1905 Moved to Berlin; studied architecture and cabinetmaking
1907 Completed six apprenticeships; received first architectural commission at age of 21
1908–10 Worked under German architect Peter Behrens
1911 Studied in Holland
1927 Opened Weissenhof Housing Settlement in Stuttgart; introduced the cantilevered MR chair
1929 Introduced the Barcelona chair
1930 Introduced the Brno chair, the Tugendhat chair, and the X-based table
1930 Designed a couch for Philip Johnson's residence; moved to Dessau, Germany as director of the Bauhaus
1933 Closed the Bauhaus
1938 Headed the School of Architecture at Armour Institute (later renamed the Illinois Institute of Technology); continued to practice architecture
1969 Died

GERRITT RIETVELD

1888 Born in Utrecht
1899 Became an apprentice to his father, a cabinetmaker
1906–8 Took evening classes in design
1908 Designed chair of oak and leather (now in Central Museum, Utrecht), which launched his furniture design career
1908–11 Studied architectural design with P. Houtzagers
1911 Opened his own cabinetmaker's shop in Utrecht
1911–15 Continued advanced architecture courses under the direction of P.H. Klaarhamer, a noted architect who later took Rietveld into his studio
1915 Designed chairs and a sideboard for Klaarhamer (now in the Central Museum, Utrecht)
1917–18 Designed his famous Rood Blauwe (Red and Blue) chair, in which he attempted to make each part a study in simplicity of form, elementary in line with the function of material used. Rietveld adopted Mondrian's approach to color in the Red and Blue chair
1918–19 Designed toys and furniture for children, including a baby carriage, a cart, and two high chairs
1919 Designed the Hoge Stoel (Highback chair)
1922 Redesigned jeweler's shop for Goud en Zilversmids Co., Amsterdam
1920–22 Designed hanging lamp of neon tube lights with cubic terminals made of ebonized oak
1923–30 Continued experimenting with chair design
1925 Designed Tafellamp (table lamp) of metal tubing varnished black, red, and blue; designed Schroeder houses in Utrecht, which were strongly influenced both by the De Stijl movement and by Frank Lloyd Wright
1930–31 Designed (with T. Schroeder) the interior of a show apartment in the Rij Huizen, Utrecht
1934 Designed Zig-Zag chair
1935 Designed crate furniture (the Krat system); originally intended for the furnishing of weekend houses, it had the appearance of being constructed from fruit crates nailed together and was made of red spruce with an untreated surface. The crate series marked Rietveld's entry into the realm of organic design

1935–64 Continued experiments with furniture design and architecture

1963 Made an honorary member of the Association of Dutch Architects and given an honorary degree at Delft Polytechnic University

1964 Died

MART STAM

1899 Born in Holland

1924 Designed a tubular steel chair employing the cantilever principle. (Stam is believed to be the first designer to achieve this, and his work influenced Breuer and Mies van der Rohe, among others.)

1939–45 Served as director of the Institute voor Kunstnijverheidsondernijs in Amsterdam

1966 Retired

OTTO WAGNER

1841 Born in Austria

1894–1912 Professor at the Vienna School of Art, where his teachings influenced an entire generation

1904–6 Merged his expertise in architecture and town planning in the design of his most important building—the Post Office Savings Bank in Vienna—which included furniture of his design, manufactured by Thonet and Kohn & Kohn

1918 Died

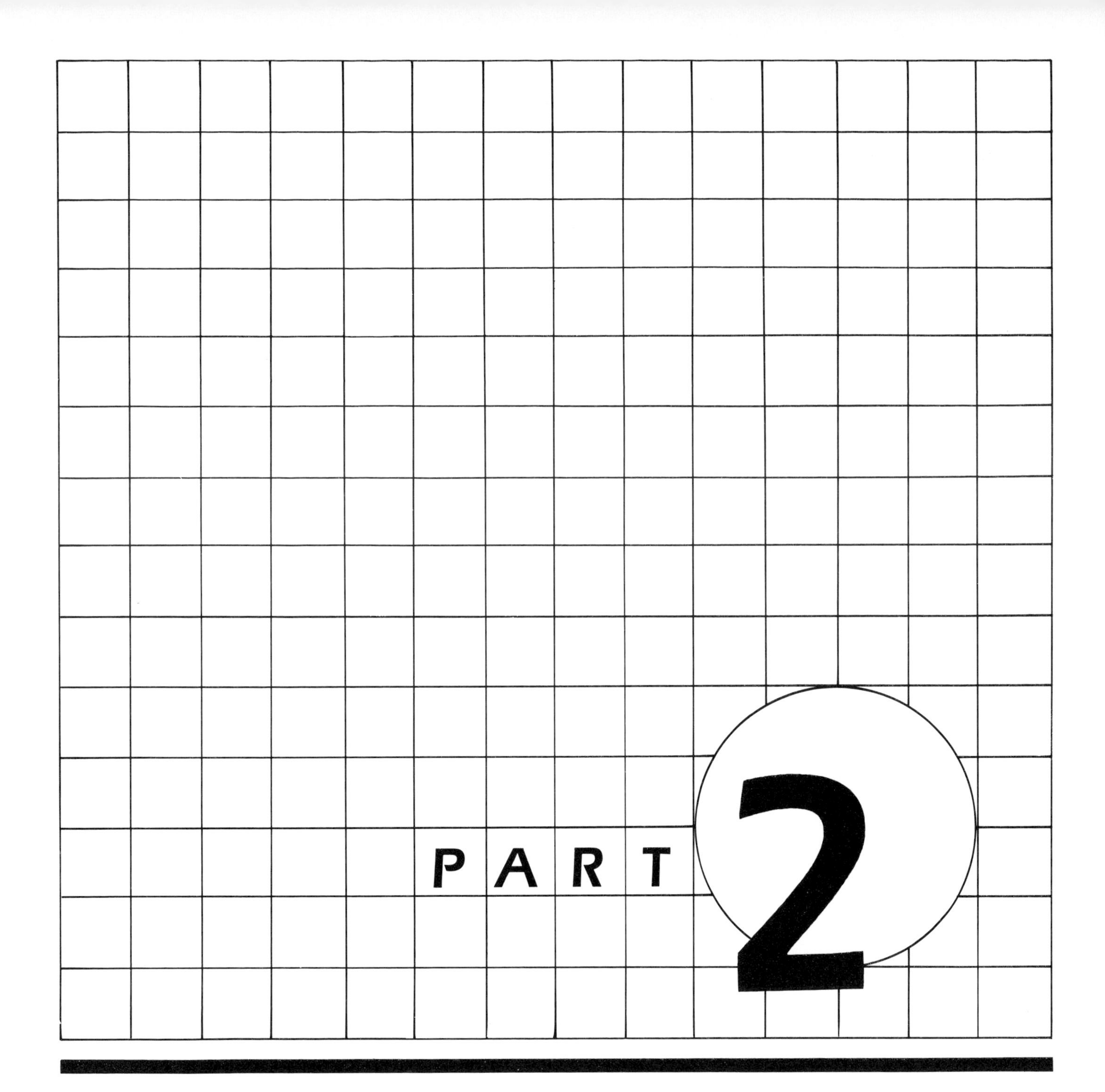

The Designers and Manufacturers

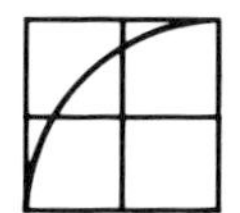

Charles Eames

Charles Eames was a mighty force in twentieth-century furniture design; he is noted for three major chair designs that influenced furniture production on an international scale. More than a mere conceptualist, his mastery of advanced technology set new standards in both design and production techniques. Eames combined original ideas with modern technology while imbuing his work with a personal and pervasive image of lightness and mobility.

More than fifty examples of Eames's work can be found in the New York Museum of Modern Art's design collection, having met stringent standards for admission. The museum's criteria for acquisition fall into two basic categories—quality and historical significance:

> An object is chosen for quality because it is thought to achieve or to have originated those formal ideas of beauty which have become major style concepts of the time. Historical significance refers to objects which, while they may not resolve problems of aesthetics and function with total success, have or will contribute significantly to the development of design.[1]

Eames's work met and in some cases far exceeded these requirements.

Eames's introduction into the museum's collection came in 1940. In that year, the museum cosponsored a contest with Bloomingdale's department store entitled "Organic Design in Home Furnishings." The exhibit was an outgrowth of the combined efforts of the museum and Bloomingdale's to encourage promising new designers in original concepts and applied production of the new technologies developed during World War II.

First prize was awarded to the architectural team of Charles Eames and Eero Saarinen. The winning chairs were three-dimensional shells that completely rejected the use of right angles. This led to their subsequent development of the series of Eames® chairs (note: Herman Miller owns the Eames® trademark) that, while based on the bentwood principles of Breuer and Aalto, represented a new sphere of sculpted furniture based on the latest technology. Most of Eames's furniture designs can be traced directly to this contest.

The Eames/Saarinen seating designs were unique in requiring an important structural innovation: all of the chairs made use of plywood shells, not bent in one direction as Aalto and Breuer had done, but molded in two directions. The resulting compound curves were three dimensional and had to be viewed in the round to be fully comprehended. Furthermore, the double curvature of the molded plywood allowed the use of thin veneers laminated to layers of glue, thereby achieving great strength. The chairs were such a radical advance in furniture design that the museum eventually installed its first one-man furniture show of Eames's work in 1946.

Receiving first prize in the Organic Design contest was an important accomplishment for Eames and Saarinen, both of whom were associated with the Cranbrook Academy of Art in Michigan (Eero was the son of the school's director, architect Eliel Saarinen). In 1936 Eames accepted a fellowship and later a teaching post at Cranbrook, after opening his own architectural office in 1930. While at Cranbrook, his colleagues included such luminaries as Florence Knoll, Harry Bertoia, Harry Weese, Ralph Rapson, and Ray Kaiser, all of whom contributed significantly to postwar architecture and design (see C1). In fact, Ray Kaiser, who had studied painting with Hans Hoffman, assisted Eames and Saarinen in preparing the 1940 competition entries. She later married Eames and played an important role in the development of his designs.

The definition of the term "organic design" by Eliot Noyes in the catalog for the Museum of Modern Art's 1940 Organic Design in Home Furnishings exhibition (see page ix), helps in understanding the conceptual motivations behind Eames's work.

As winners of the contest, Eames and Saarinen proved that exciting things were in store, even though Noyes's definition of "organic design" may have left something to be desired. Actually, while the exhibition catalog reviewed the pioneering work of several modern designers, it omitted mention of Frank Lloyd Wright, who popularized the term. Noyes seems to have overlooked Wright's concept of wholeness, focusing instead on the harmony of separate parts rather than on the concept of totality that is today being termed "holistic design." Wright's notion of wholeness required that a whole must remain a totality in both concept and construction. To remove any part of a whole destroys the part, the whole, and the harmony. The concept of "organic design" stems from living organisms, therefore precluding the possibility of interchangeable parts. It was heavily influenced by Oriental concepts of harmony with nature and utilized natural materials, primarily of curvilinear form. An ideal in organic design was the concept of a single harmonious unit of one-piece construction. This concept was later taken up by Saarinen, but Eames adhered to a different approach. Of his work he said, "I think of myself officially as an architect. I can't help but look at the problems around us as problems of structure—and structure is architecture."[2]

Eames was, indeed, trained as an architect, and his furniture designs should be viewed in this context. The Eames approach to architecture involved a cheerful acceptance of mass-produced materials. Stock window and door elements, normally used in the construction of factories, were combined with steel columns and open web joists, all ordered directly from the manufacturer's catalogs. In 1949 he and Saarinen designed a house for John Entenze, publisher of the magazine *California Arts and Architecture*. In the same year, Eames designed an adjacent house for his own use. Both buildings were in the series of case-study houses commissioned by Entenze for his magazine. The Eames house was among the most important buildings of the years following World War II, but Eames's interest in the medium of architecture soon paled in comparison to his dedication to furniture design and production techniques.

The other entry of Eames/Saarinen at the 1940 Museum of Modern Art exhibit was a group of cabinets and coffee tables, later supplemented by desk-table designs. Like those of their contemporaries, the Eames/Saarinen solution to the problem of storage called for a series of uniform boxes. However, they utilized the innovative design concept of having the boxes stack on separate benches that also functioned as seating units.

Because of the austerities of the war, production and distribution of this furniture was severely limited. In 1941 Ray Kaiser and Charles Eames were married and moved to southern California, where they worked to develop low-cost techniques for wood lamination and molding. Together they formed the Molded Plywood Division of the Evans Products Company in Venice, California. The Venice workshop remained the Eames's headquarters for more than thirty years, during which time they continued their experiments in molding and bonding techniques. They developed not only new furniture but the machines with which to make it—the KZAM! machines, so named by Eames because KZAM! was the noise they made. This research resulted in a 1942 commission from the U.S. Navy to produce molded plywood stretchers and leg splints—a project that gave the Eameses access to molding technology developed by the British for mosquito bombers.

Through their extensive research, by 1946 they had developed chairs that surpassed the promise of the 1940 competition—so much so, in fact, that the museum offered Eames a one-man show of his furniture, entitled "New Furniture Designed by Charles Eames." Eames was always intent on communicating process, so for his one-man exhibit he designed not only the exhibit itself but included a filmed display showing the transfer of energy from the seat of the chair to the leg.

The Evans Products Company was looking for a furniture manufacturer to produce the chairs from the 1946 exhibit. The Herman Miller Company was approached, but Miller's first response to Eames's designs was less than enthusiastic. The Miller company did not want to take on the task of producing the chair because the technology involved seemed too alien to them. Miller even announced, "That's never going to go into any showroom that has my name on it!"[3] But Miller relented when the Evans company offered to produce the chairs for the Herman Miller Company, thus freeing Miller from any manufacturing responsibilities but giving Miller the marketing and distribution rights. Initially, five thousand units were produced. Less than two years later, the Miller company had become a disciple of Eames's designs and was both ready and willing to buy the manufacturing rights as well. D.J. De Pree, manager of the Miller company, said of an Eames molded plywood chair, "That's beautiful, comfortable, easy to move. It's unimprovable. It's a national treasure that ought to be made available."[4] Later, Eames was to say, "There was a time when D.J. wanted to get every Hottentot into a molded plywood chair."[5]

Of the chairs included in the museum's 1946 exhibit, the shock-mounted side chair of molded plywood with tubular steel frame (Plate 39), produced in both dining and lounge heights, emerged as a totally successful and aesthetically appealing design. Practically indestructible, this chair has become a standard in offices worldwide. Among the many ingenious designs that followed it, the molded plywood and leather-padded lounge chair, and perhaps the aluminum frame lounge chair, are now also considered major achievements in the development of twentieth-century furniture.

The five-ply wood panels, molded in compound curves, are 5⁄16-inch thick. Although now made in walnut, early production models used ash, walnut, and birch. One variation used birch stained bright red or black. Originally, the tubular metal legs were equipped with rubber tips, but because these tended to fall off too easily, Eames later developed the permanently attached self-leveling nylon mounts.

Part of the elegance of this design must be attributed to the contours of the seat and, even more, those of the back panel. Eames discarded hundreds of studies because the contours of these two elements somehow did not blend well together and did not satisfy his sense of aesthetics. The back panel has been described as a rectangle about to turn into an oval, the transformation being arrested at a point midway between the two shapes. Seen as a whole, however, the shape is harmonious, without a jarring note, proving itself to be truly organic in form—a fact that might have contributed to the success of this design, if only at a subconscious level: we are often attracted to designs that relate to the natural environment, although our attraction may have nothing to do with intellect, rather being rooted in the primal, elemental forces of our origins.

During the late 1940s extreme lightness in furniture design and construction came to epitomize the American, primarily the Californian, ideal. The distinctive and memorable image of this chair is now simply referred to as "the Eames® chair." Eames's designs do not try to suppress or camouflage mechanical details but rather make them plainly visible. Yet, in doing so, they seem as natural as the skeletal shell of a tortoise being plainly visible. Hardware is pragmatically designed to do a job, rather than being overwhelming in its ornamentation.

Eames's philosophy incorporated the belief that there is an inherent good in making the greatest use of a sparse amount of materials, achieving this purpose by separating functions and defining them in the narrowest possible way, so that each requires a specific shape and material. It follows, therefore, that connectors and other hardware items were an inherent part of Eames's designs. Another characteristic of Eames's furniture is that it can be scattered or clustered in arrangements but need not be formally aligned, thereby affording a flexibility of use that has been much admired by his fellow architects and designers.

Among other variations of the lounge and dining-height chairs to enter production was a design executed entirely of wood. Few examples reveal Eames's methods and preferences more clearly. Apart from the appeal of wood for those who find metal cold and hard to the touch, the presumed advantage of the all-wood chairs was a greater uniformity of design, with a single material being used both for supporting and supported elements. Because the seat and back were molded in compound curves, their strength and rigidity were provided by conspicuously thin sheets of plywood. However, the carrying structure of the wood was much thicker than the metal tubing previously used and appeared to counteract the intended simplification.

From Eames's point of view, it was ultimately preferable to use the two different materials—wood and metal—for the two different functions, emphasizing their differences rather than trying to minimize them. However, the all-wood chairs remain among the most interesting of Eames's designs. A further variation is the wood chair with padding held in place by a veneer of leather glued along the edges of the seat and back panels.

Eames continued his experiments with molded plywood from 1941 to 1948. His objective was the resolution of technical problems, but he considered aesthetics an integral part of design. Contrary to what one might expect, Eames and his associates seldom worked from drawings. At best, preliminary sketches consisted merely of rough notations meant to indicate a general concept. Designs were actually worked out at full scale, and the curves of chair seats and backs were developed over closely spaced templates. Working directly with full-scale elements permitted Eames to test frequently for comfort. Construction drawings for the metal molds that were later to be used for mass production were taken directly from the templates themselves.

Many of the experimental chairs were discarded for reasons of function. The three-legged dining chair, for example, tipped over too easily. Other experiments, while functionally adequate, were discarded for reasons of aesthetic judgment or because they would be too costly to produce. The leather-covered armchair of 1956, which graces innumerable commercial and residential spaces today, was derived from forerunners that fit into this latter category. Even the unpadded plywood chair on its precarious metal base was subsequently developed into two distinct versions.

Perhaps one of the most beautiful of Eames's designs was an outgrowth of his work with the molded plywood chairs. He developed a simple but ingenious folding screen made of 34-inch or 68-inch lengths of plywood (Plate 40). Each piece was pressed into a flattened U-curve. The pieces were then joined to each other by a full-length canvas hinge sandwiched between the laminations. Because each section was only 9½ inches wide, the screen allowed great flexibility in its placement, much more so than conventional designs using wider flat panels. The organic undulations of the extended screen created an abstract sculptural form. Its canvas hinges were wide enough to allow the sections to fold back and nest into each other, making storage a simple matter. A few of the screens were stained bright red or black, as the molded plywood chairs had been. Unfortunately, few of the screens were made because the market did not support production.

In 1948 the Museum of Modern Art once again played an important part in Eames's progression. Almost as if on cue, the museum conducted an "International Competition for Low-cost Furniture Design." Eames entered a molded fiberglass version of his earlier laminated plywood shell chair (Plate 44), which had been developed with the help of a University of California team. The chair was the result of a collaboration between Charles Eames, Ray Eames, Don Albinson, Frances Bishop, James Connor, Robert Jakobsen, Charles Kratka, and Frederick Usher, Jr., who formed the Eames design group, in conjunction with the University of California, Los Angeles, Department of Engineering under the direction of Dean L.M.K. Boelter, Morris Asimow, Don Lebell, and Wesley L. Orr. The chair tied for second prize, the cowinning second-place entry being awarded to Davis J. Pratt of Chicago for his inflated tube chair. First-place prizes were awarded to George Leowald of Germany for a molded plastic chair and to Don R. Knorr of San Francisco for a circular chair of sheet metal that was subsequently manufactured by Knoll Associates.

By 1950 the results of the competition were in production. Since economical methods of manufacturing molded plastic (rather than metal) had been set up by the Herman Miller Furniture Company, the manufactured versions were produced in plastic, although the metal versions had been exhibited. Eames's design was so thoroughly conceptualized that the change in materials had little or no effect. Presumably, these chairs could have been constructed of any material with imperceptible visual difference other than the thickness of the edges. The chairs were manufactured with three bases: metal tube legs; a structure of metal wire (now sometimes referred to as the Eiffel Tower base); or wire with wood rockers. If any design defect can be found in these chairs, it may be in the lack of continuity between the materials of the shell and the base. Several versions of the model were produced: a side chair without arms; a stacking chair; and a version with an upholstered pad in fabric or leather.

With Russel Wright, Aalto, and Breuer, Eames is responsible for the modern sofa, but rather than adhering to the low, boxy standards set by the other designers, the Eames version has a high back broken into two horizontal slabs that fold down for shipping. The design was derived from a built-in sofa in a seating alcove of his own house, but there a solid panel closed the space between the seat and the floor. The portable production model rested on square-sectioned chrome-plated tubular steel legs with back supports of black enameled steel.

Unlike his other designs, this one is two-dimensional in that its configuration can be comprehended from a drawing of the side elevation alone, whereas it is nearly impossible to read the molded wood chairs from drawings—they must be seen in the round to be fully appreciated.

Eames's sofa design was intended primarily for commercial use and was manufactured with a vinyl covering. The design was later adapted for residential use covered in fabric rather than vinyl, accentuating the modeling details of the seat and back planes while minimizing their industrial nature. Eames did not produce a version with arms nor did he attempt a model with softer padding. The black metal supports, in contrast with the chrome legs, prove that startling asymmetry can be made to function with remarkable aesthetic appeal. (In 1984 Miller introduced Eames's last design, a soft-pad sofa designed in 1978.)

Eames broke with the tradition of the decade by designing a lounge chair that surpassed in comfort even the plump arm chairs found in English gentlemen's clubs—and he was able to do so on his own design terms while retaining his light, casual approach (Plate 46). His lounge chair consists of three rosewood shells padded with leather cushions. These are filled with a mixture of down, latex foam, and gray duck feathers. Padded armrests are encased in leather. The chair pivots on a five-pronged base of black aluminum with polished top surfaces, whose connectors support the two back shells of the same material. A matching ottoman allows the chair to function as a chaise longue. This chair is as famous as both of his molded wood chair models—a fame that is well deserved. The design of the rosewood shells is a deceptive one—curved across their width, they are flat on the longitudinal axis, and the combination of straight and curved lines is skillfully carried through to the metal hardware. The scale is also deceptive: while appearing large enough to dominate any furniture grouping, the chairs are not too large to be arranged in groups themselves. Like all of Eames's furniture, the chair's sculptural shape invites casual, clustered placement and flexible arrangement.

In 1958 Eames introduced a series of chairs known as the Aluminum group in which he repeated the thin, flat profile that had first appeared in his sofa (Plate 47). Here, the seat and back are made as one continuous plane slung between structural ribs of die-cast aluminum. An elegant design, the structure consists of six metal components in two different styles, with more structural detail concealed within the seat pad. It should be noted that the most interesting technical development is the seat itself, which is constructed of front and back layers of fabric or vinyl, between which is sandwiched an inner layer of vinyl-coated foam. This combination of materials is welded together through pressure and high-frequency current, with welds occurring at intervals (which appear as horizontal ribs on both sides of the pad).

The side rib is modeled to form a bar and is flange-cast in one piece, which terminates at each end in a cylinder. The seat pad wraps around the cylinders and is slipped into the flanges and secured in place with concealed brass nails. The supporting pedestal repeats the theme of flat bars and cylinders, carrying an intermediate stem of black steel which, in turn, supports another die-cast aluminum element sometimes referred to as an "antler." In this design, Eames seems to have come to terms with the disparate construction materials better than ever before; here, the marriage of metal and vinyl seems a completely natural one.

A variation of this chair design was developed as tandem seating for use in airports. It combines a shaped arm and back with shaped seat and leg elements connected to each other by flat steel bars painted black. Here again, the interchangeable seat and back pads are sandwiches of heat-sealed vinyl materials, but this time the welds are made in a lozenge pattern to increase strength.

All of the aluminum-group chairs are light, comfortable, and durable, making them ideal for use in both commercial and residential applications. Their comfort can be significantly increased by the addition of leather cushions in the group known as the "soft-pad" chairs. While similar in construction to their forerunners, these versions offer one seat and two or three back cushions filled with polyester foam sewn to the nylon fabric support, providing both a softer appearance and increased comfort.

Of all the modifications Eames made to his designs over a period of more than thirty years of research, the most significant was the addition of a padded surface to his original molded plywood designs. When the plastic shells of 1950 were given a padded surface to provide additional comfort, the design remained virtually intact, but the padded version of the 1946 plywood dining chair was altered so radically by the addition of padding that it seemed like a new design. In this version, a major change took place in the basic construction element, since the original molded plywood was replaced by plastic shells incorporating molded plastic housings containing metal units into which the legs and back support were bolted. The visual change came from the addition of urethane foam sandwiched between a shell and skin of fabric or vinyl. The edges of the shells were then bound with a thick vinyl welt whose dimensions approximated those of the metal rod supports that were intended to complement the lines of the legs.

Not all of Eames's designs were roaring successes. The Eames Contract Storage System (Plate 45), known as ECS, was one of the Herman Miller Company's earliest ventures into the educational market, and it was not a happy experience. ECS was a system of components that could be shipped knocked down, assembled on site in college dormitory rooms, and then attached to the wall—a requirement under federal funding regulations to deter theft of component parts. In retrospect, it appears that the ECS was a victim of bad timing. Eames had designed a product that was inexpensive, provided efficient use of space, and was durable. But in the late '50s when the product was marketed, students were already rebelling against control, and the first wave of students seeking to control their own environments was being felt. For students and planners of the day, Eames's 1950s ECS seemed a little too "1984."

Eames is also well known for his molded-shell chair designs, which suggest a precocious relationship with aviation far beyond the postwar advances of the 1940s and 1950s. Eames's designs seem to belong in the cabin of a spacecraft where comfort and utility are intrinsic design elements. As the fiftieth anniversary of their inception approaches, Eames's elegant designs remain sleek and timeless—true classics destined to move with ease and grace into the twenty-first century.

Eames's contributions to design extend far beyond the range of furniture or architecture. He was also a filmmaker, being involved with over fifty films. These include: *Blacktop* (1952); *Bread* (1952) (a study of international breads that included a special technique that actually allowed the viewer to smell the aroma of bread); *Toccata for Toy Trains* (1957), the winner of many international film festival awards; *Information Machine* (1958), made for IBM; television segments for the "Fabulous Fifties," a series produced by CBS Television (winner of two Emmy Awards); and *Powers of Ten* (1969, 1978), a physics film for general audiences. In 1959 he produced *Glimpses of U.S.A.*, a twelve-minute film for the U.S. State Department that introduced an exhibit in Moscow. It involved the use of 2,200 still and moving pictures simultaneously projected on seven screens. With the offices of Eero Saarinen, he collaborated on the IBM Pavilion for the New York World's Fair of 1964, which featured a twenty-two-screen film on problem solving.

Eames also contributed his expertise to education at the Cranbrook Academy of Art, the University of Georgia, the University of California at Los Angeles, the University of California at Berkeley, Yale University, and the Massachusetts Institute of Technology, as well as lecturing internationally.

Eames's legacy surrounds us in homes and offices, airports and museum collections. Yet perhaps Charles Eames's greatest contribution was his fine talent for problem solving and the handling of new technologies and scientific advances. Prior to his death on August 21, 1978, Eames was honored by the architectural and design community, receiving the American Institute of Architects' "twenty-five-year award" (1977) and posthumously receiving the Queen's Gold Medal for Architecture in London (1979). The following citation awarded to Eames by the American Society of Interior Designers is a well-conceived statement of his immense contributions:

> For expressing, in design, ideas that are personal and American at the same time they are public and international.
>
> For bringing to design the quality of thinking associated with the sciences, and for bringing to science the kind of imagination associated with design, and for showing us that they are inescapably part of the same process.
>
> For changing the way people sit, store things, build, play, communicate, teach, learn, and think.[6]

CHARLES EAMES

1907	Born, St. Louis, Missouri
1925	Received scholarship to study architecture at Washington University
1928–38	Employed at various architectural firms; traveled; worked independently
1938	Received architectural fellowship at Cranbrook Academy of Art, Michigan
1939–40	Joined architectural firm of Eliel and Eero Saarinen
1940	Won two first prizes in collaboration with Eero Saarinen at Museum of Modern Art, New York (Organic Design in Home Furnishings competition)
1940–41	Taught design at Cranbrook Academy of Art
1946	Had one-man show of furniture designs at Museum of Modern Art, New York; Herman Miller granted distribution rights to molded plywood designs
1948	Received research grant from Museum of Modern Art
1949	Herman Miller Company began manufacturing Eames furniture
1950–51	Zenith Plastics began producing shell chairs for Herman Miller
1952–58	Continued designing furniture; worked as furniture maker, educator, and international lecturer
1961	Awarded Kaufmann International Design award
1970–71	Held Charles Eliot Norton chair of poetry at Harvard University
1977	Received American Institute of Architects' award
1978	Died August 21
1979	Posthumously awarded Queen's Gold Medal for Architecture in London

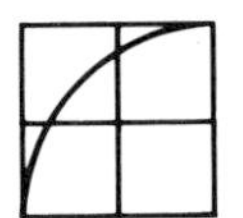

Eero Saarinen

Saarinen died at the age of fifty-one following surgery for a brain tumor, yet in his relatively short life he made an indelible mark in the fields of architecture and interior design. Design was Eero Saarinen's birthright. His father, Eliel Saarinen, was a well-known architect and educator. As such, he influenced not only Eero's career but those of Charles Eames, Harry Bertoia, and Florence Knoll, through his position as president of the Cranbrook Academy of Art.

Eliel Saarinen espoused the philosophy that spiritual function was inseparable from practical function and even went so far as to describe civilized existence itself as a search for form. Eero's early concepts of space were undoubtedly influenced by his immediate surroundings—the ninety-foot studio/living room of his parents' home in a rambling thirty-eight room house situated on a wooded bluff eighteen miles from Helsinki, Finland.

Eero's grandfather was a Lutheran minister whose beliefs were passed down through Eliel to Eero and his sister Pipsan as a capacity to overcome, to push beyond the limits of energy and resources, to pursue and to achieve. The Finnish word for this capacity is *sisu,* which Eero later translated to mean "extended guts"—a capacity for intense personal commitment in any creative endeavor.

Eero's early environment was filled with art and design. The family home in Finland was open to all manner of visiting artists, musicians, and intellectuals, including composers Jean Sibelius and Gustav Mahler, then the conductor of the Imperial Opera in Vienna. Eliel and his wife, Loja, patiently encouraged both Eero and Pipsan to explore their potential within the arts. Eero said, "I learned (to draw) while crawling around under my father's drafting table."[1] In fact, Eero was somewhat of an artistic prodigy, excelling at both drafting and free-hand drawing with either hand before he reached his early teens. He showed promise as an excellent watercolorist and at one point considered a career as a sculptor.

In 1923 the Saarinen family moved to the United States after Eliel had won second prize in the international competition for the Chicago Tribune Tower. The countryside near Detroit was to be their new home; the Cranbrook Academy to be the nurturing medium for Eero's future career.

After completing his monumental project for the redesign of the lakefront plan for downtown Chicago, Eliel was asked to join the staff of the architectural school of the University of Michigan as a guest professor. This he did, moving in the autumn of 1923 to Ann Arbor, where he first began his work as an educator. Through contacts made in this position, he was persuaded to remain in the United States and work on plans for the Cranbrook School for Boys to be built on the estate of George G. Booth, the publisher of the *Detroit News,* in Bloomfield Hills, Michigan, near Detroit.

Booth was a generous supporter of the arts and crafts in the Detroit area. He had begun by giving scholarships to young American architects and artists to study in Europe. Realizing that this reasoning was somewhat faulty, he soon conceived of the idea of establishing the Cranbrook Academy of Art to foster an in-depth understanding and nurturing of American design. His original concept for a school for boys thus rapidly grew to include a church, a school for girls and boys, and workshops for arts and crafts that evolved into the organized art center known as the Cranbrook Academy of Art. Work was begun in 1925, with additions continuing over the next few years to include the Cranbrook Institute of Science, completed in 1933.

As president of the Cranbrook Academy of Art, Eliel Saarinen outlined the completed plan for Cranbrook as follows:

> When fully developed, the Academy of Art is planned to include departments of architecture, design, drawing, painting, sculpture, landscape design, drama, music, and crafts. . . . The Cranbrook Academy of Art is not an art school in the ordinary sense. It is a working place for creative people. The leading idea is to have artists of the highest ability live at Cranbrook and execute their work there. . . . No doubt this rich and creative atmosphere will bring to Cranbrook young artists and art students who are eager to develop their talents. They will have their private studios, where they do their own work; and in being continuously in close contact with the master-artists, they can learn from them how to develop their own individualities. . . . Creative art cannot be taught by others. Each one has to be his own teacher. But connection with the other artists and discussions with them provide sources for inspiration.[2]

This open philosophy under which Eero had been raised and matured helped to foster in him a sense of freedom to try the new, the unexpected. This, in combination with the Finnish *sisu,* the sense of inner strength, formed the building blocks on which his career was based.

When Eliel took on the task of designing Cranbrook, it was more than just a personal involvement—the whole Saarinen family took part in the project. Part of the Cranbrook complex included the Kingswood School for Girls, and each member of the Saarinen family had a part in its successful completion: Loja supervised a dozen weavers to create the fabrics for draperies and upholstery; Pipsan decorated the auditorium and dining hall interiors; and Eero, then aged twenty, was responsible for the bold sculptural forms of the furniture.

Finally giving up his intention to become a sculptor after having studied in Paris for two years, Eero enrolled at the Yale University School of Architecture, graduated in 1934 with honors, and spent the next two years on a fellowship traveling throughout Europe. This was a wonderful opportunity for him to study European architecture in detail with the freshly trained eye of an architect. Upon returning to Cranbrook, Eero assumed major responsibilities both at Cranbrook and at Eliel's architectural firm.

Eero found Cranbrook infused with a new energy as a result of a group of exceptionally talented young designers that had clustered around Eliel: Charles Eames, an exponent of technological humanism; Harry Bertoia, directing metal crafts; Florence Schust (later to become famous as Florence Knoll); and Harry Weese and Ralph Rapson, who came to study architecture and city planning. Of these, Charles Eames was to have the most dramatic effect on Eero. They became close friends and collaborators who, together and separately, made invaluable contributions to the furniture industry and the American vision of interior design.

Saarinen's work built on that of Mies van der Rohe, Le Corbusier, Loos, Gropius, and the Bauhaus. While their steel-tube and laminated wood furniture provided the models for some of his own creations, Saarinen was plagued by the dissonance caused by the dissociation of the legs from the body of the chair. It was an issue that was to cause him years of experimentation, finally culminating in the Pedestal group of 1957, with which he achieved the visual unity of construction and materials he had been seeking, if not the technical unity.

In the spirit of organic design, it was Saarinen's goal to conceive a truly organic chair in which all parts—construction and materials—blended in a unity of design. He attempted this initially with Charles Eames, and the result was the winning of first prize in the 1940–41 Museum of Modern Art Organic Design in Home Furnishings competition. Saarinen and Eames jointly won first prize in category A, Seating for a Living Room, and in category B, Other Furniture for a Living Room. (For further information about the entries, see the section on Charles Eames.)

The combined approach of Eames and Saarinen revolutionized the traditional concepts of the chair, their three-dimensional molded plywood making possible the formation of seat, back, and arms in one consolidated shell. But the legs were still a problem for Saarinen. He made another attempt at unity in 1946 with his Womb chair (Plate 49), but this, again, was a compromise.

Saarinen carried the tenets of organic design even further than Charles Eames, by insisting that a chair should not only be unified as an object but should also attain unity with its user and its architectural setting. Saarinen believed that a chair was incomplete without a person sitting in it. In like manner, he considered the design of the chair in relation to the proportion and scale of walls, floors, ceilings, and the room's overall spatial proportions.

Saarinen's Womb chair is considered by many to be one of the most comfortable contemporary chairs ever made. When conceptualizing the Womb chair, Saarinen was guided by two considerations: comfort and the unity of space and architecture. Like Eames, Saarinen was intensely concerned with human anatomy and its relationship to furniture. Realizing that we no longer sit rigidly as our Victorian forebears had done, he set out to design a chair that would accommodate the way in which we really sit, not the way in which we ought to sit. Eames and Saarinen had in common the idea of designing a chair for slouchers.

It has been noted that the Womb chair was an outgrowth of the collaborative effort between Saarinen and Eames that had won the 1940 Organic Design competition. The first step was taking a molded plastic shell armchair, then upholstering it in foam rubber with loose seat and back cushions. This version was designed for Knoll Associates in 1948. Saarinen noted:

> A comfortable position, even if it were the most comfortable in the world, would not be so for very long, . . . the necessity of changing one's position is an important factor often forgotten in chair design. So, too, is the fact that an equal distribution of weight over a large surface of the body is important.[3]

Saarinen has described the Womb chair as:

> . . . [an] attempt to achieve psychological comfort by providing a great big cup-like shell into which you can curl up and pull up your legs (something that women seem especially to like to do). A chair is a background for a person sitting in it. Thus, the chair should not only look well [*sic*] as a piece of sculpture in the room when no one is in it, it should also be a flattering background when someone is in it—especially the female occupant.[4]

Saarinen's approach was quite divergent from that of Frank Lloyd Wright or Rietveld, whose main concern was the way the chair would relate to the architecture rather than to the sitter.

Hans Knoll, then the director of Knoll Associates, which manufactured the Womb chair, asked Saarinen to suggest another name for the chair, to which Saarinen responded: "I have been thinking and thinking about a printable name for that chair, but my mind keeps turning to those which are more biological rather than less biological."[5] The Womb chair inevitably retained its name because its construction encouraged the sitter to assume a fetal position. It spawned similar designs, a complementary ottoman, and an extended-width Womb chair that became a sofa. However, these lacked some of the comfort inherent in the original version.

By 1953 Saarinen was troubled by what he called the "slum of legs" in modern living-room settings. Although many designers were continuing to experiment with the concept of shell-form seating in plastics and plywood, the legs were treated as separate units, with little attempt made to unify leg and chair body. Of this jungle of legs present in most interiors of the period Saarinen said, "Modern chairs, with shell shapes and cages of little sticks below . . . became a sort of metal plumbing."[6]

Saarinen's training had led him to believe that "the great furniture of the past from Tutankhamen's chair to Thomas Chippendale's have always been a structural total."[7] He thus became dedicated to designing a chair in which body and base were a unified structure. This led to his Pedestal group of 1957, which consisted of an armchair, two stools, a side chair, and several tables (see C2). The chairs were constructed of three parts: a cast aluminum base with plastic coating matching the color of the metal; a molded plastic shell reinforced with fiberglass; and an upholstered pad of latex foam. The upholstery was zippered over the foam-rubber pad, and the pad was then secured to the steel by Velcro. Saarinen worked judiciously to calculate a base that had the stability of four legs without requiring weighting in the base of the pedestal. This was eventually manufactured in aluminum and given a plastic finish to resist marring and to present a unified appearance with the chair body, which was also constructed of reinforced plastic.

Even though the Pedestal group was visually organic in design, technically it was still impossible to construct these pieces of a single material. From collaborations with Knoll designer Don Pettit and the Knoll Research Team, Saarinen realized that the base had to be made of cast aluminum in order to support the chair, thereby eliminating the possibility of unifying construction materials. Saarinen was greatly disappointed and saw the Pedestal group as an example of unfulfilled promise; he continued to experiment until his death, searching for the one technique or material that would allow him to reach his goal of a completely organic design.

Plastics currently exist that would allow the chair to be manufactured of a single material, but even this would not fit Saarinen's requirements, for the finishes he conceptualized still cannot be achieved through contemporary plastics. Someday, a single material may be developed that will allow the Pedestal chair to be manufactured to Saarinen's original concepts. In the meantime, it continues to meet with the success of its initial impact. Saarinen's Pedestal chair has spawned dozens, perhaps hundreds of copies, although none has the graceful lines and visual unity of the original.

In combination with Saarinen's astonishing fortitude in his quest for design perfection should be considered his amazing diversity. It is hard to believe that the Deere & Company building in Moline, Illinois (1957–63) and the CBS building in New York (1960–64) could be the work of the same man—the architectural solutions are so widely ranged—yet Saarinen's ability to tackle each problem with a fresh eye, working in his methodical way, produced remarkably innovative results.

The Deere building's rural corporate headquarters is located on a heavily treed site, with the principal building of the complex being situated across the end of a large lake. Smaller buildings are linked to the center by glazed bridges, the buildings themselves being constructed of a steel alloy that develops a coppery patina when exposed to the elements. The windows are glazed with gold-tinted mirror glass, which reduces the air-conditioning load by reflecting about 70 percent of radiant solar energy.

By contrast, the CBS building is a freestanding rectangle, 491 feet in height, faced in dark granite. Saarinen referred to it as "the simplest skyscraper in New York." Its dark granite and dark-tinted window glazing are solid and foreboding by comparison to the almost eerie skeletal quality of the Deere building.

In the role of architect, Eero Saarinen's outstanding achievements include the Jefferson Westward Expansion Memorial in St. Louis, Missouri (1948–64); the General Motors Technical Center in Warren, Michigan (1948–56); the Kresge Auditorium and the Chapel at Massachusetts Institute of Technology in Boston (1953–55); the United States Embassy in London (1955–60); the United States Embassy in Oslo (1959); the Dulles International Airport in Chantilly, Virginia (1961); the Trans World Airline Terminal in New York City (1956–

62); and the CBS building in New York City (1960–64).

Throughout his career, Saarinen's work was rooted in the organic approach. He described the ideal interior as: "one that grows together with and out of the total concept of a building. In a sense, it grows the way chromosomes multiply out of the original sperm and the thinking of the total concept is carried down to the smallest detail. This organic unity is the ideal."[8]

Sarrinen was a realist who, although elevated by ideals, was not crushed by the commercialism of a society that put ideals in a position secondary to profits. He was not one to let setbacks get him down. He went on to achieve great success, in spite of the fact that for a time during his days as an architecture student he was known as "second-place Saarinen" because of his continued "failures" in competitions.

Saarinen summarized his design philosophy as follows:

> Usually the problem of interior design is limited. It begins within the existing framework of an office, apartment or ready-made house. The shells of these living and working units have to answer the needs of hundreds of thousands of people. They have become completely anonymous shells. . . . Likewise, furniture has moved from the handicraft era into a mass-production era and so, to a greater or lesser degree, have other items of the interior. The result is that the major equipment of furnishings of the interior have an impersonal character. As with the architectural shells, it is essential, in fact, that a mass-produced item must have this impersonal character. It must not be romantic, in the sense of answering a special problem or smacking of the artist's personality. It must be classic, in the sense of responding to an often recurring need, both practical and visual, and in many different situations.[9]

In coming to terms with the realistic goals of the production line, Saarinen had evolved a philosophy that enabled him to conceive of the sculptural forms of his furniture for mass-production technology.

His commitment to the inherent naturalness of organic design, regardless of the technological means used, is evident in the following statement:

> The clarity and serenity of a good interior give an absolutely marvelous feeling of strength with which to face our complicated and confused world. The fact that one has achieved this atmosphere with the form-world and technology of one's own era gives further satisfaction. And finally the psychological satisfaction of having expressed an identity is deeply rewarding. Especially in a world of standardization of people as well as things, this coherent, clear expression of one's own individuality is a necessary goal.[10]

Saarinen's approach to architecture was echoed in his approach to furniture design: "Though we use mass-produced parts in architecture, a building is custom-built to the extent it is a solution of a specific problem. In furniture design, the client is Everyman."[11]

Perhaps the most concise explanation of Saarinen's design philosophy can be found in a statement by Saarinen about Frank Lloyd Wright. Saarinen regarded Wright as the greatest architect of his time because of Wright's holistic sense. Of Wright, Saarinen said: "He did not conceive structure separately; his structure, his funny decorations, his spaces, his lighting were all one thing. Today we have all this 'icky' kind of architecture which is taken a little bit from here and a little bit from there."[12] It was this "icky" approach to design that Saarinen spent his life trying to remedy.

EERO SAARINEN

1910	Born, August 20, in Kirkkonummi, Finland
1923	Saarinen family emigrated to the United States
1925	Family settled in Michigan
1929–31	Studied sculpture in Paris
1930–34	Attended Yale University School of Architecture; traveled through Europe observing architecture
1936	Joined father's (Eliel Saarinen) architectural firm; taught at Cranbrook Academy of Art, Michigan
1939	Married Lily Swann
1940	Won two first prizes for furniture design in collaboration with Charles Eames at the New York Museum of Modern Art's Organic Design in Home Furnishings competition
1942–45	Served in the Office of Strategic Studies, Washington, DC
1946	Introduced the Womb chair
1948	Won the Jefferson Memorial competition, St. Louis
1947–55	Drake University, Des Moines, Iowa: pharmacy and dining halls
1948–56	General Motors Technical Center, Warren, Michigan (project included furniture design)
1952–55	Irwin Union Bank and Trust Company, Columbus, Indiana
1953	Divorced Lily Swann; married Aline Louchheim

1953–56 Massachusetts Institute of Technology, Cambridge, Massachusetts: Kresge Auditorium and Chapel; Milwaukee County War Memorial, Milwaukee, Wisconsin; Stephens College Chapel, Columbia, Missouri; Miller house, Columbus, Indiana

1954 Master plan for University of Michigan, Ann Arbor

1954–58 Concordia Senior College, Fort Wayne, Indiana; Vassar College dormitory building, Poughkeepsie, NY

1955–58 University of Chicago, Chicago, Illinois: dining hall and women's dormitory

1955–59 United States Embassy, Oslo, Norway

1955–60 United States Embassy, London, England

1956–59 International Business Machines building, Rochester, Minnesota

1956–60 University of Chicago, Chicago, Illinois: law school

1956–62 Trans World Airlines terminal building, New York City

1957 Introduced Pedestal furniture group

1957–60 University of Pennsylvania, Philadelphia: women's dormitories

1957–61 International Business Machines: Thomas J. Watson Research Center, Yorktown, New York

1957–62 Bell Telephone Corporation: research laboratories, Holmdel, New Jersey

1957–63 Deere & Company building, Moline, Illinois

1958–62 Ezra Stiles and Morse colleges, Yale University, New Haven, Connecticut; Dulles International Airport terminal building, Chantilly, Virginia

1958–64 Lincoln Center for the Performing Arts, New York: repertory theater and library museum in association with Skidmore, Owings & Merrill

1959–63 North Christian Church, Columbus, Indiana

1960–64 Columbia Broadcasting System headquarters building, New York City; International Airport, Athens, Greece

1961 Died September 1, Ann Arbor, Michigan

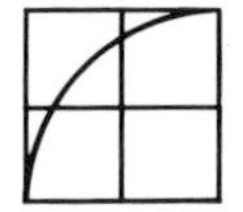

George Nelson

The most revealing discussions of George Nelson tend to focus not so much on his work as on the man himself, his design philosophy, and his remarkable lucidity. Nelson is noted for his sense of humor and his erudite literacy in relation to design, but he might best be described as being extremely selfless—that wonderful facility that gives us the opportunity to laugh at ourselves, to be serious without being pedantic.

Nelson was another of the postwar designers trained as an architect, his education at Yale University being followed by postgraduate work at Catholic University where, in 1932, he won the Prix de Rome in architecture. He then traveled in Europe for the next two years, observing the great architectural styles and interviewing the likes of Le Corbusier and Mies van der Rohe, who, while famous in Europe, were practically unknown in the United States. When he returned to America he published these interviews in a magazine called *Pencil Points* (later renamed *Progressive Architecture*), and this subsequently led to Nelson's joining the staff of *Architectural Forum* as an editor, which in turn extended to special projects for *Time* and *Fortune* publications.

From 1936 until the war, Nelson had an architectural office in association with William Hamby, but when World War II intervened, Nelson turned his attention to writing once again, producing *The Industrial Architecture of Albert Kahn* and *Tomorrow's House*, in collaboration with Henry Wright. He also worked on a special project for *Life* magazine—the development of a storage wall in which he incorporated compartmented storage into a common room partition, thus popularizing the "room divider" so prevalent in the 1950s. Once this piece of furniture was produced, Nelson never looked back in the area of furniture design. He formed an association with the Herman Miller Furniture Company that was to prove a lasting and successful one for both parties.

Following the war, Nelson tried his hand at opening an office again. In 1947 his New York office was available for both architectural and industrial design commissions.

Nelson's interests were extremely diverse; he often involved himself in many projects and experiments at the same time. Arthur Drexler of the Museum of Modern Art recalled:

> George Nelson was interested in doing many things at once . . . during the day the office devoted itself to designing chairs, among other things, made of wood. But at night the staff gathered around Buckminster Fuller and labored with him over the birth of a Seating Tool. This was made of two aluminum reflector shields of the sort used by photographers, a sheet of celluloid, and, most important, a piece of piano wire. Unfortunately, anyone sitting on this nearly invisible object completely overhung the seat and appeared to be balancing painfully on a knitting needle.[1]

Process was of the utmost importance to Nelson. His endless seeking to satisfy his curiosity led him into a seemingly infinite variety of facts, beliefs, and enthusiasms. Rather than being one to pare down or exclude possibilities, he embraced them, expanding into areas that often seemed irrelevant yet more often than not were successfully applied to his projects. This willingness to experience the unknown led Nelson into his association with the Herman Miller Company.

In 1944, following the death of Gilbert Rohde, the Herman Miller Furniture Company was suddenly left without a designer. Three names were proposed to replace Rohde: German architect Eric Mendelssohn, industrial designer Russel Wright, and George Nelson. D.J. De Pree, then heading Herman Miller, became intrigued by an article written in *Architectural Forum* suggesting that walls be used for storage. He discovered that the article had been authored by Henry Wright and George Nelson, who were also the managing editors of the magazine. When De Pree approached Nelson about designing furniture, Nelson was immediately receptive to the idea, although he freely admitted he knew nothing about furniture design. Both Nelson and De Pree, a highly religious man, were in for a shock at their first meeting: each was horrified by what the other believed about the Bible. In spite of their differences, however, De Pree was taken with Nelson's "fertile mind, his design awareness, and his ability to articulate important principles. . ."[3]

That Nelson became the design director for Herman Miller is history. However, in that capacity he went far beyond the confines of the job, not only providing the company with a corporate philosophy but formulating marketing strategy, writing frequent and relentlessly honest assessments of the company's progress, serving as corporate advisor, idea man, and a cheerleader noted for his pep talks. He was occasionally called to Zeeland (Herman Miller's Michigan headquarters) for a day or two of merely walking around the plant and talking to people—an activity that De Pree regarded as significant, if not measurable, in its effect.

Perhaps one of Nelson's more brilliant strategies was the identification of architects rather than department-store buyers as the likeliest market for Herman Miller products. Once he realized that the avant-garde nature of his designs would appeal more to those knowledgeable in design than to those buying for an uninformed public, his target population naturally took the form of his peer group.

Another of Nelson's strokes of genius was his insistence that Herman Miller should standardize whenever there was no reason not to. Prior to his intervention, all of Herman Miller's twenty-four bedroom sets had different sized drawers. Nelson also proposed that the company expand sufficiently to produce and promote the products properly. He said, "If we're going to do the things we say we want to do, then we have to generate enough cash to do them. You have to become a $2 million company."[4] At the time, Herman Miller was a $400,000 company with little thought of expansion, but following Nelson's advice, expand they did. The 1984 net sales were $402,524,000.

Nelson turned his remarkably erudite writing abilities to the production of the Herman Miller catalog, a new trend for them and for other furniture manufacturers as well. Nelson knew that fresh designs would be eagerly copied, so rather than making futile efforts to prevent this, he decided to exploit it by producing the furniture catalog. In the 1948 catalog he included all furniture dimensions, making it that much easier to copy, but he sold the catalog just as if it were a book on design—and with Nelson as the author, it was a superb one.

In the foreword, Nelson outlined the Herman Miller philosophy by setting down the following principles:

> —What you make is important. Herman Miller, like all other companies, is governed by the rules of the American economy, but I have yet to see quality of construction or finish skimped to meet a popular price bracket, or for any other reason.
>
> —Design is an integral part of the business. The designer's decisions are as important as those of the sales or production departments. If the design is changed, it is with the designer's participation and approval. There is no pressure on him to modify to meet the market.
>
> —The product must be honest. Herman Miller discontinued production of period furniture 12 years ago because its designer, Gilbert Rohde, had convinced the management that imitation of traditional designs was insincere aesthetically.
>
> —You decide what you will make. Herman Miller has never done any market research or any pretesting of its products to determine what the market "will accept." If designer and management like a solution to a particular furniture problem, it is put into production. There is no attempt to conform to the so-called norms of "public taste" nor any special faith in the methods used to evaluate the "buying public."
>
> —There is a market for good design. This assumption has been more than confirmed, but it took a great deal of courage to make it and stick to it.[5]

The 1948 catalog was not only a specifications guide but a trade reference work. It sold remarkably well at $5.00 and a second edition was soon produced at $10.00.

Nelson's original furniture designs were highly innovative: a headboard that tilted so you could lean against it and read; a coffee table fitted with a lift-out tray; and a completed version of the storage wall that had first brought him to the attention of De Pree. Nelson's early designs for Miller were compatible enough with those of his predecessor, Gilbert Rohde, that the transition was a smooth one. Nelson's best-known works include a daybed (Plate 70); a residential desk (Plate 60); handmade miniature cabinets; steel-frame cases; modular seating; the Marshmallow sofa (Plate 63); the Coconut chair (Plate 66); the comprehensive storage system (Plate 68); the sling sofa (Plate 65); and the Kangaroo chair (Plate 64), all of which will be discussed further in Part 3, "Materials and Methods of Construction." (See also C3 and C4.)

Of his work Nelson noted: "What we designed became best sellers, but they were always made best sellers by other manufacturers who knocked them off, not by Herman Miller."[6] However, Nelson made a tremendous contribution to the steel furniture industry with his MMG (Modern Management Group), a line of wood, steel, and Micarta desks that incorporated architectural detailing and color into the design and was intended for corporate use. Unfortunately, the Herman Miller company was unable to profit from the designs due to technical and economic difficulties, and the MMG was quickly dropped from production. Steelcase, General Fireproofing, and others quickly picked up Nelson's idea and, because of better marketing and production methods, revolutionized the office interior. Nelson, though, must be remembered as the originator of this concept.

In addition to his own innovative contributions, Nelson's infallible eye and sense of curiosity brought to his attention the work of other talented artists and designers whom he attracted to Herman Miller. Paul Laszlo, Isamu Noguchi, and Charles Eames all owed a debt of gratitude to Nelson for his farsighted recognition of their abilities.

In establishing the Herman Miller Company's goals and progress, Nelson expressed a kind of holistic thinking aligned with that of the other organic designers. Speaking of the role of the designer in society, he said with typically irreverent humor:

> In any organized society people have to do things for each other, and the esteem they enjoy depends on the society's evaluation of the services performed. . . . Anyone who offers the prospect of unlimited wealth and/or unlimited disaster is quite a guy—or if you prefer, quite a profession. Obviously such a professional will find himself higher on the ladder of status than one who merely offers an increase in creature comforts. Nobody really cares anyway if the missile with the atomic warhead has been subtly color-styled by Zilch Associates to look its very best just below the ionosphere. The color of the bomb going off is prettier and has greater impact on more people. . . . It is a curious fact, and one generally ignored, that the least imposing occupations have frequently proven the most durable. . . . Take for example the case of Buddha. Who remembers how much money Buddha's father had? Or the name of India's military leader of the time? What we do remember is that Buddha has affected the lives of hundreds and hundreds of millions of people, that he did this by sitting in a cave and saying something once in a while, and that the name of his most powerful contemporary is not even a whisper.[7]

According to Nelson's philosophy, the artist/designer should be a purveyor, not of comforts, but of truths. "You can always tell when his communication comes through because in the shock of understanding the message there is also the feeling that you had known it all your life. . . . Truth is a most important quality in design of any dimension and people tend to recognize it when they see it."[8] In like manner, he defined "good design" as "neither a book of etiquette, nor a social register [but] one of many attempts to remove the heavy hand of authority from what should be an area of personal enjoyment."[9]

More than his accomplishments as a designer, an arranger of spaces, or a corporate figure, Nelson's design philosophy was instrumental in leaving its mark on his body of work. He once wrote: "I believe enlargement of our vision to be the most significant problem in design and architecture." Through this "enlargement of vision" Nelson believed it imperative for the designer to expand his or her awareness and perception of the world. He proposed that the twentieth-century world in which we live, the world we look at all the time, is not formed from twentieth-century concepts but from a "series of outdated inherited images of earlier periods. Our vision is cluttered with retained images and it is too narrow."[10]

This narrow way of thinking he termed "atomistic"—meaning that ideas were perceived as separate, static concepts, unrelated to the whole at large. He urged a reformed way of thought. "The modern way of seeing things starts with the assumption of a dynamic rather than a static situation, and it proceeds from this assumption to a growing understanding that relationships can take us closer to the truth about things than the things themselves."[11] This statement perhaps illustrates more clearly than any other his direct agreement with the principles of organic design.

All life is in constant jeopardy of annihilation. The subconscious fear of dying, our ability to respond to the subtle, ever-present threat of imminent danger, is inherent in our survival mechanisms. Yet, as Nelson pointed out, for the first time in history we live with the knowledge that we have created the threat ourselves. The plagues and famines that have taken the lives of millions throughout history were chance occurrences over which man had little or no control, but with Hiroshima everything changed. "The Bomb was programmed, designed, built and exploded by people who presumably knew exactly what they were doing. It is, I think, this new sense of intellectual mastery over the physical world that is making us so acutely and unhappily aware of the world over which seemingly we have no mastery at all."[12]

He considered "enlargement of vision" an essential force in the physical and spiritual survival of humankind. He stated: "Modern relationships are an expanding network that links even enemies like Siamese twins. Beating the other man to the draw was once a workable technique for survival, but for Siamese twins it is not."[13]

Relating his philosophy to the area of design, Nelson noted that assuming the image of the world carried in the mind of the average person is preconceived and preconditioned by outmoded thinking, then the concepts and insights of freethinking artists and designers cannot help but be highly disturbing and, therefore, threatening to those whose thought processes have not adjusted to a holistic view of the universe.

Nelson proposed that future humans, the ones for whom designers will be designing, and for whom "every major development in his very dynamic world, whether under capitalism or communism, in peace or war, will act to foster him as a type," are the prototypes of the noncompetitive man. His vision of future humankind is that of a society where "individuality" becomes absorbed into the larger organism, but in which this absorption brings no sense of loss, rather a sense of gain. In a sense, humans will equate themselves with the unity of cell colonies, synchronized and cooperative, with a new comprehension of constructive relationships between the individual and the group. Out of this, Nelson's vision extended to see architecture and design forgoing "individuality" in exchange for a noncompetitive form of architecture/design that will

> ". . . express the human values which fostered the Acropolis and the Gothic cathedrals. It is because this magnificent possibility seems to me to fit so clearly in the picture of the unfamiliar world that is taking shape that it is essential that we learn how to see it. . . . No society can build beyond the range of its vision. The vision of a materialistic society is a materialistic vision.[14]

Because of his architectural training, it was natural for Nelson to be involved and concerned with more than the interiors of spaces. His interest carried over to urban planning as well as to the sculptural forms of architecture. Nelson saw the need to deal with urban blight as the biggest problem facing cities in the postwar years. With typically clear insight, he compared the decay of cities to natural decay:

> Decay in nature is not a disaster. It is part of an organic process of change. Many of our most valuable mineral resources are the result of decay. Any gardener making a compost pile knows that the decayed vegetable matter will enrich his soil. So with our cities. Blight occurs in cities at almost the exact places where building should be cleared out anyway to make room for sun, air, and automobiles.[15]

Nelson invented the shopping mall in his "grass-on-Main-Street" concept, which included changing congested blocks into verdant shopping promenades by planting sod in closed-off former streets; by including large planned parking areas to provide easy access to downtown commercial areas; by eliminating traffic congestion with appropriate mass-transit systems and by replacing noisy congested streets with pedestrian shopping malls, sidewalk cafes, landscaped recreation areas, and arcades to protect shoppers from inclement weather and so encourage commerce. He also visualized the expansion of small businesses—grocers, pharmacies, dry cleaners, and so on— in residential areas providing convenience facilities close to home.

Nelson was not satisfied with his views merely being pipe dreams. He encouraged public involvement in urban planning, stating:

> It is not too soon to start thinking and planning now for such a transformation of your city's shopping center once the war is won. By obtaining a plan of your own city as it is now, you and your neighbors and friends could begin discussing the possibilities of a project like this, and become perhaps the moving force behind such a civic improvement.[16]

Perhaps one of Nelson's most intriguing theories relates to the use of interior space. After numerous observations, he noted that people, when given the choice of a large open recreational space and one that is small, with cozy nooks and corners, invariably chose to avoid the more spacious room in favor of the smaller, more cramped space, which he termed a "dead-end room," with only one way in or out and corners where people can group. He explained this phenomenon by relating it to our human visual apparatus. Because human eyes are frontally set, we are blind to at least 180 degrees behind us, making us particularly vulnerable to attack from the rear. Considering man in the light of the primitive, subject to attack each time he left his cave, it is feasible to assume that ancient protective mechanisms come into play in our selection of rooms and spaces in which we feel comfortable.

A wall at our backs and the protection of corners give us an unconscious feeling of security. Nelson believed that dim racial memories continue to play an important role in the fabrication of interior spaces and that architects should definitely take these memories into consideration when designing. "In the history of house design there are many examples to support the notion that surprisingly often modern man acts like a defenseless animal in search of protective shelter. . . . Complaints leveled against the first modern house usually resolved themselves into one sentence: 'Who wants to live in a goldfish bowl?' "[17]

Nelson went on to say that goldfish have no problem in living in a goldfish bowl because their eyes are so constructed that they cover a full 360-degree circuit. Since fish have no blind spots, there is no need for a protective wall, but with humans he considered such a wall essential to comfort and security. Nelson credited Frank Lloyd Wright with an intuitive knowledge of this, since his work often included dead-end rooms. Following studies of spatial relationships in Wright's houses, Nelson concluded that

> ". . . the size of the room is not one of the psychological factors determining its comfort. . . .

> Wright's clients have been conspicuous for their enthusiasm about their houses, and without discounting the many other important factors which contribute to their feeling, I am convinced that one reason is that Wright always finds a way to put walls at their backs.[18]

The need for protective cul-de-sacs and alcoves affording privacy, whether large or small, is an essential human need. Nelson warned of the potential dangers in indiscriminate open planning when rendered without sufficient thought to basic psychological needs. Too often, buildings are constructed as mammoth sculptures, with too little thought given to the people who will inhabit them. Nelson's solution? "It couldn't be simpler. All we have to do is keep in mind that people still remember, however dimly, those far-off days when a cave felt like a good place to live."[19]

With Nelson's premise in mind, it is interesting to note the number of glass-walled buildings (particularly residences) that are sealed off from the world with opaque draperies or blinds as the occupants attempt to find privacy and a sense of security. Yet, such structures continue to be built in amazing numbers. One cannot help but wonder when human needs will be taken into consideration.

True to the principles of organic design, Nelson was a humanist first and foremost. As such, he abhorred the postwar trend of interior decoration:

> Modern decoration is in its present appalling state because it *is* decoration. By decoration I mean what most people mean by decoration—the piling of assorted objects into a space until the occupants are no longer made uneasy by its emptiness. . . . It is far easier and safer to follow a formula than to develop a principle. This is why modern decoration, so-called, is largely a matter of plywood and rubber plants and why it is so devastatingly boring—although there is nothing wrong with either plywood or rubber plants. . . . I think it possible that when a room is full, in the sense of decoration as defined, the emptiness may show up in the lives of its occupants.[20]

Nelson's sense of design was highly sophisticated, relying on the premise that everything should be simultaneously meaningful and decorative—essentially, a restatement of the "form follows function" principle. Tongue in cheek, he continued the above discussion:

> How would you design a room to express the thoughts and activities of your clients if their activities were canasta and gawping at a video screen and their thoughts were non-existent? You could do it, of course. It would be a room with walls, floors and ceiling painted one color, a card table (inlaid with plutonium if they were real rich) at one end of the room, and pews at the other end where everyone could kneel when the Milton Berle show went on. . . . The fault, dear Brutus, lies not in our clients. . . . Come to think of it, I never did run into a client who asked for plywood and rubber plants.[21]

Nelson's concepts were light-years ahead of his time. Even today, as his designs are freely copied and adapted, few of his imitators have the intellectual capacity to grasp the deep meaning behind his work. His vision, his designs, were meant for a kind of human not yet completely formed. He saw beyond the materialistic, fearful archetype of the twentieth century to what we are capable of becoming, to the noncompetitive trusting human of a new age, and in a thousand different ways he warned us through his work that we have no choice in becoming this new type of human; if we do not, we will face annihilation.

Through the utter, stark simplicity of his designs he reflected the Japanese taste, yet he always incorporated the necessary practicality to be functional for the way we live. Perhaps in trying to understand Nelson, we have taken a step toward becoming the kind of human he envisioned. Whatever judgments posterity may make about George Nelson, his brilliance cannot be disputed. As Arthur Drexler said: "He was his own best design."

GEORGE NELSON

1908	Born, Hartford, Connecticut
1928–31	Trained as architect, Yale University
1932	Won Prix de Rome in architecture
1932–34	Became fellow of the American Academy in Rome
1935–49	Served as editor and consultant to *Architectural Forum*
1936–37	Wrote series of articles for *Pencil Points*
1936–41	Opened architectural offices in New York with William Hamby
1942	Developed grass-on-Main-Street concept of pedestrian malls
1945	Introduced his Storagewall concept; wrote *Tomorrow's House* with Henry Wright
1946	Appointed design director of Herman Miller
1947	Opened industrial design firm and associated architecture firm in partnership with Gordon Chadwick, which produced Bubble lamps, clocks for Howard Miller, and plastic dinnerware for Prolon

1952 Publication of *Living Spaces* (George Nelson, ed., New York)

1953 Publication of *Chairs* (George Nelson, ed., New York); *Display* (George Nelson, ed., New York)

1954 Publication of *Storage* (George Nelson, ed., New York)

1957 Wrote *Problems of Design;* introduced Modern Management Group

1959 Introduced Comprehensive Storage System (CSS); designed American national exhibition in Moscow for United States Information Agency

1963 Introduced Catenary furniture group

1964 Introduced Sling sofa and Action Office; designed Chrysler exhibition and Irish pavilion at New York World's Fair

1976 Designed "USA '76" for American Revolution Bicentennial Administration

1977 Wrote *How to See*

1979 Wrote *George Nelson on Design*

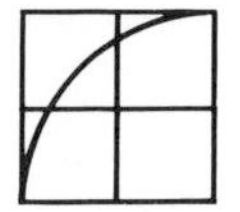

Harry Bertoia

In 1950 Harry Bertoia began working for Hans and Florence Knoll in a capacity that can only be termed an artist's dream. He was given an entirely free hand to work in his own way, to experiment inside or outside the furniture field; if he came up with a furniture design in the process, so much the better.

Bertoia's life began in San Lorenzo, Udine, Italy in 1915. In 1930 he and his family moved to the United States where, in 1937, he enrolled on a scholarship at the Cranbrook Academy of Art. There he met Florence Schust (later to become Florence Knoll), Eero Saarinen, and Charles Eames, who were to have an immense influence on his career in furniture design. Bertoia's scholarship took the form of a work/study program in which one of his duties was to oversee the metalworking studio in a teaching-assistant capacity. Bertoia had graduated from Cass Technical High School the year before and had briefly attended the school of the Society of Arts and Crafts, where his work came to Cranbrook's attention.

In 1938 Bertoia began teaching full-time at Cranbrook, having been appointed Metal Craftsman. In addition, he was encouraged to do his own work, which at that time consisted primarily of innovative experimental metalware and jewelry produced with a light, spontaneous touch. Often, his pieces were created on the spot at his workbench.

Bertoia became fascinated with creating inexpensive, well-designed objects from nonprecious materials and with combining precious and nonprecious materials, as in his Kamperman silver service (in the collection of the Detroit Institute of Arts), which features the striking combination of silver and lucite, and the 1940s silver tea set with cherry wood handles, which was influenced by Eliel Saarinen's silver globular urn of 1934. Other experiments led to objects of brass and pewter and a polished bronze vase of so flawless a finish that the only ornamentation necessary was the play of light on the deeply buffed surface.

By 1942 Bertoia was trying out different possibilities for surface decoration, such as textures and irregular biomorphic forms. Bertoia's later work in design and sculpture superseded his early delvings into jewelry, but the experiments in jewelry—his ambiguous statements in organic forms—were forerunners of later designs. Perhaps one of his better-known jewelry pieces is the Centipede (1942), fashioned of brass, which simultaneously seems to be both animal and vegetable. It so thoroughly epitomizes a fusing of plant and animal natures that it suggests a primal microscopic form.

Like most of the other designers of his era, Bertoia did not go untouched by the war. In 1942 the shortage of metals interfered with the metalcraft program at Cranbrook, so Bertoia was forced to teach graphics. Shortly thereafter the metalcraft program was discontinued entirely for the duration of the war.

On Bertoia's application to Cranbrook he wrote, "I can use any tool or machinery with dexterity."[1] Time proved that statement to be no hollow boast. His dexterity, paired with his fine sense of form and craftsmanship, were much too strong to let World War II intervene for long.

In 1943 Bertoia married Brigitta Valentiner, daughter of William Valentiner, then director of the Detroit Institute of Arts. The elder Valentiner undoubtedly had a marked effect on Bertoia's adoption of an abstract style, as he had a private collection of works by Kandinsky, Klee, and other German Expressionists, and the two men often discussed abstraction at length. Bertoia's early monoprints show Paul Klee's influence, and his later mixed-media experiments with ink-coated pieces of metal and wood in geometric compositions pressed into paper show a relationship to Kandinsky's later works. These experiments in abstraction were the forerunners of the geometric metal screens created by Bertoia in the 1950s.

Shortly after Bertoia's marriage to Brigitta, Charles and Ray Eames, also recently married, invited the Bertoias to move out to the West Coast to work with them in developing the Organic Design Competition's prizewinning molded plywood chairs into a form suitable for mass production. At first Bertoia worked well with the Eameses, but after about three months of experimentation he expressed the opinion that the project was doomed to failure, saying that "it was forcing plywood into a shape it did not want to take."[2] On hearing this, Eames suggested that Bertoia go ahead and try out his own ideas.

Bertoia then proceeded to work from the premise that a chair was not merely sculpture but must relate to the body and its skeletal behavior. He considered such issues as how long the chair would be occupied, reasoning that lengthy sitting would require more seating area to accommodate shifting body movements. Within a period of three weeks he had produced about a dozen designs, but always their basic interest in materials differed: Eames preferred wood; Bertoia preferred metal. Their compromise turned out to be the first of the Eames® chairs—a plywood seat and back on a three-legged metal frame.

The designs were initially intended to be the result of a group effort, with credit and problems being equally shared. In reality, however, things did not work out quite that way. The spirit of camaraderie spawned at Cranbrook began to dissolve. While the precise reasons for the breakup are probably known only to those directly involved, Eames finally put the Eames® chair into production through Herman Miller in 1946; Saarinen, who also worked on the initial design, went on to manufacture his designs through Knoll.

After a year of working together, Eames and Bertoia parted as a result of artistic differences. Bertoia took a position in the publicity department of the Naval Electronics Laboratory in San Diego. This must have been a difficult time for him, seeing his contemporaries achieving success while his career appeared to have reached a standstill. But things were soon to improve, for Bertoia received an invitation from Hans and Florence Knoll to come work for them. Bertoia was reluctant to leave the West Coast at first, but Brigitta sent the Knolls a postcard saying, "Harry is happy to come." Later, when Bertoia received a telegram from the Knolls thanking him for accepting the position, he was astonished. Brigitta claimed she had simply "forgotten" to tell him of the invitation.

Fortunately, Brigitta's deception worked out well. In 1950 the Bertoias came to Pennsylvania and Knoll. The Knolls provided Bertoia with a studio that was a small room at the factory near the railroad tracks where "there was not a single pair of pliers, a hammer, a grinding wheel, nothing."[3] Bertoia wrote of this period that rather than taking a traditional research approach to furniture design:

> [I] began to rely once more on my own body. I began to think in terms of what I would like as a chair. I started very slowly, but things were beginning to shape up. . . . When it came to rod or wire, whether bent or straight, I seemed to find myself at home. It was logical to make an attempt by utilizing the wire.[4]

Bertoia's wire chairs (Plates 72–74) had become a reality by late 1952, and by early 1953 prototypes were being produced by Knoll. Of his work Bertoia said:

> In sculpture, I am concerned primarily with space, form, and the characteristics of metal. In the chairs, many functional problems have to be satisfied first, but when you get right down to it, the chairs are studies in space, form, and metal too. My sculpture is made up of a lot of little units, and these rectangles or hexagonals or triangles are added together and produce one large rectangular or hexagonal sculpture. The same with the chairs. The chair has a lot of little diamond shapes in its wire cage and they all add up to one very large diamond shape, and this is the shape of the whole chair. It is really an organic principle, like a cellular structure.[5]

In the early 1950s, at a time when Eero Saarinen was designing the General Motors Technical Center in Warren, Michigan, he visited Bertoia in his studio and saw Bertoia's work with the metal screen sculptures. Bertoia utilized geometric units similar to those of his monoprints and positioned them at regular intervals to form spatial constructions of metal planes and connecting rods coated with molten metals. Saarinen saw the possibilities of using Bertoia's screens as interior architectural elements, and Bertoia was subsequently commissioned to create a metal screen thirty-six feet long and ten feet high, which served the utilitarian purpose of being the formal entrance to the staff cafeteria at the General Motors center.

In 1954 Bertoia designed another welded metal screen for the Manufacturers Hanover Bank in New York, measuring seventy-two feet long, sixteen feet high, and two feet deep. The sculpture served a dual purpose: since it was installed on the second floor of the bank, it was simultaneously the focal point of the interior and a functional division between the public areas and private offices.

Additional Bertoia experiments took the form of "floating sculptures," which he related to early paintings from his Cranbrook years. Of these works Bertoia said:

> I used to make paintings on the most transparent paper I could find—paint just a shape here, leave a lot of space around it, and then another shape and color them. Then I would stretch the paper on a frame, and hang it up against the light. The colors would float in the air, some closer, some farther back. I started to get interested in all these space experiments long ago—at Cranbrook after I had been there for a little while.[6]

These "floating sculptures" formed the basis of his sculptures used as reredos for the Chapel at the Massachusetts Institute of Technology, designed by Eero Saarinen. Saarinen wanted a focal point above the altar that could also partition off a staircase to the sacristy from the nave.

Bertoia also became involved in sound sculptures, exploring the relationships between sound and motion in the sculptural medium, in a somewhat similar manner to the works of Alexander Calder. The sounds produced by his metal rod sculptures resembled the sounds of nature: the rustling of leaves; waves breaking against rocks. Bertoia's intensive study of sound properties related to metal produced a full range of tonalities. The film *Sonambient: The Sound Sculpture of Harry Bertoia,* directed by Jeffery Eger (Kenesaw Films, 1971), credits Bertoia's lifelong interest in kinetic sculpture to a band of gypsies that passed through his native village of San Lorenzo when he was a child. They brought with them shiny metal cooking utensils which they sold, and to attract business they beat the metal objects with small implements, producing a variety of sounds—a memory that remained with Bertoia well into adulthood.

Shortly before his death, Bertoia was in Denver for an exhibition of his "singing sculptures," which involved the use of sounds as an integral part of the work. He spoke of his interest in sound and of his desire to experiment in other areas:

> I would like to pursue sound a while longer until something happens to it. I would like to enter into the investigation of space and color. That is a field which has been almost neglected; very little has been done. Some color in space has been achieved by projection with laser beams, gases, but that is not quite enough. I would like to take a solid material, colorful, and multiply it to the point where it actually produces an atmospheric color, so there is a play of sunlight and a play of matter.[7]

His death, in 1978, prevented experimentation in the color/space dimension, but his wire chair remains a classic, its chromium-plated steel-rod frame having a skid-type leg structure that has been freely copied by other designers.

Bertoia, like his contemporaries Eames and Saarinen, created timeless designs that appear as contemporary now as they did when they were conceptualized in the era of organic design. Perhaps their greatest contribution was not the designs themselves but the truth they understood so well: unity transcends all.

HARRY BERTOIA

1915	Born, San Lorenzo, Udine, Italy
1936	Graduated from Cass Technical High School, Detroit
1936–37	Attended Art School of the Society of Arts and Crafts, Detroit
1937	Accepted as a student at Cranbrook Academy of Art
1938–43	Taught metalwork at Cranbrook Academy of Art; taught graphic arts when metal shop was closed
1943	Married Brigitta Valentiner; moved to California to work with Charles and Ray Eames as furniture designer
1946	Received U.S. citizenship
1950	Moved to Pennsylvania; began producing designs for Knoll Associates
1953	Wire chair introduced by Knoll Associates; continued work on major sculptural projects
1978	Died

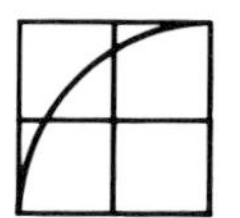

Hans and Florence Knoll

Today, Knoll International is a major force in furniture design and manufacture, but back in the early 1940s it was little more than a dream in the mind of Hans Knoll. Knoll was born in Stuttgart, Germany, on May 8, 1914. His father, Walter C. Knoll, had pioneered furniture manufacturing in Weimar Germany, with his production of some of the Bauhaus designs for Gropius, Breuer, and Mies van der Rohe. From an early age, Hans showed an interest in furniture design, but Hans and his father were of different worlds and different minds. Hans hated the rigid old-school ways of his father, being more of a visionary, with a highly developed sense of foresight. He broke away from his father by going to England, where he established an interior design firm called Plan, Ltd. By 1937 he had moved to New York where he was in business as the Hans G. Knoll Furniture Company.

Hans realized that modern architects would eventually want to use modern furniture in keeping with the innovative structures being built. Based on this belief, he formed an alliance with Jens Risom, a Dane who had been designing textiles for Dan Cooper in New York, and together they began designing basic, simple furniture. Prior to doing any designs, though, Knoll and Risom went on a four-month tour of the United States, talking to architects and designers about their needs. Their initial line included chairs of soft wood and army surplus webbing or parachute cloth, which was readily available from the short supplies of wartime.

Knoll's first catalog was published in April 1942 and consisted of gray boards pasted up with twenty-five photographs of the "600" line, enclosed in a brown folder. Fifteen pieces of the "600" line were Jens Risom designs executed in cherrywood—cabinets, bookcases, tables, chests, and a few chairs. Several overstuffed pieces from the early "200" and "800" series were also included—these were primarily the designs of Ernest Schwadron of Vienna, a friend of Hans's family.

Gradually, other designers were invited to join the Knoll collective on a royalty basis: Abel Sorenson of Denmark; Ralph Rapson, a former student of Saarinen at Cranbrook and architect in Saarinen's offices; Franco Albini of Italy; Hans Bellman of Switzerland; and Pierre Jenneret, Le Corbusier's cousin. Hans also handled marketing in the United States for the Hardoy or "butterfly" chair of canvas or leather slung on a metal tube frame, a design that has become a legendary symbol of the '50s (Plates 75, 76).

The Hardoy chair is one of the most widely copied pieces of furniture on an international scale, with as many as five million produced in the United States alone since 1950. The chair is generally considered to have been designed by Argentinian architect Jorge Ferrari Hardoy, although there is considerable conjecture as to its conceptual origins. It has been attributed in part to architects Antonio Bonet and Juan Kurchar and to an English patent filed on March 22, 1877 by civil engineer Joseph Fenby. Royalties and rights of ownership have been nearly obliterated. Knoll filed a lawsuit test case against one of the many copiers of the Hardoy chair but he lost the suit, and the "butterfly" chair copies were soon being turned out at an astonishing rate. One estimate suggests that 3,000 copies a week were being manufactured by independent producers in the Los Angeles area alone.

At about this time Risom was drafted, but Hans avoided the draft because of an early bout with tuberculosis. When Risom returned from service he found a few changes at Knoll. Hans had met Florence Schust, whom he would later marry, and her design influence was already being felt.

Florence, nicknamed "Shu," once referred to herself as a "meat and potatoes" furniture designer. She said of herself:

> People ask me if I am a furniture designer. I am not. I never really sat down and designed furniture. I designed the fill-in pieces that no one else was doing. I designed sofas because no one else was doing sofas. Eero and Bertoia did the stars and I did the fill-in. . . . I did it because I needed the piece of furniture for a job and it wasn't there, so I designed it.[1]

However, like Charles Eames, Eero Saarinen, Harry Bertoia, and others of the organic movement, Florence tried to relate interior design to architecture, furniture, and human scale (see C5).

Florence had been trained at the Cranbrook Academy, where she formed associations with Eames, Saarinen, and Bertoia that were to be of long-range influence. Of her Cranbrook years she writes:

> We used to work from early morning until lunch time, then we'd break for lunch, go back to work, go off at four o'clock and have a touch football game out in the fields, or walk or something, then back to work until dinner. Then after dinner we'd all go back to work 'till ten o'clock, when we'd go have a hamburger at the local diner. . . . That was just standard procedure.[2]

Following Cranbrook, Florence received her degree from the Architectural Association in London, but since she was required to have a degree from an American school in order to practice in the United States, she studied with Mies van der Rohe for a year at the Armour Institute in Chicago. She then went to work for Walter Gropius and Marcel Breuer in Boston. Later, while she was with the offices of Wallace ("Wally") Harrison in New York, she was offered the opportunity to work with Hans Knoll in the design of an office for Henry L. Stimson, secretary of war. After the project was completed, Florence continued to see Hans and, in fact, did quite a bit of moonlighting for his company, designing unitized wall elements, chests, files, desks, counters, display cases, room dividers, and seating. Two years later, in 1943, they formed a business partnership, and in 1946 they were married.

By the end of the decade, Knoll Associates had a remarkably avant-garde team of international designers working on projects. By 1951 Knoll International had expanded to France and Germany, and by 1955, the year of Hans's untimely death as the result of an auto accident, there were subsidiary companies in Belgium, Canada, Cuba, Sweden, and Switzerland. But their success was the result of hard work and considerable good fortune.

Both Hans and Florence were perfectionists, he in the areas of marketing and promotion, she in design and production. They had the intelligence and foresight to foster a nurturing, creative environment in which the designers could work, but creativity was never confused with sloppiness or lack of discipline. Their work was characterized by a seriousness of mind and a desire to produce the very best product available. Quality was a key concept at Knoll, as was attention to detail. The smallest details were executed with care, even down to fuse-box covers being finished in the same surfacing material as walls—an innovation for its time (see C5, C6).

Howard Meyers, then editor of *Architectural Forum*, was highly instrumental in the Knolls's success. Meyers was noted for his parties at which creative people had the opportunity to meet and exchange ideas: a typical Meyers party might include the likes of Philip Johnson, Frank Lloyd Wright, or Isamu Noguchi. Howard Meyers and his wife Louise helped the Knolls by introducing them to influential people and bringing them in contact with potential clients. In fact, Louise Meyers later became the first showroom manager of Knoll in New York. Meyers even promoted the Knolls's first major breakthrough into the interior design business by securing them the design of the Rockefeller family offices on the fifty-sixth floor of 30 Rockefeller Plaza.

Much of the company's success must also be attributed to Hans's drive and determination. He was the motivating force behind the company. Murray Rothenberg, an employee who worked closely with the Knolls for years, said:

> Hans was a superlative salesman. He could sell almost anything. He was always selling—himself, his product, the company. You would do almost anything for him. He had the ability to get you to work for him. You would also hate his guts sometimes. . . . He always had a reason. When you worked with Hans you knew he never did anything just for the sake of doing it. He was a casual, impeccable individual, relaxed in his appearance. A difficult guy to get along with, no question; but you admired him, respected him.[3]

Richard (Dick) Schultz, another employee who had attended the Chicago School of Design with Rothenberg, gives a slightly different view of Hans. Schultz was hired right out of design school to help Harry Bertoia with his experimental wire chairs. He recalled the excitement of knowing right from the beginning that Bertoia's chairs were going to be extraordinary. Knoll was noted for his dedication to producing good designs, for not cutting corners, and most importantly, for hiring well-trained, creative people to whom he then gave free rein. Knoll's staff were not professional engineers but design school graduates who had been trained to think creatively. But although Hans Knoll promoted good design, he was also a businessman, as Schultz recalls: "In those days I don't think anyone thought about money because everybody loved Knoll. Most of them could have made more money someplace else, but Hans used to pat you on the back. You'd get to the point where you were going to quit, and he'd come and pat you on the back and you felt so great that he didn't have to give you a raise."[4]

In the mid-1940s Knoll formed the Knoll Planning Unit, a milestone for its time, described in a 1946 issue of *Interiors* magazine as "a proving ground for a group of young designers with architectural and engineering backgrounds who refuse to compromise with the taste of a dictatorial public. A loose collaborative arrangement [that] has benefitted both designers and manufacturers."[5]

The "young designers" referred to included Jens Risom, Abel Sorenson, Ralph Rapson, Eero Saarinen, George Nakashima, and Florence Schust, who at the time was moonlighting for Hans while still working for the architectural offices of Wallace Harrison.

In the beginning, there was a reluctance on the part of the public to accept the new designs. They were used to the period styles that dominated the early 1940s. Florence explained their domination:

> Prior to World War II, most nonresidential interiors were either designed by the architects for the buildings or were not designed at all. More often than not, the building itself was at violent odds with its interior requirements. While the structure might be neo-classical, the functional requirements of the interiors were frequently modern in the extreme, so that either the interior spaces would match the exterior (and thus not function at all), or they would be made to function reasonably well, in which case the furnishings were not likely to match the style of the building. . . . This inherent conflict was resolved by a number of pioneer architects in the early part of the twentieth century [who] designed and built commercial and industrial structures in which exterior form and interior space were completely integrated. . . . To achieve this they had to design the furniture as well as the actual building. As a result, almost all the really significant early innovations in modern furniture design were carried out by architects. . . . The reason these architects had to design their own interiors down to the lighting fixtures and doorknobs was obvious: the "interior decorators" of the time had no knowledge of modern architecture—or, if they had, they were generally out of sympathy with it.[6]

According to Florence, the typical office of the postwar period was usually comprised of "a diagonally placed desk, with a table set parallel behind it, a few chairs scattered around the edges of the room and a glassed-in storage bookcase. The table behind the desk generally became an unsightly storage receptacle."[7]

Knoll Associates set out to remedy this situation by implementing space planning. They began an individual analysis of each client's requirements including space, furniture, equipment, color, fabrics, art, graphics, and accessory items (see C7). This was arrived at through a series of interviews with both executives and clerical staff, designed to evaluate a client's true needs. Today, this is a standard industry practice, but in the mid-1940s it was revolutionary.

Florence had very definite ideas about the role of space planning. "Because of the high cost of building, every square inch of space must count. . . . The object is not to make rooms smaller simply to reduce the cost, but to make them the size they reasonably should be to fulfill their function."[8]

To illustrate their expertise at space planning, the Knolls's own offices became their best sales tool. Hans's private office was only 12 × 12 feet but so effectively planned that it enlightened many executives to the ways of effective use of space. Florence believed strongly that an office should reflect the personality of its occupant. Speaking of Hans's office she said, "His office was a radical departure from the vapid greens that were then usual—light teak furniture, white walls except for the one behind his desk, which was matte black, and natural Indian silk curtains which set off his blonde hair and ruddy complexion."[9]

The Planning Unit was responsible for a multitude of projects including residences, executive offices, research centers, and restaurants. Perhaps its most memorable project was the design of the CBS offices at their Sixth Avenue building under the architectural direction of Eero Saarinen (Plates 87–91). Originally, the project was to be totally Saarinen's, but his sudden death required Florence to come out of retirement to do the interiors. The project was completed in 1964.

As time progressed, Florence became Knoll's official "tastemaker." Murray Rothenberg remarked:

> Everything was controlled by Mrs. Knoll. Everything, everything the public saw—letterhead, business cards, stationery, graphics—it doesn't matter. She saw it and she approved and that maintained a very high level all the way through. In other words, she didn't have good design and lousy stationery, if you know what I mean.[10]

Florence was a perfectionist when it came to design, trying things dozens of times, having prototypes made again and again before a design measured up to her standards. Bob Longwell, quality-control manager for fifteen years said:

> Having worked with Shu, I knew what a stickler she was. She had the greatest design eye of anybody in the business. . . . After all was said and done and she finally agreed on it, it was letter perfect. It was absolutely perfect. She had that ability to critique a design, to tear it apart and put it back together again. . . . She was something else.[11]

In the early 1950s the Knolls put into production pieces designed by Mies van der Rohe in the '30s. Since Florence had studied with Mies at the Armour Institute (now the Illinois Institute of Technology), she was familiar with and an admirer of his work. As Knoll grew, it became apparent that furniture suitable for public spaces and lobby areas was needed. She turned to her former teacher, asking for the rights to produce his Barcelona chair and ottoman. The production model was an immediate success, so much so that it has become almost a cliche of every new entrance lobby. By 1951 Harry Bertoia's line of wire chairs was going into production, and 1957 saw Saarinen's Pedestal group reaching public attention (see C8). In 1968 Breuer's line was introduced.

As well as nurturing modern furniture design and production, Knoll was responsible for promoting textiles. In 1947 they opened a Knoll showroom on East 65th Street in New York, solely devoted to textiles, and announced the inception of a Knoll Textiles Division directed by Arundell Clarke. Their textile line included men's suiting fabrics, which Florence had been using as upholstery fabric through the Planning Unit, having despaired of the quality of available upholstery materials.

Many innovations came out of the Knoll Textiles Division that had an industry-wide impact, including the blending of handweaving crafts with machine looms. Largely responsible for this were Marianne Strengell and Evelyn Hill, hired as consultants to the Knoll Textiles Division. They provided original designs and worked to solve technical problems in developing textiles durable enough for the long, hard wear of contract applications. Knoll also introduced prints and native cloths from the Philippines that became a Knoll trademark as wallcovering and furniture panels. As 1947 progressed, further innovations were to come from the textile showroom. Florence, in conjunction with Herbert Matter, invented the fabric "tree" and the fabric "wall" as presentation devices. These soon became industry standards. Also, fabric samples sandwiched between lightweight cardboard identifying tags—now an industry universal—were first conceived at Knoll (see C9).

Eszter Haraszty became director of Knoll Textiles in 1949, a position in which she remained until 1955. A Hungarian immigrant, she had been living with the Breuers when Knoll discovered her, and she was to have a marked effect on contemporary fabrics and the use of color. She introduced the Knoll stripe, the first print used by Breuer (now in the Museum of Modern Art design collection), and "Transportation Cloth," which she described as "the first industrial fabric, the first one that stood all the tests. It was used widely by Detroit . . . the first pure linen in the American (industrial) market. It was my greatest design success."[12] Eszter also introduced the combination of orange and pink.

Knoll Nylon Homespun soon followed. It was discovered almost accidentally by Eszter's assistant, Suzanne Huguenin (later the head of Knoll Textiles from 1955 to 1964), when a Swiss woman came in with a small experimental sample she had been working on. According to Huguenin, "it exploded. . . . That was the most exciting fabric that had come on the market for years."[13]

Florence Knoll attributes Knoll's far-reaching and influential success to its organization—all the products and creative talents necessary for the solution of an interior design problem were accumulated in one place—but Knoll's attention to proportion and quality, drive for perfection, and dedication to the highest principles of design must surely have played a major role.

More than collecting designers, the Knolls began a design dynasty. Florence Knoll and associate designers were collectively awarded an overwhelming number of honors. Individually, Florence received three Good Design Awards from the Museum of Modern Art, a First Award from the American Institute of Decorators, and a Gold Medal from the American Institute of Architects, in addition to many others. Knoll's associates also distinguished themselves in the field. Marcel Breuer was the first architect to have a one-man show of his work at the Museum of Modern Art. The Museum of Modern Art produced an exhibit dedicated solely to the furniture and designs of Ludwig Mies van der Rohe, as well as to the early collaborative work of Eero Saarinen and Charles Eames (although Eames's designs were produced by Herman Miller).

In 1955 Hans was killed when a runaway truck smashed into his car while he was visiting a subsidiary company in Havana, Cuba. Surviving him were Florence and two children from a former marriage. Florence took over the presidency of Knoll. With Hans's death, people assumed the company would liquidate, but for two years previous to his death, Hans had been making plans to transform the company from an individually operated base into a solid organization operated by a well-trained staff. Knoll continued, although it underwent some changes.

In 1958 Florence married Harry Bassett, a Florida banker, and in 1959 she sold her interests in Knoll to Art Metal, a large manufacturer of office furniture. In 1960 she retired from her position as president and became a consultant, retiring entirely from the company in 1965. Art Metal was bought by Walter E. Heller International Corporation of Chicago in 1968, and Knoll was part of the package. In 1977 Knoll was purchased by Stephen C. Swid and Marshall S. Cogan under the name of General Felt Industries. Both Swid and Cogan had an active interest in the arts and set about to restore some of the personal involvement and vitality that had been lost at Knoll during the late '60s and early '70s. Swid and Cogan wanted to achieve an "explosion of creative energy." A 1979 issue of *Industrial Design* magazine commented that since Swid and Cogan's ownership, Knoll had created twenty new design jobs and tripled its staff. Today, Knoll continues in its tradition of quality and in searching out the creative talents of new designers, in keeping with the original concepts set down by Hans and Florence Knoll.

Lewis Butler, who was one of the first to work at the Planning Unit, said of Hans: "He felt, by combining the professional and manufacturing facilities, he could develop a group that could teach the profession what constituted good furniture on contract deals." Of Florence he said: "She was a driving force, extremely creative. She could target in on one thing, whether it be fabric, catalogues, or furniture development. She had a strong, basic design philosophy."[14]

Of the Knolls's many contributions to interior design, their most important was their ability to seek out and nurture creative talent. They provided a forum for avant-garde ideas and, through their business acumen, were able to successfully merge profit-making with creativity. In so doing, they enlarged the scope of the interior design profession immeasurably.

HANS AND FLORENCE KNOLL

1914	Hans Knoll born
1917	Florence Schust Knoll born
1937–38	Hans G. Knoll Furniture Company established in New York
1941–42	First Knoll chair produced—a Jens Risom design
1942	First Knoll catalog produced
1943	Hans Knoll and Florence Schust formed business partnership as Knoll Associates
1946	Hans Knoll married Florence Schust
1947–65	Production of Eero Saarinen's Grasshopper chair
1947	Knoll Textiles Division showroom opened in New York
1948	Knoll produced the Barcelona chair and ottoman
1949–55	Eszter Harastzy was director of Knoll Textiles
1950	Harry Bertoia joined Knoll; Diamond chair was introduced
1950	Knoll marketed the Hardoy chair
1951	Knoll International expanded to France and Germany
1954	Florence Knoll won A.I.D. First International Design Award
1954	Isamu Noguchi rocking stool introduced
1954–57	Firm designed the interiors of Connecticut General Life Insurance Company, Hartford, Connecticut
1955	Hans Knoll killed in automobile accident; Florence Knoll took over presidency of company
1957	Introduction of Eero Saarinen's Pedestal group
1958	Florence Knoll married Harry Bassett
1959	Knoll International sold to Art Metal
1960	Florence Knoll retired from presidency
1964–65	Interiors of CBS Headquarters in New York
1965	Florence Knoll Bassett retired
1968	Introduction of Breuer line
1977	Knoll International purchased by General Felt Industries
1979	Knoll Textiles became a separate division of Knoll International

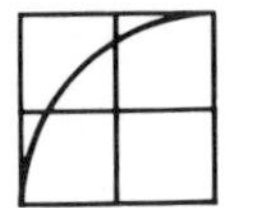

Gilbert Rohde

Gilbert Rohde is not technically a postwar designer, since the main body of his work was done in the '20s and '30s. Yet, while his furniture designs never became particularly popular with the public, he had a profound influence on those who were subsequently to become the prominent American designers of the postwar period, including Eames, Saarinen, and Nelson. Gilbert Rohde's contribution was that of a catalyst, a pathfinder who prepared the way and promoted modern design as a major feature of the furniture industry.

Rohde's designs immediately broke with the furniture industry's inclination to rely on historical reproductions as the basis for furniture production. In the summer of 1930 Rohde changed the course of the Herman Miller Furniture Company, and in so doing, changed the course of furniture design in the United States.

Like many other designers, Rohde's breakthrough into design consciousness came during his 1927 visit to Europe, where he was exposed to innovative design developments close up. He had formed a close personal relationship with Gladys Vorsanger, who encouraged him to go to Paris, and he married her there during the summer of 1927. On returning to New York, Rohde produced some custom work for Norman Lee's penthouse on Sheridan Square in New York City. These early works were to form the basis for his later space-saving furniture designed for mass production.

Nineteen thirty found Rohde in Grand Rapids, Michigan, then the furniture manufacturing capital of the United States, where he had taken his designs in the hopes of selling his modern furniture concepts to some of the big companies. He had few takers, but the one small company that did listen to him was Herman Miller. The Miller company was not Rohde's first choice, but nobody else would give him credence. Rohde's track record in furniture design was less than exemplary, as his designs for other companies had all ended in closeouts. But Jimmy Eppinger, a Herman Miller salesman during that period noted:

> All of the art moderne designs in the late twenties were closeouts. Publicists for the fashion industry and people like that would go to Europe on department store business assignments and come back with modern fashions in furniture. But the trouble was that nobody believed in contemporary furniture. The forms were unacceptable and they were not accepted.[1]

Rohde's background was not that of an architect, unlike many prominent furniture designers of the time. He was trained in advertising and display illustration. Rohde was born in New York City on June 1, 1894. His father, Max Rohde, was a cabinetmaker who had come from East Prussia. After his father's death in 1901, Rohde was raised by his mother and an aunt. He attended schools in New York, including the Art Students League and the Grand Central School of Art. Following graduation, he worked in the early 1920s as a political cartoonist, a stringer for New York newspapers including the *Bronx News*, a drama and music critic, an illustrator, a copywriter, and a professional photographer. His background gave him a strong grounding in the selling, merchandising, and advertising techniques that were to play an important role in the marketing of his later designs and were to lay the foundation for Herman Miller's innovative sales approach.

In the late '20s Rohde was among the vanguard of industrial designers in the United States, on a par with Walter Teague and Raymond Loewy. In 1929 he opened his own industrial design office, where he introduced new merchandise and acted as a consultant to manufacturers such as General Electric, Rohm and Haas, Kroehler Manufacturing, Simmons, the Hudson Motor Car Company, and the Herman Miller Furniture Company.

Rohde came into his own in the '30s, during which time he began his association with the Miller company and received considerable exposure and recognition for his designs. In 1933 he designed the interiors of a house in the "Design for Living" exhibit at the Chicago World's Fair Century of Progress exhibition. He also served on the committee of architects and designers for the New York World's Fair of 1939. During this period his work was shown frequently in publications such as *Architectural Forum*, and in 1934 his work was exhibited by the Metropolitan Museum of Art at a show of contemporary American art. From 1936 to 1938 he directed the Design Laboratory, an industrial art school in New York established under the Federal Arts Projects of the WPA, and from 1939 to 1943 he directed the Industrial Design Department of the School of Architecture at New York University. He was also a founding member of the Society of Industrial Engineers and a member of the American Designers Institute.

When Rohde first came to Herman Miller he had little hope of selling his ideas based on his background. He had no training in furniture design and little to sell but concepts, so he promoted himself as a "student of living," claiming, "I know how people live and I know how they are going to live. Modern living calls for smaller houses with lower ceilings and this in turn calls for a different kind of furniture."[2] He was able to convince D.J. De Pree, founder of the Herman Miller Company, that he could indeed design such modern furniture for a fee of $1,000 per group. At that time, Miller was hiring the most expensive furniture designers of the time for a comparatively small fee of between $100 to $300 per group, for which the designer not only made detailed working drawings but also chose the materials and supervised the production process. After some negotiating, Rohde finally agreed on a 3 percent royalty arrangement because Miller was such a small company that they had no cash available to pay his requested figure.

Rohde's arrival at Miller was both providential and prophetic, for it heralded the arrival of a new force in design, changing Miller from an obscure company to a giant commanding respect in the international design community. When Rohde came to Miller, the company's staple product was an expensive, highly ornate, seven-piece bedroom suite. Rohde responded with a design consisting of four basic large pieces, eliminating turned posts and ornament, reducing the amount of wood, and relying heavily on plastics.

De Pree was not quite ready for Rohde's approach. He protested that the designs were too plain and needed surface ornament. Rohde responded that Herman Miller was not obligated to produce his designs, but that if they did then they must produce them exactly and without change. Rohde won.

De Pree, a devoutly religious man said:

> I came to see that the starting point of our design had been immoral. It was immoral chiefly in its pretense, but that pretense hid other immoralities: moldings and carvings were used to conceal sins of sloppy workmanship, for instance. With his simplicity, Rohde had taken away our means of covering up. We had to learn new manufacturing techniques, such as how to make mitered joints in a very precise way.[3]

Rohde continued in his "student of living" philosophy by convincing DePree that Herman Miller was not just making furniture but providing a way of life, and that in order to succeed with the designs they must get closer to the user and more fully understand consumer requirements.

De Pree felt that Rohde introduced the idea of modern storage spaces that save space and increase storage capacity. De Pree also credited Rohde with inventing the sectional sofa and with promoting the concept of modular furniture. Rohde's Executive Office group (EOG) (Plates 102, 103) had fifteen components, out of which four hundred combinations could be made.

Rohde's ideas were outrageously innovative for their time and therefore very hard to sell to a public whose design awareness was still in the nineteenth century. As a result, Rohde was reluctant to burden the Miller company with his EOG line, since they were having enough trouble trying to promote his residential line. However, after unsuccessful attempts at selling the samples to other manufacturers, the Miller company finally became the producer of Rohde's EOG line.

When Rohde approached Miller, he had no audience and needed Miller's backing. Fortunately for Rohde, Miller had no line and needed Rohde. Pushed to the wall, the normally conservative De Pree was willing to take a gamble. To play it safe, De Pree also hired Freda Diamond to design a traditional line for the company, just in case Rohde's designs failed. Diamond reworked traditional designs such as Chippendale into more contemporary versions, while retaining the safeness of the familiar. Later, she branched out by designing a Shaker line for Herman Miller that was more in keeping with the modern concepts of Rohde's designs.

Rohde's arrival at Miller brought about major changes in the company. Prior to Rohde, Miller had only made case goods. Rohde introduced seating, but since the company had no experience in manufacturing upholstery or metal articles, everything that was not wood was farmed out at first.

It was during 1934 that Herman Miller, under Rohde's guidance, instituted an important principle by establishing innovative merchandising techniques to sell its new lines of Rohde's designs. Calling on his background in marketing and promotion, Rohde suggested that salesmen receive training in how to sell the new furniture by being taught to understand the concepts on which it was based and its functional qualities. Prior to that, Miller's salesmen were typical of the time—more concerned with "friendly persuasion" than in understanding the product they were trying to sell. The new sales techniques were successful, but the salesmen resisted using them, since it meant they actually had to learn about the lines, and the buying public was hard to sell because the designs were so new, so different, that the consumer tended to shy away.

Rohde's greatest contribution to the Herman Miller line was his sectional modular furniture, a concept which up to that point was new to the American furniture industry and had never been available to a large market. After moderate success with sectional pieces, Rohde introduced his living-dining-sleeping group, which permitted interchangeable pieces to be used in any room of the house. Prior to this, of course, the furniture industry had been keyed into furniture suites specifically manufactured for living rooms, bedrooms, and so on, and only intended for use in the rooms for which they had been specifically produced.

Rohde then made his mark on commercial design with the introduction of his Executive Office group. In taking on that project, Herman Miller was the first manufacturer of residential furniture to move into the area of office and commercial design.

Simultaneous with his arrangement with the Miller company, Rohde contracted with the Troy Sunshade Company of Troy, Ohio to produce his designs for tubular-steel outdoor furniture. At the same time, while most of Rohde's major designs were manufactured by Miller, the Heywood-Wakefield Company of Gardner, Massachusetts produced one of his better known and most commercially successful chairs—his side chair, created in 1930 and heavily inspired by the work of Alvar Aalto.

This chair, originally created as one of a pair (one of which is now in the collection of the Metropolitan Museum of Art), represented Rohde's experimentation with laminated and bentwood furniture for mass production. It was based on Rohde's belief that furniture for the modern consumer should be both excellently designed and inexpensive enough to be readily available to the average buyer. The chair was made of walnut with rose-colored vinyl upholstery and vinyl gimp held in place by brass tacks. The unified back/seat shell was of a single piece of wood, separate from the bent laminated wood supports. As was the case with Rohde's other modular and sectional designs, the chair was conceived as a multipurpose piece for use in any room of the house.

Rohde made his design philosophy known in an early (1933) written statement that accompanied an exhibit of his work:

> Modern furniture is our expression of the ancient and simple desire to make beautiful and useful things, suited to their purpose and to the materials and tools available. Great changes have come about in the last two generations. The development of electricity, power, air-travel, rapid transit, the automobile, motion picture, the radio, have all resulted in changed ways of living. The apartment house has come; rooms are fewer and smaller. The modern creative artist tries first to satisfy our living needs. Often the same room must serve two purposes, so he designs furniture to meet these needs. We find that by careful designing, chairs can be made just as comfortable as the huge clumsy ones we formerly had. There is no excuse for a "modern" chair not being as comfortable as an older chair of the same type. If chairs are low, it is not because sitting near the floor has anything to do with the idea of modern chairs.
>
> You will notice . . . that in every case the furniture is shown against ordinary simple backgrounds such as are found in the interior of the average home. Another reason that "Art Moderne" came to an early end was that it was shown against elaborate and costly architectural backgrounds, and people naturally thought they had to build a new home to use it. We need no special architecture whatever in order to use modern furniture. A perfectly plain wall is best, which is just what is found in the average apartment.
>
> The walls can be plain, painted, or be covered with wallpaper of simple modern designs. Draperies and upholstery material can be plain or have simple patterns: the wallpaper and textiles should, of course, never have patterns that are strongly characteristic of other periods such as Jacobean or Renaissance. Primitive patterns, whether of French, Swedish, Central European, or American Indian origin are very useful in modern decoration on account of their simplicity.[4]

Rohde's greatest design successes came during the depression years, but with World War II and the accompanying depletion of materials and lack of opportunity to introduce new lines, Rohde's commissions soon shrank. Suddenly, the war took prominence in the headlines, and publicity for furniture design was scant. Much of his staff was drafted or laid off due to the decline of business, and Rohde was forced to take over the running of his office almost single-handedly.

When he died on June 16, 1944, a new wave of designers had already begun to replace him. Eames and Saarinen had won the Organic Design competition at the Museum of Modern Art, and Nelson was waiting in the wings, soon to become Rohde's successor at Miller. By the time the war ended, people were anxious to forget it and all of its associations. In doing so, it seems they also forgot Gilbert Rohde. Nevertheless, his contribution to the furniture industry was indelible.

GILBERT ROHDE

1894	Born, June 1, in New York City
1927	Married Gladys Vorsanger in Paris
1929	Opened own industrial design office, New York
1930	Began association with Herman Miller Furniture Company; chair produced by Heywood-Wakefield Company

1933 Exhibited at "Design for Living," Chicago World's Fair
1934 Work exhibited at Metropolitan Museum of Art, New York
1936–38 Director of Design Laboratory, New York
1939–43 Director of Industrial Design Department, School of Architecture, New York University
1942 Introduced Executive Office Group (EOG)
1944 Died, June 14

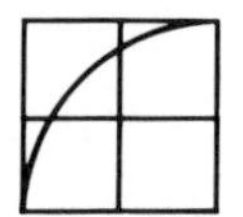

Isamu Noguchi

Like Harry Bertoia, Isamu Noguchi brought the sculptor's art to postwar furniture design, creating his legendary Noguchi table (Plate 105) for the Herman Miller Company as well as original lighting concepts and furniture for Knoll. Noguchi's link to the era is perhaps even more significant than that of Bertoia, because he epitomized the blend of East and West that was represented in so much of postwar design, not only through his work but in his physical being as well. Noguchi typifies the tortured artist—a man trapped between two cultures, searching for a means of communication and consumed with a need to create that often puts him at odds with society. Half Japanese, half American, he spent a childhood split between the two countries—a split that contributed to lifelong internal conflicts.

In 1906, at the age of two, Noguchi was taken by his mother from America to Japan. His father, Yonejiro Noguchi, was a poet and professor of English at Keiō University. He wrote many books in English on Japanese art—on Sesshu, the Shosoin, Korin, Hiroshige, Hokusai, Saraku, Utamaro, and the Ukiyoe primitives. Of him Noguchi said, "He was like a bridge between Japan and the West but, like others, he was swept up in the nationalism of the war."[1]

Isamu's mother was Leonie Gilmour, an American of Irish descent. As a young man, Isamu went by the name of Isamu Gilmour, adopting the name Noguchi only after he had decided on sculpture as a career.

As a child, Noguchi was extremely dependent on his mother, a fact that eventually led her to send him back to the United States to enter a boys' school—a move that she hoped would help him assert his independence. This move occurred at the critical age of thirteen, a time when Noguchi had ". . . become a typical Japanese boy, knowledgeable in the ways of nature; such as how to skin the young willow to make whistles, or where to find eels."[2]

Noguchi said goodbye to his mother and traveled to Indiana, where he attended summer camp at Interlaken School on Silver Lake, a school where boys "learned by doing." The war intervened, however, and the school did not open that fall as planned. Instead, it was turned into a motor truck training camp. Noguchi entered public school in the town of Rolling Prairie, and during this period he led a wild existence. No one was in charge of him. He camped out in the deserted faculty buildings in the company of two caretakers. Each morning at four o'clock, Noguchi rode out on a horse to fetch the mail and food, returning in time to make breakfast.

The following summer, Dr. Edward A. Rumley, founder of the Interlaken School, took him under his wing and brought him to board with the family of Dr. Samuel Mack in LaPorte, Indiana, where he lived for the next three years until graduating from high school. These were difficult years for Noguchi. In addition to the usual conflicts of adolescence, he constantly fought the strong feelings of abandonment that were beginning to permeate his life. He constantly worried about his mother in Japan and developed a loathing for his father.

When he finished high school, Dr. Rumley asked him what he wanted to do. Noguchi replied without hesitation that he wanted to be an artist, although the answer surprised him. Since coming to America, art had been far removed from his life, and he did not show any particular aptitude for it at the time. Further, he had gone out of his way to avoid art because it reminded him of his father who was a poet, and therefore, in Noguchi's opinion, an artist. Yet as Noguchi stated, "My first instinctual decision was to become an artist."[3]

During this time, when Noguchi's inner conflicts were beginning to turn into a search for communication through art, Dr. Rumley had other ideas and guided Noguchi into medicine, but he also arranged for him to apprentice with his friend, sculptor Gutzon Borglum in Connecticut. Borglum's plan was either to carve the granite of Stone Mountain in Georgia into Confederate soldiers or, if that failed, to blast the faces of various ex-presidents into Mount Rushmore, North Dakota. Noguchi's only chance at sculpture turned out to be a head of Lincoln, but in working with Borglum, he had the opportunity to meet some Italian plaster casters who taught him casting. Borglum had little faith in Noguchi's chances of becoming a sculptor and advised him to enter medical school instead. In January 1923 Noguchi entered Columbia University. His tuition was paid by Dr. Rumley, but he worked at night in a restaurant to meet other expenses.

In the mid 1920s Noguchi's mother returned to America, settling in New York where she planned to open a small business, importing goods from Japan. Noguchi returned to live with his mother at a time when he seemed to be struggling simultaneously toward and against becoming a sculptor. He also found that his attachment to his mother had been broken, that his resentment at being abandoned was by far the stronger feeling. It was at this point that he adopted the name of Noguchi, giving up the name Isamu Gilmour.

Noguchi's close attachment to his mother never

returned. The more she tried to make up for lost time by mothering him, the more he resented her and turned away from her attentions. By this time, Noguchi had become thoroughly Americanized; there was no hint of Japan about him. His mother was well aware of the conflicts Noguchi was experiencing, not only about his parentage, but about his need to become an artist rather than a doctor.

One evening, she casually mentioned to him that she had noticed the Leonardo da Vinci Art School in a converted church near their apartment. She suggested that Noguchi take a few classes there. Noguchi took her advice, reluctantly at first, and stopped in to see the school director, pretending that he was not really interested in sculpture at all. He was persuaded to make a copy of a plaster foot as an entrance examination and was offered a full scholarship. He enrolled in evening classes but soon found that his schedule of attending university, working at the restaurant, and taking art classes was just too much. Something had to give. Fortunately, the school director offered Noguchi a job as a sculptor, which enabled him to give up his restaurant job. "How could I resist?" Noguchi said. "I became a sculptor, even against my will. I shall always be grateful to him and the Italian community in New York."[4]

Noguchi's philosophy of sculpture, later to be recognized in his furniture designs, was made apparent in a statement of application for the Guggenheim Fellowship:

> It is my desire to view nature through nature's eyes and to ignore man as an object for special veneration. There must be unthought of heights of beauty to which sculpture may be raised by this reversal of attitude. . . . Indeed, a fine balance of spirit with matter can only concur (sic) when the artist has so thoroughly submerged himself in the study of the unity of nature as to truly become once more a part of nature—a part of the very earth, thus to view the inner surfaces and the life elements. . . . My father, Yone Noguchi, is Japanese and has long been known as an interpreter of the East to the West, through poetry. I wish to do the same with sculpture."[5]

This philosophy is made visible in the Noguchi table produced by Herman Miller (see C11 and Plate 105). Its organically shaped plate-glass top reveals the sculptural base, which strongly resembles jointed bones. When asked to draw a picture of the Noguchi table for a recent issue of *Reference Points*, a catalog of early designs now being reproduced by Herman Miller, Masami Hirokawa said:

> When I opened the box and unpacked it, and saw how this table was made, it reminded me of how long ago it was first produced (1947). Our thought processes have changed a lot since then. Our products, and maybe even our people, are more "processed." That is, they are not as open to feeling.[6]

Being a man of intense feelings, Noguchi was not afraid to explore his emotions through either his sculpture or his industrial designs. Noguchi received the Guggenheim Fellowship and in 1927 began a three-year period of work and study in Paris and the Orient. He experimented with various techniques and materials that were to play a major role in his furniture and lighting designs. Of this period, Noguchi wrote:

> With the work I was doing in sheet metals, I was interested in getting a certain plasticity of form, like something alive—and I wanted it to imply a certain imminent motion. Joints, if possible, were never fixed (no welding) but grooved, held by gravity or tension. . . . From sheet metal things in balance to hanging things in tension and balance was only a step. I made an arrangement in "discontinuous" tension and compression. Two pieces floating in air, not touching, but balanced in tension. A concept I had not heard of and so considered an invention. What were my influences? The Russian constructivists; and Picasso, of course, who had by then made some compositions of metal rod and wire. Behind may have been childhood memories of paper use in Japan. . . . Everything was sculpture. Any material, any idea without hindrance born into space, I considered sculpture. I worked with driftwood, bones, paper, strings, cloth, shell, wire, wood, and plastics; magnesite, which I had learned to use at the World's Fair.[7]

Unfortunately for Noguchi, things did not go as smoothly as he had hoped. His third-year fellowship was denied, and he was forced to return from France to the grim realities of trying to earn a living in New York. A show of his small pieces at Eugene Shoen's gallery was critically acclaimed in *The New York Times*, but nothing sold. Noguchi was forced to earn his bread and butter by doing small portrait busts on a commission basis. Through this he made many valuable contacts, including Buckminster Fuller and Martha Graham. By the following spring, Noguchi had accumulated enough funds to continue his plan and return to the Orient and self-discovery.

Once again, though, he was to be disappointed. Just before his arrival in Japan he received an unpleasant surprise from his father—a letter asking that he not use the name of Noguchi when he came to Japan. He was crushed, and instead of going directly to Japan he spent eight months in Peking. Just as his money was about to run out, he decided to tackle

Japan. The strained relationship between Noguchi and his father was worsened by the trip. While his father was polite, he remained firmly distant. Noguchi received some help from his uncle, but the times cannot have been easy for him. He moved into the cottage of a ditchdigger in Higashiyama and devoted his time to making terracottas and to discovering the beauty of gardens and the Japanese countryside. He has said that "I have since thought of my lonely self-incarceration then, and my close embrace of the earth, as a seeking after identity with some primal matter beyond personalities and possessions. In my work I wanted something irreducible, an absence of the gimmicky and clever."[8]

On returning to New York in 1932, he renewed his friendships with Buckminster Fuller and Martha Graham, both of whom Noguchi credits with being of major importance in his intellectual and artistic development. He found Fuller's ideas refreshing and marveled at the way Fuller influenced him while leaving him free to seek out his own course. Martha Graham was to give him the opportunity to express himself in set design.

During 1932 Noguchi exhibited his abstract aluminum sculpture, named "Miss Expanding Universe" by Buckminster Fuller, at the Reinhardt Gallery in New York. The sculpture, which is thirty inches long, is now in the collection of the Toledo Museum of Art. At this time Noguchi also came into contact with Leo Theremin, who had invented an electronic musical instrument whose tone and pitch are controlled by moving one's hands through the air in varying distances from two projecting antennae. Noguchi tried to persuade Theremin to produce a new form of music with his instrument, based on the Japanese Gagaku records in Noguchi's collection. Noguchi suggested that Theremin rods be placed at different points on the stage to become activated as a dancer moved. The dancer he had in mind was Martha Graham, but nothing came of his idea. Noguchi was searching out new ways of expressing himself. He said, "I wanted other means of communication—to find a way of sculpture that was humanly meaningful without being realistic, at once abstract and socially relevant. I was not conscious of the terms 'applied design' or 'industrial design.' My thoughts were born in despair, seeking stars in the night."[9]

Exhibits of his work followed but very few sales. Then, in 1935, Martha Graham asked Noguchi to do his first stage set for *Frontier*. Of this opportunity he wrote:

> It was for me the genesis of an idea—to wed the total void of theater space to form and action. A rope, running from the two top corners of the proscenium to the floor rear center of the stage, bisected the three-dimensional void of stage space. This seemed to throw the entire volume of air straight over the heads of the audience. At the rear convergence was a small section of log fence, to start from and return to. The white ropes created a curious ennobling—of an outburst into space and, at the same time, of the public's inrush toward infinity. This set was the point of departure for all my subsequent theater work: space became a volume to be dealt with sculpturally.[10]

Noguchi's excursions into set design led him from his first experience with the theater in 1926—making papier-mâché masks for the Japanese dancer, Michio Ito—through his friendship with Martha Graham and his first set for *Frontier*, to a long association with the theater. In 1939, *Chronicle* was produced; in 1940, *El Penitente*. In 1944 he began a major series of collaborations with Martha Graham, including *Appalachian Spring*, *Herodiade*, and *Imagined Wing*. Others soon followed:

1946 *Dark Meadow* (Music: Carlos Chavez)
Cave of the Heart (Music: Samuel Barber)
1947 *Errand into the Maze* (Music: Gian Carlo Menotti)
Night Journey (Music: William Schuman)
1948 *Diversion of Angels* (Music: Norman Dello Joio)
1950 *Judith* (Music: William Schuman)
1953 *Voyage* (Music: William Schuman)
1955 *Seraphic Dialogue* (Music: Norman Dello Joio)
1958 *Embattled Garden* (Music: Carlos Surinach)
Clytemnestra (Music: Halim El Dabh)
1960 *Acrobats of God* (Music: Carlos Surinach)
Alcestis (Music: Vivian Fine)
1962 *Phaedra* (Music: Robert Starer)
1963 *Circe* (Music: Alan Hovhannes)
1966 *Cortege of Eagles* (Music: Eugene Lester)

Altogether, Noguchi did nearly twenty sets for Martha Graham, and even today, some are still presented, including his props and jewelry.

In the depression years, Noguchi tried to get a commission to work for the WPA (Works Progress Administration), but the artist and society were in conflict. He sculpted a head of the wife of the New York director of the Art Section, at her request. The sculpture was very unflattering and Noguchi earned her hatred and lost himself a job with the WPA in the process. He tried several times to work for the WPA but was consistently turned down as being too successful to qualify. He considered this refusal as further proof of the discrimination against him. He appealed to the WPA, explaining that he did not want to be forced into continually sculpting portrait heads to make a living; he wanted to create a ground sculpture, covering the entire triangle in front of Newark Airport, to be seen from the air. His proposal was laughed at. In total despair, Noguchi left New York for Hollywood, where he earned enough money doing portrait heads to make an exploratory trip to Mexico. He said of this trip: "How different was Mexico! Here I suddenly no longer felt estranged as an artist; artists were useful people, a part of the community."[11]

It was in Mexico that Noguchi was given the opportunity and the freedom to do his first major work, a wall in the Indian Market of Abelardo Rodriguez. Entitled *History Mexico*, it was made of colored cement on carved brick, two meters high and twenty-two meters long. He was paid by the meter and ended up receiving only half of the money ($88.00) owed him by the Mexican government. Of the experience, Noguchi noted that while the Guggenheim Foundation had loaned him only $600 for his trip, and he had to sell his car to get back, he never regretted having had the opportunity of executing what was for him "a real attempt at a direct communication through sculpture with no ulterior or money-making motive."[12]

Noguchi was depressed at returning to New York. His means of survival was, again, sculpting portrait heads. To keep himself going artistically, he entered every competition that came along. He was willing to do anything to get out of his rut, to find the means to practice his art without having to sell his work. He had come to think of commercial art as less contaminated than one that appealed to vanity. In 1937 he produced a strictly industrial design called the "Radio Nurse," an intercom device that would allow parents to keep tabs on the nursery, as a precaution against kidnapping (a matter of great concern at the time, as a result of the Lindbergh case). The "Radio Nurse" was produced by the Zenith Radio Company. Jean Michel Frank, the French furniture designer, suggested that Noguchi design furniture for him, as artist Giacometti was doing. Following up Frank's idea, Noguchi designed a nightclub in a church for which he got Arshile Gorky and Misha Resnikoff to design large murals.

In 1938 Noguchi's luck began to change. He finally won a competition—a commission to do the bas-relief over the entrance of the new Associated Press Building in Rockefeller Plaza—nine tons of stainless steel, the largest casting of its kind. Then came the shock of Pearl Harbor in 1941. Noguchi was suddenly thrust into the position of being a stranger in a strange land:

> With a flash I realized I was not just American, but Nisei. A Japanese-American. . . . I sought out those of us who were sympathetic and with whom I thought I could work to counteract the bigoted hysteria that soon appeared in the press. I organized a group called "Nisei Writers and Artists for Democracy." All to no avail.[13]

However, the notoriety he received with his group brought him to the attention of Frank Lloyd Wright, who offered him the use of Taliesin West in Arizona if he could run it with twenty or so talented Nisei.

Eventually, the situation returned to a more even keel. Noguchi said, "The deep depression that comes with living under a cloud of suspicion, which we as Nisei experienced, lifted, and was followed by tranquility. I was finally free of causes and disillusioned with mutuality. I resolved henceforth to be an artist only."[14]

In addition to the Noguchi table, Noguchi is also noted for his lighting designs. He had begun toying with the idea of light sculptures in the early '30s, and by the early '40s he was producing his series of Lunar light sculptures composed of magnesite, cork, and other media, all of which were illuminated from within. Knoll produced a small version, and imitations were soon being manufactured. Noguchi had neglected to patent his invention, so he had no recourse. He was most disturbed by the bastardization of his designs saying,

> Plagiarism, of which I have been a constant victim, is not as painful when a thing is copied outright as when it is distorted and vulgarized in an attempt to disguise the theft.
>
> One day, somebody told me of a sign in a window, "Noguchi-type lamps." The manufacturer, to whom I complained, said he had "Calder-type" and "Moore-type" lamps as well. If I didn't like mine, why didn't I design him one? When I devised what I thought was a contribution, all he could say was, "Sorry, that's not a Noguchi-type lamp."[15]

Theft of Noguchi's ideas was rampant in other areas of his work as well. He went to Hawaii in 1939 to do an advertisement with Georgia O'Keeffe and Pierre Toy. As a result of this, he met Robsjohn Gibbings, the furniture designer, who asked him to do a coffee table. (Noguchi had previously designed a table for Conger Goodyear.) Noguchi set out to design a small model in plastic and heard no further before he went west. He was surprised, to say the least, when he saw his design for the table published as a Gibbings advertisement. When Noguchi complained, Gibbings told him that anybody could make a three-legged table. Noguchi would not be beaten. He said, "In revenge, I made my own variant of my own table, articulated as the Goodyear Table, but reduced to rudiments. It illustrated an article by George Nelson called 'How to Make a Table.' This is the coffee table that was later sold in such quantity by the Herman Miller Furniture Company."[16]

In 1944 Noguchi designed a lighting fixture for his sister, consisting of three legs with a cylinder around them. Noguchi said, "Hans [Knoll] decided he would like to make it and sell it. It came to nothing because everybody copied it."[16] He continued his work on light sculpture, in 1952 creating "akari," (the Japanese name Noguchi coined for his new light sculptures), which means both illumination and lightness—the illumination of lighting a space, the illumination of awareness, and lightness as opposed to weight. The akari lamps were based on traditional Japanese lantern designs of paper and bamboo, with a feeling for the quality and sensibility of light. When not in use they could be folded away; in use they could be pinned to a wall, clipped to a cord, or left on a surface such as a table or floor. Noguchi's akari lighting-fixture concepts have been so freely copied that we now tend to think of them as generic, often forgetting to credit their inventor. Nineteen fifty-two was also the year Noguchi married Japanese actress Yoshiko (Shirley) Yamaguchi—a marriage that ended in divorce in 1955.

In addition to his industrial designs, Noguchi achieved international fame as a sculptor; his work graced numerous garden settings, playgrounds, and architectural applications. Tragically, however, Noguchi was seldom given credit for the art he created. His name went unmentioned in both the dedication of the Beinecke Rare Book Library at Yale University and that of the Chase Manhattan plaza, for example. Noguchi had been commissioned to do an abstract sculpture "garden" for the Beinecke library. He worked on the project from 1960 to 1964, creating a symbolic garden of white marble geometric shapes in a sunken court. He borrowed his ideas from the sand mounds often found in Japanese temples, but soon the image of the astronomical gardens of India intruded, as did the more formal paving patterns of Italy. Noguchi referred to the Beinecke sculpture as a "landscape of the imagination."

In the Chase Manhattan Bank plaza (1961–64), Noguchi created an environment of sparse, powerfully sculptural water-smoothed rocks that interacted with the curved, concentric lines of a mosaic pavement. The rocks are found objects, a concept rooted in Japanese tradition. The patterned pavement symbolizes the raked sand gardens of Japan. In the Chase Manhattan sculpture garden, Noguchi used rocks in a nontraditional way—he intended them to appear to burst forth from the ground and seem to levitate. In both the Beinecke garden and the Chase Manhattan plaza, Noguchi's name was certainly worth mentioning.

Isamu Noguchi, a bicultural man, spent much of his life trying to reconcile East and West within himself and in his work. Yet, as is often the case in art, it is perhaps the struggle itself that shaped the artist. Indeed, Noguchi recognized this in saying:

> My own contradictions, enhanced perhaps by my mixed parentage, are probably shared by most artists to some degree. We all look to the past and to the future to find ourselves. Here we find a hint that awakens us, there a path that someone like us once walked. I have been fortunate in the people I met at critical junctures who inspired my choices. Were they chance? After each bout with the world I find myself returning chastened and contented enough to seek, within the limits of a single sculpture, the world.[17]

ISAMU NOGUCHI

1904	Born, United States
1906–17	Lived in Japan
1918–26	Studied in the United States
1927	Received Guggenheim Fellowship
1933	Play Mountain project for New York Park Commission
1935	Designed sets for Martha Graham's *Frontier*
1937	Designed "Radio Nurse" for Zenith Radio Company
1938	Sculpture for Associated Press Building, Rockefeller Plaza, New York
1939	Designed playground equipment for New York Parks Commission
1939–66	Designed stage sets for theater
1941	Designed the Contoured Playground
1944	Knoll introduced lighting fixtures
1946	Work exhibited at Museum of Modern Art, New York
1947	Noguchi table introduced by Herman Miller Company
1951	Designed Reader's Digest Garden, Tokyo, Japan
1951–52	Project for Two Bridges, Hiroshima, Japan
1952	Project for Memorial to the Dead, Hiroshima; project for garden and ground floor of Lever Brothers Building, Park Avenue, New York (Architects: Skidmore, Owings & Merrill)

1952 Playground project for United Nations Headquarters, New York (model exhibited at Museum of Modern Art)

1956–57 Gardens for Connecticut General Insurance Company, Bloomfield Hills, Connecticut (Architects: Skidmore, Owings & Merrill)

1957 Ceiling and waterfall for 666 Fifth Avenue, New York (Architects: Carson and Lundin)

1956–58 Gardens for UNESCO, Paris (Architect: Marcel Breuer)

1960–61 Plaza for First National Bank, Fort Worth, Texas (Architects: Skidmore, Owings & Merrill)

1960–65 Playground for Riverside Drive Park, New York (Architect: Louis I. Kahn)

1961–62 Fountain for John Hancock Insurance Company, New Orleans (Architects: Skidmore, Owings & Merrill)

1961–64 Marble Garden, Beinecke Rare Book Library, Yale University (Architects: Skidmore, Owings & Merrill); garden for Chase Manhattan Bank Plaza, New York (Architects: Skidmore, Owings & Merrill)

1964 Gardens for headquarters of IBM, Armonk, New York (Architects: Skidmore, Owings & Merrill); study for the tomb of President Kennedy, Washington, D.C.

1965–66 Playground for Kodomo No Kuni (Children's Land), Tokyo, Japan; sculpture gardens for the National Museum, Jerusalem, Israel

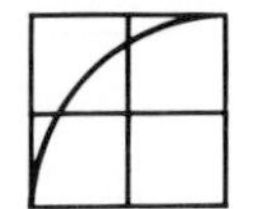

Arne Jacobsen

Arne Jacobsen was born in Copenhagen on January 11, 1902. Like Eero Saarinen, he first had aspirations tending toward the fine arts rather than architecture. He wanted to become a painter, like Saarinen showing an early talent for drawing. His father, Johan Jacobsen, a practical wholesale merchant, had other ideas, however, and influenced Arne to take up the study of architecture. Jacobsen enrolled at the Architectural College of the Academy of Arts, where he soon came under the influence of his teachers, Kay Fisker, Ivar Bentsen, and Kay Gottlob. Gottlob was of particular importance in Jacobsen's training because of the emphasis he placed on the study of architectural history and classicist art and because of the travel/study trips Gottlob organized, which gave Jacobsen an opportunity to study the art and architecture of France and Italy with a considerable amount of personal involvement.

In 1925 Jacobsen won the Silver Medal at the Paris World Exhibition, where he exhibited a book cover and a chair. During the same year, he paid a visit to the International Exhibition for Applied Arts in Paris, where he saw Le Corbusier's "Pavillion de l'Esprit Nouveau." Le Corbusier's work was far ahead of its time and quite a bit beyond Jacobsen's ability to comprehend. Still a student at that time, he had not yet gathered enough knowledge and expertise to appreciate it, but it nevertheless made an impact, as did the works of Mies van der Rohe and Gropius, to which he was exposed in Berlin during the period 1927–28.

While still a student at the Academy, Jacobsen had already worked in architectural offices with the likes of Thorkel Hjejle and Niels Rosenkjaer, who were well known for their designs of detached houses. Jacobsen's first independent work was exhibited while he was still a student at the Academy. In 1928, only one year after the completion of his studies, Jacobsen was awarded the Minor Gold Medal for the design of a museum to be built in Klampenborg Cottage Park in Copenhagen.

Jacobsen built himself a house at Gotfred Rodesvej, Ordrup, of conventional Danish building materials—brick and timber—in a cubic style, with whitewashed outer walls and flat roof. In 1929 he was awarded a First Prize in collaboration with Flemming Lassen in the Copenhagen Academic Association of Architects "House of the Future" competition. The house was circular in shape, of two stories, and even had the innovative touch of a helicopter landing pad on the roof.

An artistic breakthrough occurred in 1930, when Jacobsen was commissioned to build a large residence for wealthy lawyer Max Rothenborg in Ordrup. In the Rothenborgs, Jacobsen was fortunate to find clients who were receptive to new ideas and willing to allow him creative freedom. This afforded Jacobsen the opportunity of designing furniture for the house so that the interior design and architecture were compatible. The Rothenborg house is considered the most significant work of Jacobsen's early years. It is a great pity that subsequent conversions and remodeling attempts essentially destroyed it.

In general, competitions had a marked effect on Danish architecture and design from the 1920s through the 1950s, most of the important public buildings being awarded as a result of them. Thus, in the 1930s and 1940s Jacobsen gained most of his major commissions by responding to competitions, designing the Bellevue Lido, Klampenborg; the Bellavista housing estate (1933); the Bellevue estate (1934–35); the Hellerup Sports Club tennis hall (1934–35); the Novo Medical Factory (1934–35); the stadium of the city of Gentofte (designed 1936; built 1941–42); and what is considered one of his masterpieces, the gas station at Skovshoved Harbor (1936–37), a structure that is just about as elegant as gas stations can get, sporting a circular concrete roof resting on a central column and connected to the cubic building behind it. The mushroom-shaped concrete awning carries the lighting, which is directed upward to reflect from the underside of the roof and, on a darker note, is reminiscent in shape of the mushroom cloud of an atomic explosion, perhaps *the* symbol of the war years.

Jacobsen was another of the holistic thinkers, showing a great sensitivity both to landscape design in relation to architecture and to architecture in relation to interior design. In 1937 he built himself a summer cottage at Gudmindrup Lyng on a site of sloping wooded dunes. His unorthodox plan included a living-room wing placed on one of the dunes, with the wing curving slightly to follow the natural curve of the terrain. He placed the bedroom wing so that it was protected from winds at the bottom of the dune.

Throughout the '30s and '40s Jacobsen continued to win competitions, sometimes in collaboration with other architects, sometimes independently, including those for town hall designs. In 1943 the politics of war intervened, forcing Jacobsen to seek refuge in Sweden. He was welcomed there, and while having to curtail his architectural activities slightly, he was offered a commission to work on designs for the architectural offices of the Swedish housing association. During this period, Jacobsen began experimenting with wallpaper and textile patterns, using nature as the basis for his designs of wildflowers and leaves. His wife, Jonna Jacobsen, a trained textile printer, was instrumental in producing these designs, which met with great success. In 1942–43 he designed "Rush" (also called "Reed"), a pattern for wallpaper and fabric, plus "Crown Imperial," "Dockleaves," and "Foxtails"—all floral textile prints. Other fabrics were produced under the names "Trapeze," "Waves," and "Collier." These were geometrics with a '60s op-art quality. "Hotbed" and "Hyacinth" were hybrid patterns incorporating both geometric and floral forms.

When Jacobsen returned to Denmark in 1945, he found that the war had hit him hard. The business of his architectural firm was practically nonexistent, and even worse, the war had caused a severe restriction on Denmark's building activities that was to persist for several years. He plunged right into entering competitions, however, and won two first prizes for projects that unfortunately failed to materialize.

An unexpected turn of events in educational philosophy affected Jacobsen in the 1940s. Prior to that time, Denmark (like most western countries) built schools on a monumental scale. In a sense, they were contemporary castle forms paying homage to the "overlord" of education. During the early 1940s a subtle change in educational philosophy proposed that children would learn better if their school environment were less forebidding. Suddenly, a "friendlier" atmosphere was called for, and people were immensely concerned that schools be more in scale with the children, even at the expense of the teachers and administrators. There followed a rash of competitions for school buildings of the bungalow type, and the architectural community answered the call. The Munkegårds school, built in 1952–56, was one of the first of this type, and is considered one of Jacobsen's principal works.

From the beginning, Jacobsen had several strikes against him with this project: an awkwardly shaped site and a group of unattractive houses in the immediate vicinity. The Munkegårds school was an elementary school for children from seven to fifteen years old. As a solution to the various housing and storage problems, Jacobsen designed a group of self-contained buildings with the classrooms arranged in pairs and combined with anterooms and storage rooms of their own linked by bright "friendly" corridors. The school comprised fourteen standard classrooms of the pavilion type, connected by a simple system of parallel corridors that also allowed access to the assembly hall and faculty room. The gymnasium and bicycle sheds were designed as separate buildings.

Each classroom grouping was provided with its own patio area. Jacobsen distinguished the patios from one another by using flagstone paving and landscaping as well as individual sculptures placed in the outdoor patio areas to beautify and identify each classroom section. He was originally asked to decorate the building itself, but instead he chose to acquire a large number of reproduction classic and modern sculptures that he used in the patio areas, mounted on simple wooden or marble cube-form pedestals. One of the patios even had a pool of water with aquatic plants, another had showy floral displays, and another had topiary shrubbery clipped in the shapes of animals. Jacobsen continued the "friendly" feeling by incorporating yellow brickwork, white-painted timber, and aluminum roofing, which kept the appearance light and airy.

Furniture and fittings inside the school were given the same care and attention to detail as the architecture and landscaping; the result was a totality of concept in keeping with the tenets of organic design. Initial worries that the children would soon destroy the delicate-looking school proved to be unfounded; the children rose to the challenge. In fact, after many years of use, the school remains in excellent condition, showing it to be a success both in artistic design and in its ability to capture and maintain the children's respect. Munkegårds school has been regarded as a milestone in international school architecture, being both functional as a school and providing an intimate, holistic environment in touch with nature. It was extremely important in influencing school architecture of the '50s and '60s, although few recent schools have achieved the totality of concept of the Munkegårds school.

Following the war, eyes turned to the United States for inspiration. Frank Lloyd Wright exercised a strong influence on Danish postwar architecture, his concept of organic unity manifesting itself in the detached houses of the Danish upper class. Jacobsen was influenced by Wright and to a greater extent by Mies van der Rohe. Like Wright, Jacobsen preferred to design in the vein of conceptual holism, creating not only the architecture itself but the landscaping, interior furnishings, and lighting fixtures, so that all parts would be in harmony. As a result, he worked in diverse areas of design, creating furniture, textiles, lighting fixtures, stainless steel flatware, wallpaper, bathroom fixtures, and even package designs for his own products.

While the Scandinavians are noted for working primarily in wood and natural materials, it was not always so. Jacobsen had a great impact on postwar styles. His three-legged plywood 3100 chair (Plates 110, 111), introduced in 1952, is a classic. In addition to working with plywood, he also pioneered in the use of molded plastics. In 1958 he introduced two chairs of upholstered or leather-covered plastic—the Egg chair (Plate 117) and the Swan chair (Plate 118)—both of which featured metal bases with well-balanced form-fitting bodies. Jacobsen's furniture designs were and still are manufactured by Fritz Hansen of Denmark.

The Serie 7 chair (also known as the Series 7) consists of five models with identical seat/back shells made in molded plywood (Plates 112, 113). The base consists of chromium-plated steel-tube legs. There is also a pedestal version that can be affixed to the floor with concealed screws and (by special order) a swivel base with automatic return. The chairs are also available with such accessories as stainless-steel ashtray, seat and row numbers, and transport trolleys for ease of stacking and storage. A linking device is also available for auditorium seating. The Series 7 is available in three types of padding: total padding; seat padding; or a choice of seat/back padding.

The 3100 chair, similar in appearance to the Series 7, is also constructed of a molded plywood shell with a chromium-plated steel-tube base in either a three-legged or a four-legged version. Like the Series 7, the four-legged version is available with accessories that include a linking device for auditorium seating, ashtray, seat and row numbers, and transport trolley. Both the 3100 (three-legged) and the 3101 (four-legged) are available in natural beech plus seven colors. (For additional details, refer to Part 3, "Materials and Methods of Construction.")

Jacobsen's Swan chair is available in two versions, a high and a low chair with optional fabric, leather, or vinyl upholstery. The Egg chair is also available in fabric, leather, or vinyl and is equipped with a loose seat cushion applied over a shell of molded polyurethane reinforced with fiberglass on which is glued molded latex. Both versions swivel, and the high Swan chair (model 3322) is equipped with a pneumatic height adjustment.

The Egg chair was originally designed for one of Jacobsen's major works, the SAS Royal Hotel and Air Terminal in Copenhagen (1958–60). The SAS Hotel is located in central Copenhagen and consists of a long two-story building and an eighteen-story high-rise hotel tower of reinforced concrete framework with a curtain wall of gray anodized aluminum sections with gray green glass panels. The hotel lobby is banked on either side by shops that are also accessible from the street. The design called for pale gray marble slab flooring, with a ceiling of dark green sprayed oil paint. Jacobsen designed all the furniture, lighting fixtures, and carpets, including the famous Egg chair. Adjacent to the hotel lobby, Jacobsen designed a two-story-high conservatory of double glass walls with orchids suspended between them.

The first-floor bar had rosewood wall paneling, a bronze bar counter, and lighting fixtures of smoke-colored Plexiglass. Seating was covered in olive green worsted fabric. Circular domes in the restaurant ceiling were designed to admit natural light but also contained suspended smoke-colored glass lighting fixtures resembling downturned wine glasses. The carpet and draperies were of a design that incorporated gold threads in a grid pattern. Hotel hallways were paneled with light oak, and the elevator doors and interior walls were veneered with Wenge wood (a wood native to Scandinavia), as was all paneling and built-in furniture in the hotel rooms.

Jacobsen's original designs for the hotel rooms consisted of drawer units mounted on the walls, one of which was intended to be a dressing table, another providing the call buttons for staff and wired for radio, lighting, and so on. Lighting fixtures above the low wall units were fitted on tracks so that they could be moved as required. All tabletops were specified in gray blue Formica. Drapery panels were hung so that the bedroom section of each room could be separated from the seating area to assure privacy. The Egg chair was included in every room.

Jacobsen was so prolific and diverse that it is difficult to keep track of all his accomplishments. His furniture was designed for Fritz Hansen of Allerød, Denmark; his stainless steel flatware (1957) for A. Michelsen (Plate 121), by appointment to His Majesty the King of Denmark; his carpets were produced by the Gram Carpet Factory of Denmark; his 1967 line of Cylinda stainless steel ware was produced by Stelton of Copenhagen, winning the Danish Industrial Design Prize of that year. (Jacobsen also designed the packaging for his Cylinda line.); his lighting fixtures were manufactured by Louis Poulsen & Co. of Copenhagen (1953 on); bathroom fixtures were made by I.P. Lund of Denmark; and a door handle was designed for Carl F. Petersen of Copenhagen in 1956. In addition to this, his design for a loudspeaker for Paul Lehmbeck was awarded the Silver Medal at the Triennale in Milan, 1957, while 1955 found him designing a showcase for the H-55 exhibition at Halsingborg and an exhibition stand for Lavenda knitting wools for the British Exhibition in Copenhagen. In 1952, the year in which his 3100 chair was introduced, he also designed a writing desk for the American-Scandinavian Foundation in New York, consisting of metal-tube legs supporting a metal top, with a single pedestal file cabinet that appeared to float beneath it. An attached typewriter support stand was created from cantilevered steel tubing and platform-suspended from one of the steel-tube legs. This desk was manufactured by Rudolf Rasmussen, Cabinetmaker. Coming almost full circle from his beginnings, in 1956 he was appointed professor at the Copenhagen Academy of Arts.

Of Jacobsen it has been said:

> Arne Jacobsen's qualities do not lie in the application, to his well-designed works, of any special originality or any unusual wealth of imagination. But he is a highly gifted architect who has a supremely sure touch in working out his designs, who is extremely neat and clear in his architecture and who, in his simplified compositions, is always aiming at a harmonic overall solution.[1]

ARNE JACOBSEN

1902	Born, January 11, in Copenhagen
1925	Won Silver Medal at Paris World Exhibition
1927	Completed studies at Architectural College of the Academy of Arts, Copenhagen
1928	Won Minor Gold Medal for museum design in Klampenborg Cottage Park
1929	Awarded First Prize in collaboration with Flemming Lassen in Copenhagen Academic Association of Architects "House of the Future" competition
1930	Rothenborg House in Ordrup
1933	Bellavista housing estate
1934	Dragør South Lido
1934–35	Tennis hall of Hellerup Sports Club, Hartmannsvej, Gentofte; Bellevue estate
1935	Juncker's tennis hall, Mathegårdsvej, Gentofte
1936	Stadium, city of Gentofte (built 1941–42)
1936–37	Gas station at Skovshoved Harbor
1937	Summer house at Gudmindrup Lyng
1939–42	Århus town hall (with Erik Møller)
1940	Ibstrupparken No. 1 housing estate, Hørsholmvej Jaegersborg, Gentofte
1940–42	Søllerød town hall (with Flemming Lassen)
1941–42	Gentofte Stadium, Jaegersborg, Gentofte
1943	Relocated to Sweden; introduced textile designs
1945	Returned to Denmark
1946	Ibstrupparken No. 2, Smakkegårdsvej, Jaegersborg, Gentofte
1947	Hørsholmvej housing estate, Jaegersborg, Gentofte
1949	Yacht harbor, Vejle (design completed; project not carried out)
1950 & 1955	Søholm housing estate, Klampenborg, Gentofte
1951	Islevvaenge housing estate, Rødovre; C.A. Moller house, Badbaek; Hårby Central School, Hårby, Fyn Island
1952	Apartment building at Alehusene, Jaegersborg Alle, Gentofte; designed writing desk for American-Scandinavian Foundation; Massey-Harris display room, Roskildevej, Glostrup; introduced plywood 3100 chair
1952–56	Munkegårds school, Vangedevej, Gentofte
1953	Introduced lighting fixtures for Louis Poulsen & Co.
1954	Henning Simony house, Geelsvej, Jolte
1955	Showcase for "H-55" Exhibition at Halsingborg; Rødovre town hall; office building for Jespersen & Co., Copenhagen
1956	Ruthwen Jurgensen house, Vedbaek; door handle design for Carl F. Peterson, Copenhagen; design for Landskrona Sports Hall (project not built); Carl Christensen Factory, Ålborg; appointed Professor at Copenhagen Academy of Arts
1957	Kikfelt summer house, Tisvildeleje; house Sjaellands Odde, Odden Havn; won Silver Medal at Triennale in Milan for loudspeaker design; terrace houses at Ørnegårdsvej, Jaegersborg, Gentofte; Marl town hall, Germany; introduced stainless steel flatware through A. Michelsen of Denmark
1958	Glostrup town hall; extension of Cologne town hall; introduced Egg chair and Swan chair
1958–59	Novo Industri A/S Factory, Gladsaxe
1958–60	SAS Royal Hotel and Air Terminal, Copenhagen
1959	Erik Siesby house, Prinsessestien, Lyngby; Onderlinges Headquarters building, The Hague; Rødovre School
1960	Edwin Jensen House, Mosehøjvej, Ordrup; headquarters building of the World Health Organization, Geneva; apartment building at Rødovre; St. Catherine's College, Oxford, England

1961 National Bank and Bill Printing Plant, Copenhagen; Tom Chocolate Factory, Ballerup; Gertie Wandel House, Ordrup; Novo Industri A/S Factory, Hillerødgade, Copenhagen; Rødovre Library

1962 Landskrona sports hall; competition project for Essen town hall, Germany; Parliament building at Islamabad, Pakistan; headquarters building for the Hamburg Electricity Supply Company

1963 Designed furniture for St. Catherine's College, Oxford, England

1967 Designed Cylinda line of stainless steelware for Stelton of Copenhagen

(Note: some of the architectural projects listed were never constructed.)

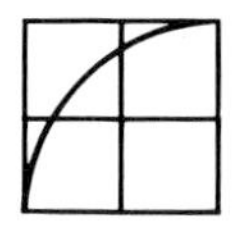

Børge Mogensen

Børge Mogensen is noted for his consumer-oriented designs. His ideas never grew out of preconceived artistic concepts. Rather, he utilized what he termed the "workshop method," which involved a sorting and classifying of all the practical and technical demands into a synthesis of extremely simple forms. This method was employed by other designers and architects and in Mogensen's case can be traced back to the furniture designs created by the Danish architect Kaare Klint, one of Mogensen's teachers. Klint's teaching advocated the use of scientific investigations of furniture function as the ultimate basis for design rather than notions derived from aesthetically biased personal observations. Mogensen had the insight and ability to take the dreams of former generations and turn them into practical realities; Klint's scientific investigations became the essentials of Mogensen's furniture designs.

As far back as 1917, Klint had conducted numerous studies on the relationship of furniture proportions to human anatomy. These studies resulted in the design of shelving and storage systems based on prefabricated units totally devoid of extraneous decoration. Klint, however, was a bit too far ahead of his time, and his projects were not produced as planned. But three decades later, Børge Mogensen's sectional bookcase was the physical proof that Klint's innovative concepts had indeed been on the right track, even though society was not ready for them when they were first introduced. Spurred on by the acceptance of Mogensen's work, however, Klint began to experiment again with a set of "ideal" dimensions for office furniture—writing desks, shelving, bookcases, filing cabinets, and the like—based on parameters established by paper sizes. He then proceeded to design around the demands imposed by three-dimensional objects, developing storage spaces for typical family needs based on the objects needing to be stored: cups, dishes, cooking utensils, flatware, and so on. By taking precise measurements of a large number of Danish and foreign kitchen items, he quickly found that size variances were minimal. It was then possible to establish measurement norms for storage units of a multipurpose nature that could easily be adapted to fit individual user needs. This, in combination with a set of measurements devised from the dimensions of the human body, enabled Klint to establish a basis for a set of design criteria based on utilitarian measurement that echoed the "form follows function" philosophy of Sullivan, et al.

Børge Mogensen was involved with Klint in these studies both as an employee in Klint's office and as his assistant at the School of Furniture Design of the Royal Academy of Fine Arts, Copenhagen, where Klint was a teacher. Klint's studies were of such major significance to Mogensen's work that it is impossible to consider his contributions without also acknowledging Klint's influence.

Klint was in opposition to the Bauhaus in that he believed in the importance of tradition. He felt that ignoring the old was throwing out the baby with the bath water and that bypassing established norms prevented a designer from benefiting from the experiences accumulated throughout centuries of trial and error; Klint saw the futility of constantly reinventing the wheel. Mogensen shared Klint's view, and his work reflects this philosophy in his use of traditional motifs, some of which were inspired by English Windsor chairs and American Shaker furniture, others by Chinese and Spanish influences. This adherence to traditionalism gave Mogensen's work an internationally homogeneous, untrendy appearance.

Mogensen's designs stemmed not from the mind and training of an architect but from that of a cabinetmaker wholly engrossed in perfecting his craft. The vast majority of his furniture was executed in wood, with a little dabbling in steel. He completely shunned plastics and fiberglass in his work, preferring instead a long-term commitment to wood, leather, and natural fibers. His early work showed a proclivity toward daring massiveness, as evidenced by the solid oak library table manufactured by Karl Andersson & Soner of Sweden. His later tables continued this trend of sculptural strength in both dimension and detail. Most of his furniture was first produced for the Copenhagen Cabinetmakers' Guild exhibits prior to industrial production.

Throughout his career, Mogensen often collaborated with other designers. In 1939 he made his design debut at the Copenhagen Cabinetmakers' Guild exhibition where, in collaboration with Aage Windeleff, he displayed simple, practical furniture for a "student's den." In the same exhibition, he displayed original designs for a dining/work area. This multipurpose approach was to become his hallmark. For his dining/work furniture, Mogensen chose Oregon pine for the tables and Cuban mahogany for the chairs.

In 1942 Mogensen was appointed head of the drafting office in the Design Department of the Danish Cooperative Wholesale Society. This organization had just embarked on a project to produce unpretentious good-quality furniture at reasonable prices. Danish designer Steen Eiler Rasmussen had been hired to head the project, and it was at Rasmussen's request that Mogensen was hired. Within two years they had arrived at a series of furniture designs able to meet the needs of an average family. The pieces were based on the unitized modular concept that allowed the formation of harmonious groupings from units that were coordinated in terms of measurement, materials, and design. According to an individual's budget, basic pieces could be purchased and others added as finances permitted.

Because of the war's strict limitations on materials, Swedish pine and Danish beech were the only options open to Mogensen at the time. With the consumer in mind, he designed furniture that would withstand hard use, take up minimal space, and be light enough to move for easy cleaning.

The humanistic, personal approach adopted by Mogensen in his furniture designs was expressed by the subtle "homey" names he chose for his exhibition interiors: Hanne's attic (1940) and Peter's bedroom (1943), for example. In these designs and in the design of a two-room apartment model for newlyweds, his furniture consisted of light chairs, sturdy tables, shelves, chests, and wardrobes in simple geometric shapes executed in Danish beech, cherry, pine, and larch.

Another collaboration occurred around 1945, this time with Hans J. Wegner. They created furniture designs for a relatively spacious three-room apartment, with Wegner designing the dining-room furniture, Mogensen designing the bedroom, and the living room being designed as a joint effort whereby Wegner conceived the upholstered sofa and Mogensen designed a high chest and a stick-back sofa.

Like Klint, Mogensen's aim was to create functional furniture. In 1936, when he was working in the drafting office of Mogens Koch, he designed modular furniture for the administrative offices of a hospital in Skive, Denmark. After continuous refinement, by 1950 the system had been expanded and adapted for manufacture in beechwood after the simplification of construction details brought down production costs. One cost-cutting factor was the use of mahogany veneer for tops instead of the solid mahogany boards originally conceptualized. Mogensen's sectional units were based on Klint's functionalist theories, and as such, human anatomical measurements were taken into consideration in the scale of the pieces. Mogensen also designed the units so that the maximum height from units in combination with each other would not exceed the height of an average door. In this he achieved a relationship between architecture and furniture, much as Eero Saarinen had sought to do.

In the late '40s Mogensen abandoned the safe forms and traditional materials that had become his standard for a more experimental approach. In an exhibition of 1949 he displayed a low table cut from the cross-grain knot of a giant sequoia, allowing the natural shape of the wood to determine the shape of the table. Instead of using underframing to support the top, he devised a supporting element of four sets of legs having the appearance of vertically split isosceles triangles.

The chair he designed to accompany his sequoia table is vaguely reminiscent of Eames's molded plywood chair in its curves and graining, but Mogensen's chair, which was shown at the Copenhagen Cabinetmakers' Guild exhibition of 1949, was made of cherry wood and certainly lacked the perfection of line and the grace of Eames's chair.

Mogensen set up his own offices in 1950, determined to design a series of inexpensive consumer-oriented furniture based on his previous work with sectional units. His experiments led to standardized construction modules similar in concept to those of Kaare Klint. Mogensen's work, sometimes referred to as festive and impudent (due to his unconventional use of color and pattern), raised a few eyebrows in 1953 when he intentionally ignored the traditions of cabinetmakers who were aiming at the wealthy client and instead prepared an exhibit of a multipurpose room, frankly rejecting the presumptuous poses that had become the norm. In doing so, he produced reactions ranging from delight to outrage.

For the exhibit, he designed chairs in a combination of molded plywood on solid wood frames. For the portable furniture units he chose teak and mahogany combined with storage units of deal painted bright yellow and orange in front. Bright awning canvas was selected for the upholstery fabric, and all furniture, with the exception of chairs, was designed to be bolted to the walls so that everything could be folded out of the way to make room for dances or large groups of people. This exhibit proved Mogensen's theory that an unpretentious arrangement in combination with excellent craftsmanship could "steal the show."

Nineteen fifty-three also found Mogensen accepting a position as the artistic consultant to A/S C. Olesen's Cotil Collection, one of Denmark's major textile firms. In another collaboration, this time with the weaver Lis Ahlmann, he had a great influence on the production of upholstery fabrics, drapery fabrics, and carpets. These textile designs were extremely simple, relying for the most part on stripes and checkered patterns in a limited range of colors. As usual, Mogensen tended toward traditional design elements that remained unadulterated by trendy influences.

One of Mogensen's best-known works was the Boligens Byggeskabe series (named for the firm for which it was initially designed), first presented at the Copenhagen Cabinetmakers' Guild exhibition in 1954 (Plates 123–126). He had begun developing the series in 1952 in collaboration with Grethe Meyer, producing a system of sectional units designed to meet every imaginable storage need in the average home.

The system utilized a floor-to-ceiling, wall-to-wall storage approach, favoring permanently installed shelving and cupboard systems over stackable modular units. With this system, the storage facilities became an architectural element rather than furniture and therefore an integral part of the building structure itself.

The "BB" system, as it is sometimes called, was based on comprehensive investigations of an average Danish family's storage requirements. The wardrobe unit's construction was well conceived and detailed to perfection. Doors were hinged in such a way that they only had to be opened ninety degrees before the drawers could be pulled out. Keyholes were countersunk to prevent clothing from catching on the hardware and to prevent damage to neighboring walls when the doors were opened. The BB system was highly avant garde, bearing a strong visual resemblance to "innovative" closet storage systems of the present.

The BB system's measurements were as carefully conceived as any of the design details. With the average Danish ceiling height being 250 cm, after the average height of baseboard and ceiling molding were subtracted, the remaining height of 237.6 cm was divided into thirty-six sections of 6.6 cm each, so that all storage measurements were then based on multiples of 6.6 cm. Cupboard widths were established based on the length of an adult's bed—30 cm × 6.6 cm—allowing for the storing of folded garments or for hanging clothing at right angles to a suspension bar.

By using Mogensen's system, it was possible to have an immaculately ordered clothing storage system. Even the drawer units were divided into sections based on a detailed study of the measurements of a wide variety of clothing articles in both flat and rolled positions. The measurements taken were incredibly thorough, anticipating every possible combination of storage needs and providing grooved partitions so that the user could determine the most appropriate configurations for individual needs.

Another attractive feature of the BB system was the ease with which it could grow and change in the form of add-on units, so adaptable that even objects unimagined at the time of its construction can be readily accommodated.

Frame construction was of solid Oregon pine with rabbeted doors of plywood veneered with Oregon pine or teak. The sides, tops, and shelves were of gray-painted masonite on frames with brass mounts. Bases were complete with self-leveling screws to allow for uneven floors.

Mogensen remained primarily a first-rate cabinetmaker, undertaking very few interior design commissions. He preferred to concentrate his energies on furniture design solutions. In 1959, however, he designed the classroom buildings of Krogerup High School in collaboration with architect Erling Aeuthen Nielsen. In 1964 he completed the interior of the cloister at Løgum Church. In both cases he utilized furniture designs already in production. But in 1958, when he worked on the Royal Danish Yacht Club, overlooking Copenhagen Harbor, he was forced to produce an entirely new series of furniture for this application.

In his Øresund designs (1955–67), Mogensen expanded on his work with the Boligens Byggeskabe storage system. As in the case of the BB storage groups, Øresund elements could be used separately or in combinations to form shelf and cupboard units encompassing an entire wall. When installed in this way they became architectural elements and a dominant feature of any room. Manufactured in Oregon pine, oak, and teak, later versions of the Øresund elements were adapted to kitchen use where, in 1967, they were fitted with such special features as wire shelves, wire baskets, cutting boards.

The work of Mogensen that most links him to the Organic Design Movement is a series of chairs from the early '60s that were designed to be suitable for the long hours of sitting in school. In conjunction with the recommendations of physiotherapist Eigil Snorrason, he arrived at a solution in collaboration with Ebsen Klint (a son of Kaare Klint). They produced chairs in four different sizes, the smallest for use in kindergarten classes, the two middle sizes suitable for elementary school use, and the largest for high schools and colleges. The chair frames were of beech, with the seats and backboards of padouk. These chairs were designed to facilitate three basic sitting positions: (1) the writing position, when the sitter is bent slightly forward; (2) the relaxed upright position; and (3) the listening position, when the sitter is leaning back. The backboard was thus molded in accordance with anatomical considerations, being inclined at an angle of 100 degrees at chest level and at 105 degrees to the horizontal plane at the small of the back.

On the whole, Børge Mogensen's work cannot be classified as innovative when compared to the work of Eames or Saarinen, yet his meticulous attention to detail and his precise dedication to consumer-oriented design have certainly earned him a place as a strong design influence on the postwar era.

BØRGE MOGENSEN

1914 Born, April 13, in Ålborg, Denmark

1934 Certified as a journeyman cabinetmaker

1936–38 Studied furniture design at the College of Arts and Crafts in Copenhagen

1938–41 Studied at the School of Furniture of the Royal Academy of Fine Arts, Copenhagen

1938–42 Worked in various architectural drafting offices, including those of Mogens Koch and Kaare Klint

1939–62 Was a regular exhibitor in Copenhagen Cabinetmakers' Guild exhibits and the Danish Society of Arts and Crafts

1942–50 Served as head of the Design Department of the Danish Cooperative Wholesale Society

1945 Became a member of the Danish Society of Academic Architects; awarded the Bissen Bursary

1945–47 Served as teaching assistant at the School of Furniture Design of the Royal Academy of Fine Arts, Copenhagen

1950 Opened independent design firm; awarded the Eckersberg Medal for furniture design and craftsmanship

1953 Awarded the Silver Medal of the Danish Trade Fair; began as artistic consultant to A/S C. Olesen

1958 Awarded the Annual Prize of the Copenhagen Cabinetmakers' Guild

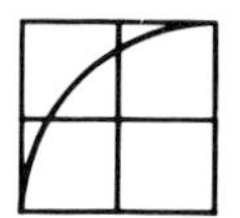

Hans J. Wegner

When asked if he had received early preparatory training as a furniture designer, Hans Wegner first answered, "No," then added mischievously, "I played!"[1] His simple statement may well hold the key to creativity itself—focused play—the creative impulse unhampered by the linear thought processes of contrived planning.

Born Hans Jorgensen Wegner on April 2, 1914, in Tønder, Denmark, the little boy who played with wood scraps from the cabinetmaker two houses away from his father's shoe repair shop was one day to see the products of his "play" in international museum collections. Wegner's designs are calm and restrained, produced primarily from natural materials, all with a simplicity and functionalism that is distinctly Scandinavian.

His furniture designs are light-years removed from those so often associated with '50s kitsch and, in fact, they exemplify the purity and understated elegance representative of the postwar period prior to the intervention of unscrupulous manufacturers who "ripped off" many of the best designs of this era and produced copies in which the original purpose and concepts were totally lost.

By his early teens, Wegner had become quite accomplished at wood carving and began a four-year apprenticeship in a local cabinet shop where he learned the basics of furniture construction. It seemed likely that he would one day open his own workshop, since the amount of poorly designed furniture being produced in Denmark at the time pointed to a need for change. With this in mind he continued his studies, first honing his skills at the Danish Institute of Technology in Copenhagen, then enrolling at the Kunsthandvaerkerskolen—the Copenhagen School of Arts and Crafts,—a leading center of advanced design at the time. There he studied fine arts, taking courses in drawing, sculpture, painting, and art history, as well as furniture design, which required him to make detailed studies of the furniture in the Arts and Crafts Museum collection.

His instructors were so impressed with his artistic abilities that he was encouraged to give up the idea of designing modern furniture (which was then thought to provide only a marginal living at best) and instead to turn his attention to becoming a professional portrait painter. But Wegner stuck to his original goal and found a champion in his furniture design teacher, O. Mølgaard-Nielsen, who eventually recommended Wegner to the famous Danish architect Arne Jacobsen. While still a student, Wegner was commissioned to design some furniture for Jacobsen's summer house. His work must have been quite pleasing to Jacobsen, for in 1938 Wegner joined the architectural office of Arne Jacobsen and Erik Møller as a full-time employee in the drafting section. In this capacity, Wegner was given a great opportunity to prove himself as a furniture designer—he was assigned to design the furniture for the town hall of Århus, based on the traditional concepts of Kaare Klint. Yet, even while Wegner's Århus designs did adhere to accepted traditions, he incorporated his own unique sensitivity and individuality.

Nineteen forty was a big year for Wegner. He married Inga Helbo in November and met the man who was to become the single most important influence in his career—Johannes Hansen. Hansen, a businessman, was also a well-respected and established member of the design community, being one of the founders of the Danish Cabinetmakers' Guild exhibitions intended to promote interest in excellent craftsmanship. The guild also served as a showcase for progressive designers and new techniques, giving the participants an opportunity to show their talents to the architectural community and the public at large. Hansen and Wegner formed a manufacturer/designer relationship, and Hansen began producing Wegner's designs, an association that continues today through Poul Hansen and Fritz Hansen, Eft.

In 1942, Wegner completed the Århus project, but the war's travel restrictions prevented him from returning to Copenhagen, so he spent a great deal of his time on further studies of furniture design, analyzing historical styles and experimenting with function. He became quite enamored of the Oriental approach to simplicity in design and to the equally simple, practical forms of Shaker and Windsor. By 1944, he had integrated his ideas into his Chinese chair (Plate 127), which was manufactured by Fritz Hansen. During the same year, he was admitted to the Royal Association of Danish Architects and also experimented with lighting, flatware design, office furniture, and children's furniture.

On returning to Copenhagen in 1946, Wegner accepted a teaching position at the School of Arts and Crafts, a position that he held until 1953. During his spare time he worked with Palle Suenson on restoring the woodwork and furniture on a salvaged ship.

Everything seemed to have been building to a climax for Wegner, and it occurred in 1947, when his now famous Peacock chair (Plate 128) was shown at the Cabinetmakers' Guild exhibition of that year. Nineteen forty-eight brought him further recognition when he entered the New York Museum of Modern Art's International Competition for Low-cost Furniture Design and won an honorable mention award for his molded plywood armchair. The guild exhibits of ensuing years assured Wegner a place in history as a furniture designer, with 1949 bringing forth the Classic chair (Plates 129, 130) and the folding chair (Plate 131) and 1953 the Valet chair (Plates 144, 145).

While Wegner's projects covered a wide area, he is best known for his seating designs. He spent years studying the human form and concluded that sitting is a uniquely human activity that requires proper support if the body is to be comfortable. From observing people sitting, he noted that considerable shifts and movements took place in short periods of time as the sitter tried to find a comfortable position. Because of this, Wegner designed spacious seats with rounded back rails to accommodate position changes. Another hallmark of Wegner's work is armrests that relieve some of the body weight from the spine.

Wegner eventually came to realize that there was no one perfect chair type, due to the range of human variables to be considered—height, weight, age, and physical flexibility among them. He did discover, though, that certain anatomical measurements fall within a specified range, and it was on this theory that he based most of his designs. For example, in most human adults the measurement from the small of the back to the tip of the coccyx (tailbone) is quite similar. From this he determined the placement of the support rail for the back. Also, he generally left the space beneath the rail open so that the sitter could nestle back into the chair for a proper upright body position. Taking a cue from the Orient, he reasoned that it was less comfortable for a short person to sit in a high chair than for a tall person to sit in a low one, so he designed chairs with seat heights lower than the norm.

Wegner's concepts were usually tested and developed in his own home. First he did preliminary sketches, next came scale models, then revised scale models constructed from pine or plywood. Finally, after making the necessary corrections, a prototype was constructed that was tried out at home. If needed, further revisions were made; then, once the design had been approved, manufacturer's drawings were made, and the piece went into production under Wegner's supervision.

Wegner designed both for mass production and for handcrafting, with the mass-produced designs being manufactured by Fritz Hansen and the handcrafted pieces by Johannes Hansen. Currently, however, much of the hand labor has been replaced by machine techniques.

Wegner's Peacock chair of 1947 was based on early hoop-back Windsor chair designs. The Peacock chair featured a large hoop back with radiating spindles, four splayed legs braced with side stretchers, and a centered cross-stretcher. The flattened cattail-shaped spindles in the back were carefully conceived to conform to the sitter's back. The scale of the Peacock chair was typically Wegner—roomier than a traditional Windsor—and the chair sported a resilient woven seat. For additional strength, the hoop was formed from a solid piece of laminated wood instead of bentwood—an ash rod sliced into four strips, then relaminated and shaped. This permitted better control during the molding process and produced a smooth, evenly curved hoop. The chair was constructed from wax-finished ash, except for the arms, which were made of oil-finished teak so that the natural oils from the user's skin would eventually create a fine patina. This is typical of Wegner's attention to detail.

Wegner's Classic chair of 1949 broke all the rules. It was designed to be handmade at a time when mass production was de rigueur. Its construction was of traditionally joined wood rather than machine-produced structuring, and it embodied an almost primitive simplicity. What is more, the sculptural joining of the chair's component parts was new to contemporary design, making Wegner's Classic chair a trendsetter for future designs.

Wegner's design philosophy extended both to his work and to his ideas about education. He believed that both training and design concepts should result from a "bringing out" of what is already within the individual, rather than from a forced learning of accepted concepts. This is, of course, education in its purest form. (Indeed, the word "educate" is derived from the Latin, *educare* meaning to lead or draw out that which is already there. This is something Wegner fully understood and practiced both in his own work and in teaching his students.)

Wegner followed the well-established Scandinavian tradition of quality above quantity, and his work shows a high regard for detail, technical skill, and finishing. Whether intentional or not, his work epitomizes the "form follows function" dictum—there is not a speck of unnecessary ornamentation to be found in Wegner's designs. Each component part serves a purpose, and each part is crafted to perfection.

The Classic chair was derived from his earlier Chinese chair of 1944, but with the Classic chair he achieved a remarkable economy of form while retaining user comfort. In all the years since its construction, the Classic chair has undergone only minor revisions from the prototype. At one point,

Wegner modified the shape of the arm to taper more gradually—this is the version that continues in production. Another slight change came in the joining process. In the prototype, Wegner used exposed mortar-and-tenon joints to connect the three-piece back rail. But it became apparent that humidity and aging of the wood caused the joints to separate slightly. Also, Wegner was dissatisfied with the rectangular outline of the joint, thinking it a distraction from the chair's sculptural lines. So, the 1949 modified version called for the back to be wrapped with rattan as camouflage. By 1950, however, Wegner had conceived a sawtooth joint whose zig-zag shape eliminated the need for the dishonesty of camouflage. Thus, the rattan version was discontinued except for custom orders.

Another problem occurred with the seating material. Due to climatic differences between Denmark and the United States, the caned seating material tended to sag in some geographical areas, so an upholstered version was introduced in which a leather seat became an option.

Wegner's original title for the Classic chair was the Round chair because of its rounded shape, but the name Classic chair soon caught on and was advocated by its admirers, who often referred to it as The Chair. Wegner designed this classic when he was only thirty-five years old and tended to be a little reticent in accepting the honor of having designed The Chair, believing that he had not at that point reached the height of his creative powers and was therefore not deserving of such an honor. But whether deemed The Chair or the Classic chair, it is one that will long be remembered.

Wegner's Folding chair of 1949 was the result of a long fascination with folding furniture. His earliest attempt at a folding chair came in 1937, but the design was never manufactured. Wegner was intrigued by the challenge of designing for compact living spaces; he theorized that there were always times when additional seating was a necessity and that a well-designed, comfortable folding chair that could easily be stored when not in use would be a marketable reality.

Certainly his reliance on the principle of X-shaped folding furniture was not new, having been around for centuries in the form of easily transportable campaign furniture for the military (and used by wealthy travelers as well). Wegner, however, took the original concept and improved on it, the major change being a better distribution of body weight. Wegner accomplished this by integrating the seat surface, the front leg, and the seat's front brace into the design in a fashion that transferred pressure from the seat almost directly to the floor. This, coupled with the lower sloping position for seat and back surfaces, resulted in a chair that was more comfortable and more stable than its predecessors.

Wegner's innovative use of the seat brace also resulted in easy storage. To close the chair, one had only to draw the front edge of the seat and the chair back together. This released the supporting brace, allowing the chair to be compacted. It could then be turned upside down and hung on the wall from the brace's cross-stretcher by a specially designed hook. Wegner's folding chair became so popular that it was seldom used only as a utility item to be stored when not in use; more often, it became a permanent part of a room's furnishings.

The 1951 Valet chair was a solution to one of the problems created by changing times. The days of the "gentleman's gentleman" were over. The middle classes could no longer afford valets, and too often the day's clothing ended up piled on a chair each evening. Wegner decided to design a chair that could double as a place where a man could hang his clothes before going to bed.

His first step was to rethink the chair back. Noting that ordinary chairs deformed a jacket's shape, he incorporated the concepts of hanger and chair back into one beautifully sculptured unit on which a jacket could drape properly. The seat height and angle were carefully conceived to be suitable for removing shoes. Also, the seat was hinged in front and could be raised at a ninety-degree angle, which both allowed the seat to be used as a rack where a man could hang his trousers and provided a small storage space under the seat for keeping jewelry and the contents of pockets. Not only was the Valet chair eminently practical in these ways, it was also remarkably comfortable when simply used as a chair, owing to its formfitting wooden seat and back.

Wegner first designed the Valet chair with four legs, but before it went into production in 1953, he altered the design to a three-legged version, thus simplifying the lines and making it easier to walk around the chair when hanging up a jacket.

All of Wegner's designs bore his unmistakable stamp, being visually light forms reduced to basic essentials. They were hand carved from solid woods such as ash, oak, or teak, with an oil or wax finish that enhanced the wood's natural beauty and allowed a gradual patina to develop with aging. While best known for his designs in wood, Wegner worked in various media, including steel; his tubular-steel and leather Bull chair (1960) is one example. However, he found it hard to gain acceptance when working in media other than wood. He once commented wryly, "A lot of my stuff never sees the light of day. . . . Many of [them] are attempts to break new ground. But I'm not allowed to. Wegner has to look like Wegner."[2] In spite of this, his designs in solid wood, molded plywood, laminated wood, and steel can be found in residences, dormitories, conference and office spaces, and hospitals throughout the world.

HANS J. WEGNER

1914	Born, April 2, in Tønder, Denmark
1927–31	Apprenticed at cabinetmaker's shop in Tønder
1936	Began studies at Copenhagen Institute of Technology and later at the School of Arts and Crafts (Kunsthandvaerkerskolen) in Copenhagen
1938–42	Worked as furniture designer for Århus project in the offices of architects Arne Jacobsen and Erik Møller
1940	Became associated with Johannes Hansen; married Inga Helbo
1943	Opened own firm in Gentofte
1944	Introduced Chinese chair, his first chair for mass production (Fritz Hansen); accepted as a member of the Royal Association of Danish Architects
1946–53	Taught at School of Arts and Crafts, Copenhagen
1947	Introduced Peacock chair
1948	Won honorable mention award at New York Museum of Modern Art Low-cost Furniture Competition
1949	Introduced Classic chair and folding chair
1953	Introduced Valet chair
1960	Introduced Bull chair and ottoman

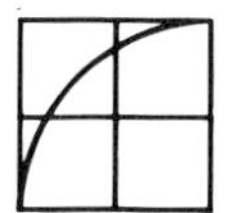

Russel Wright

Russel Wright has been called America's answer to the Bauhaus. Wright was born in Lebanon, Ohio on April 3, 1904 to a Quaker family. This, in combination with his attraction to things Oriental, formed the basis of his design sense. The Quakers favored directness and lack of ornamentation, which meshed well with Oriental simplicity. Wright's designs for dinnerware, housewares, and furniture were conceived in the straightforward "meat and potatoes" language readily accepted by an era of Americans who had been brought up to consider Bauhaus doctrine as the last word in design but who could not afford to buy the expensive imports of Breuer, Mies van der Rohe, or Le Corbusier in the economically lean years surrounding the depression. During the 1930s, 40s, and 50s, Russel Wright's designs could be found somewhere in nearly every American home. In the postwar years, Wright's name was a household word. With his simple, sophisticated, scrupulously marketed consumer goods, Wright played a major role in leading middle-class America toward an understanding of modern design.

Wright was a designer of varied talents but is best known for his American Modern dinnerware, recognized for its organic lines molded in simple, rimless forms (see C12). Although he had never before tried designing dinnerware, he was compelled to attempt it because he disliked the way food looked on the traditional china of the day. Around 1937, he began a series of photographic studies comparing the appearance of food placed on a variety of shapes and colors. His experiments proved to him that food looked best on neutral, unornamented surfaces of black, brown, or gray. The resulting American Modern dinnerware was unique and spectacularly innovative, being totally without stylistic predecessors. In fact, American Modern was so innovative that it was immediately rejected.

Wright offered his finished designs to a number of factories, all of which turned him down with barely a glance. The dinnerware was too different, too strange to take a chance on during the depression. Wright then approached several major New York department stores but met with the same disappointment. During a two-year period of trying to find a buyer for his dinnerware line he met with nothing but rejection. Then a small ray of light appeared; a buyer for the J.L. Hudson department store of Detroit liked Wright's design and made attempts to persuade the Steubenville Pottery Company of Ohio to produce it. The firm accepted the challenge—but only if Wright agreed to finance the production costs himself. Feeling that he had no alternative, Wright agreed.

At first, the negative response Wright had experienced in trying to get American Modern produced was echoed in his attempts to sell it. Professional buyers totally rejected it with the familiar cries of "too strange; too radical." Spurred on by his economic investment in its production, Wright persisted in trying to find markets for his "strange" new product. Finally, a few stores agreed to try American Modern on a limited basis. Almost magically, the jinx was broken. The American consumer accepted American Modern immediately. It became a phenomenon unparalleled in the industry before or since.

Public demand for American Modern dinnerware was so great that when department stores in several cities announced the arrival of shipments, the police had to be called in to prevent pandemonium because the crowds were so huge. *Home Furnishings Daily* ran a headline, "Mob Scene over Modern," to describe the more than 1,500 people who stormed Gimbels department store in New York, clamoring for Wright's dinnerware. American Modern broke all sales records. Between 1939 and 1959, over 80 million pieces of the dinnerware were produced, making it the most popular mass-produced pattern ever sold. To date, more than 350 million pieces have been sold. American Modern was so popular that by 1952 there were over 90 imitations being produced.

Wright borrowed heavily from Oriental aesthetics, proposing harmony of design in table settings. In keeping with this philosophy, he believed that glassware, linens, flowers, and dinnerware must be given equal consideration and coordinated to produce visual unity.

Wright proved to be a genius at marketing. To promote his ideas he prepared audio-visual demonstrations to accompany his displays at department stores, illustrating ways in which the average consumer could achieve dramatic table settings. Wright had worked with ceramic engineers at Alfred University to develop his unusual glazes. The mottled, muted colors of Seafoam Blue, Bean Brown, Granite Grey, and Chartreuse Curry had not been seen on western tables before. His colors were not only individually distinctive but could be successfully mixed in combinations to give additional scope to his dinnerware line. He encouraged consumers to experiment within his color line by combining hues within the same table setting to suit their own tastes.

Wright preferred the neutral earth tones of black, brown, and medium gray to display food with maximum visual impact and shunned white, which he thought made food look lifeless and opaque. Eventually, though, he did expand his color line to include white as well as Cedar Green, Black Chutney, and Coral.

Wright's brilliance at marketing led him to introduce the idea of the "starter set," which made available sixteen pieces of dinnerware at near-cost price in the hopes of seducing buyers into purchasing additional place settings and serving pieces at a later date. Based on sales figures, the idea was an obvious success. Within two years, the factory simply could not produce enough American Modern to keep up with the demand.

American Modern was not without its problems, however. Its soft clay body broke and chipped easily, the overhanging lips on some of the pieces were nearly impossible to clean, and a few of the shapes were not suited to their intended function. For example, it was annoyingly difficult to get sugar from the sugar bowl, and the neck of the water pitcher was too narrow for ice cubes. Cup handles were too small for most men's fingers, and the rimless plates sent peas and gravy spilling over the edge.

Wright corrected many of these problems in later modifications and in other designs. In 1948 he created a line of ceramic ware for hotel and restaurant use in colors such as Straw Yellow, Suede Grey, Cedar Brown, and Ivy Green. Because of their commercial application, these pieces were less delicately shaped and visually weightier than American Modern. Along the same lines, he designed Casual China for residential use. The glazes were smoother and less mottled than the commercial line, and Wright eliminated the fragility that had been a problem in American Modern. The starter sets of Casual China offered a full replacement guarantee against chipping and breakage in normal use. Because the body was of superior quality to that of its predecessor, it was also suitable for stove-to-table use. In 1951, Wright added the Highlight line to his dinnerware designs, its innovation stemming from a combination of pottery and white-flecked snowglass used in the same table setting. The White Clover line—his first patterned dinnerware—also appeared that year for the Harker Pottery Company.

Russel Wright was a complex amalgam of contradictions. By nature reclusively shy, he nevertheless made regular personal appearances to promote his work. He was independent and fiercely guarded his privacy yet sought out the guidance of his wife and close friends. His indifference to business matters often verged on hostility, yet he achieved a high degree of financial success. He was disorganized and absent-minded yet paid the strictest attention to every detail of his complex design projects.

In like manner, Wright's career mirrored the extremes of his personal life. Although the American Modern dinnerware was an industry phenomenon, similar marketing techniques used to promote his home furnishings line, the American Way, designed in 1940, resulted in crushing failure. On the other hand, Wright's early experiments with furniture had been successful. In 1934 he introduced a sixty-piece group at Bloomingdale's department store in New York, manufactured by the Heywood-Wakefield Company of Gardner, Massachusetts. The store displayed room settings of Wright's designs that included furniture, carpets, draperies, lighting fixtures, upholstery fabrics, and accessory items. With this line, he was also marketing the concept of a coordinated line of furniture and accessories by one designer—a unique approach at the time. The individual pieces of the early Heywood-Wakefield line showed little ingenuity. The furniture was boxy and heavily upholstered. Wright did show ingenuity, however, in his emphasis on flexibility; all the pieces of furniture and accessories had been designed so that they could be grouped according to individual taste (in much the same manner as his later American Modern dinnerware). Another unique touch from this line was Wright's design for the first sectional sofa—an invention much copied in later years.

The American Way disaster was in part predicated by Wright's inconsistency in business affairs. His client relationships were usually volatile, and even when covered by rigid contracts, he was involved in many lawsuits. Perhaps some of Wright's distrust about business came from his unpleasant experiences with American Modern. Wright had formed a partnership with Irving Richards in 1935 under the name of Russel Wright Associates. Wright organized the partnership in such a way that he could be free of business involvement and spend his time designing. In 1939, just as American Modern was becoming established, he sold his interests in the partnership to Richards. Later, he suffered from the sale in seriously reduced revenues from this immensely successful line. True to his contradictory nature, Wright wanted both to be free of business responsibilities and to maintain control. With this dichotomy firmly entrenched in his professional life, Wright embarked on his American Way promotion.

Wright's concept was to package a complete line of home furnishings designed and produced by a cooperative of sixty-five American craftsmen and manufacturers, to be sold through major department stores under the name of the American Way. His intention was to demonstrate the quality and uniqueness of American design, to make average Americans more aware of their environment, and to show the world that American design could compete successfully with anything that Europeans could produce.

Wright and a small staff traveled throughout the United States screening and selecting designs for the American Way line and negotiating contracts for their manufacture. The American Way included some powerful allies: Raymond Loewy, Walter Teague, and Gilbert Rohde agreed to provide designs; John Curry and Grant Wood were to provide textiles and framed reproductions of their works; Wright's dinnerware and aluminum line were also to be included. Wright received support for the American Way from its board of directors, which included Edgar Kaufmann, Jr., architects John Root and Edward Stone, and Macy's vice president Edwin Marks.

The American Way line was displayed as room settings in department stores, just as Wright's previous furniture lines had been, the emphasis being on harmonious design relationships and color combinations. The model rooms were intended only as guides, and consumers were encouraged to express their own tastes through individualized groupings. Wright's goal was "to provide unity with freedom to make our own choice—the American Way!"[1]

In an attempt to overcome the public's reluctance to accept the coldness of modern design, Wright stressed functionalism and traditionalism in arranging his products by geographic areas. His marketing genius came to the fore again when he arranged to have Eleanor Roosevelt cut the ribbon at the American Way opening ceremonies at Macy's New York store. The American Way advertising promotion was on a monumental scale. There was wide press coverage, and initial public response was enthusiastic. But trouble lay just around the corner.

While it is difficult to lay the failure of the American Way on any specific cause, two major problems were logistics and quality control. It became nearly impossible to coordinate the deliveries from sixty-five suppliers, some of whom were quite small and erratic in their production schedules. Keeping the products of an even quality was a larger task, and Wright tried to solve the problem by forming a nine-member panel to revise and upgrade the level of selections. All furniture was produced in a single finish in an attempt to promote unity. But Wright's attempts at saving the American Way were to little too late. Supply and distribution problems, aggravated by wartime shortages, disappointed both Wright and consumers alike. In 1942 the American Way line was liquidated.

Several years passed before Wright was ready to tackle such a large-scale design project again. In the meantime he turned his attention to promoting his ideas through writing. In 1950, Wright and his wife Mary published the *Guide to Easier Living* in which they defined their design credo. Some of their suggestions were rooted in common sense, others were quite daring for the time. For example, they exhorted their readers to:

> . . . develop routines for chores; involve the whole family in cooking and cleaning; space out cleaning to different days; cut down on dish washing with one-dish meals; add casters to furniture for easier moving; ask your guests to help with party clean-up; drastically reduce the number of your possessions to make maintenance easier; replace sit-down meals with "family cafeteria" service; use only throwaway paper plates for most meals; redecorate your home, replacing old-fashioned fabrics and surfaces with easy-care plastics.[2]

While the Wrights' book seems to carry utilitarianism to extremes in some of its advice, its primary aim was to break with the bonds of the "gracious living style" then being touted as *the* way—a style the Wrights considered nothing but a sham. They believed the democratic way of life inherent in the Easier Living plan far more suited the American way of life than an old-fashioned life with servants.

During the '50s, Russel Wright also turned his attention to experiments in design with innovative materials. Years earlier he had worked with spun aluminum, bringing out a line of stove-to-table ware in the early 1930s that popular magazines had publicized as the wave of the future. Indeed, his early work in spun aluminum had led the Metropolitan Museum of Art to invite him to exhibit in its Contemporary American Industrial Art show of 1931. In 1945 Wright had been asked to design a set of dinnerware using the newly developed thermoplastic, Melamine, developed by American Cyanamid. It took the company four years to find a manufacturer for Wright's designs, but in 1949 General American Transportation produced the line under the name Meladur. Further experimentation with Melamine led him to design Residential in 1953 and Flair in 1959, both manufactured by the Northern Industrial Chemical Company of Boston.

All of Wright's Melamine dinnerware is organic in form, playing up the intrinsic curves of its molded shapes in integral handles and grips. In 1955, he also added a touch of whimsy in designing a line of polyethylene dinnerware for the Ideal Toy Company and a matching line of miniature reproductions of his American Modern line as children's toys. Wright's plastic designs were immediately adopted by the foodservice industry and for the first time represented a viable alternative to china for residential use.

By early 1950, much of the bitter taste left by the failure of the American Way had faded, and Wright felt ready to embark on another major marketing program. The publication of the *Guide to Easier Living* seemed the perfect time to bring out a line of merchandise in keeping with the philosophies put forth in the book. The Easier Living furniture line was based on fifty pieces manufactured by the Statton Furniture Company of Hagerstown, Maryland, constructed of solid, natural-finished sycamore. These designs demonstrated many of the multipurpose ideas mentioned in the book: a lounge chair with one arm that could fold to make a writing surface and another arm that formed a magazine rack; a coffee table with a sliding top that opened to hold insets for food and beverages; beds with tilting headboards as supports for reading and concealed storage compartments; a magazine stand on casters for ease of mobility; slipcovered furniture for ease of cleaning; a nightstand with extendable shelves for eating in bed. The line also included coordinated accessories including lighting fixtures, rugs, draperies, and upholstery fabrics.

In spite of the massive promotion effort and its moderate pricing, the Easier Living line flopped just as the American Way had done; Wright had lost touch with the public taste. In the postwar years, the public wanted furniture to express a renewed prosperity, while the Easier Living line reflected the austerities of war. Its excessive utilitarianism smacked of institutionalism, of which the American people had already had their fill.

After his success of the 1930s and '40s, the '50s were disappointing years for Wright. In a speech to the Society of Industrial Designers in 1976 he recalled:

> About 1953, "contemporary" began to be defeated. My religion, which I had pioneered for twenty years, was losing. I wanted to convert the masses—to design for middle- and lower-class Americans a way of life expressive of what I thought was basic American taste. Now with postwar affluence. . . Easier Living, my book and design group have failed.[3]

The '50s brought another loss to Wright. His wife Mary, who had been his right hand, died of cancer. Her death caused much of the fire to go out of him, and he sought solace in isolation. Gradually, he withdrew from his New York City design practice and spent increasing amounts of time at Dragon Rock, his eighty-acre estate overlooking the Hudson River. It is ironic that at a time when Wright's design practice was in decline, he received his greatest recognition by the design industry. From 1950 to 1955 his work was regularly exhibited in the "Good Design" exhibitions of the Museum of Modern Art. He was included in the Society of Industrial Designers' annual exhibits of 1950 and 1951; and in 1951, his work was included in the Museum of Modern Art's "Design for U.S.A." exhibit. The Albright-Knox Art Gallery of Buffalo showed his work in their "Good Design Is Your Business" show of 1947 and again in the 1959 "Twentieth Century Design: U.S.A." exhibit. In 1952, Wright was elected president of the American Society of Industrial Designers, and in 1959, a *Fortune* magazine poll selected American Modern dinnerware as number 22 of the "100 Best-Designed Products."

This sudden flurry of notoriety led to a renewed prestige for Wright, which, in turn, led to a series of lectures at college campuses and design schools. In 1955 he was commissioned to design folding metal outdoor furniture for Samsonite. The furniture was available either in bent plywood or with painted and molded aluminum seats in green, chartreuse, aqua, or coral. A matching table was also available. After five years of successful sales, Samsonite commissioned Wright to design a line of school furniture that enabled him to become an innovator once again.

Prior to Wright's designs, color had been banned in school furniture as a distraction to learning. After visiting schools and talking with educators, Wright formulated a theory that color would have an enlivening effect on the school environment. He set about to design a line of school furniture that was what he termed "friendly"—sturdy, comfortable, and easy to move. He designed his line in steel tubing with plywood and reinforced plastic writing surfaces. The innovation came in his use of color, with four separate subdued shades available in place of the traditional schoolroom gray. It is highly likely that anyone attending school in the United States from this time on has sat in a desk of Wright's design.

During this period, he also tried his hand at various challenges, including a commission from Du Pont to select colors and create the pattern design for a line of vinyl upholstery fabrics; he designed a ceramic-faced wall clock for General Electric (1952), and a decanter and box for Calvert Reserve Whiskey. In 1959 he designed a reusable jar for Big Top Peanut Butter and in 1960 a ketchup bottle for Hunt Foods.

By the '60s, Wright had taken up full-time residence at Dragon Rock and become closely involved in local community activities and studies of the park system, which resulted in the "Summer in the Parks" program launched in 1968 in which trips, crafts, instruction, concerts, and sports were organized on a neighborhood level.

Throughout his life, Wright had struggled to resolve the conflicts of efficiency and aesthetics. He tried to produce designs in which the machine and nature could exist together in harmony. Until the time of his death from cancer in 1976, he never gave up that dream.

RUSSEL WRIGHT

1904 Born, April 3, in Lebanon, Ohio

1921–24 Attended Princeton University; worked as theatrical designer

1927 Married Mary Small Einstein, who influenced Wright to turn toward designing for the retail market

1929–35 Designed service pieces in pewter, aluminum, and chrome

1932 Designed piano, accordion, and radios for Wurlitzer; redesigned street floor of Gimbel Brothers, New York; designed showroom of Wright Accessories, New York

1933 Designed experimental silver flatware set; designed cocktail lounge interior, Restaurant de Relle, New York

1933–34 Introduced upholstered furniture line, manufactured by Heywood-Wakefield Company, Gardner, Massachusetts

1935 Introduced Modern Living line of furniture (later renamed American Modern), manufactured by Conant Ball Company, Gardner, Massachusetts; introduced Oceana line of wooden serving pieces, manufactured by Klise Woodenware, Grand Rapids, Michigan; designed office interior for George Bijur, New York

1936 Introduced Blonde Modern furniture line; designed showroom of Wilkes-Barre Lace Company, New York

1937–39 Designed American Modern dinnerware, manufactured by Steubenville Pottery, East Liverpool, Ohio (marketed until 1959)

1939 Designed showroom of International Handkerchief Company, New York; designed exhibits at New York World's Fair (Focal Food exhibit; Mental Hygiene exhibit; Guiness Stout exhibit; Fashion Show; New York Department Stores exhibit)

1939–51 Designed various lighting fixtures for Wright Accessories/Raymor, New York; Mutual Sunset Lamp Company, New York; Acme Fluorescent, New York; Amplex Corporation; Fairmount Lamps, Philadelphia

1940 Introduced Old Hickory furniture line for American Hickory Company, Indiana; introduced American Way furniture and accessories

1942 Introduced Knockdown furniture line for Sears Roebuck, Chicago, Illinois

1942–55 Designed various appliances for Silex Corporation, General Electric, Cornwall Corporation, Peerless Electric, Ladge Electric, and Amtra Trading Corporation

1943–46 Designed "art" ceramics for Bauer Pottery Company, Atlanta, Georgia

1944 Designed interior, fourth floor, Sak's, New York

1945 Designed folding metal furniture for Colgate Aircraft Corporation; designed prototype of Melamine dinnerware for American Cyanamid, New York

1946–48 Introduced stove-to-table line of serving pieces

1946 Introduced Casual China, manufactured by Iroquois China Company, Syracuse, New York (design modified in 1950 and 1959)

1946–57 Designed fabrics and carpets for: Lecock and Company, New York; Cohen, Hall, Marx, and Co., New York; Hedwin Corporation, Baltimore, Maryland; Frank and Sadev, New York; Simtex Mills, New York; Art Loom Carpets, Philadelphia; Everfast Fabrics, New York; Comprehensive Fabrics, New York; Lumite Division, Chicopee Manufacturing, New York; Aristocrat Leather, New York; Patchogue Mills, New York; Foster Textile Mills, Chicago; Edson, Inc., New York; Du Pont, Wilmington, Delaware; American Olean Tile, New York (tile)

1948 Designed vitreous hotel china for Sterling China Company

1949 Designed Meladur melamine dinnerware, manufactured by General American Transportation

1950–51 Coauthored *Guide to Easier Living* with Mary Wright

1950 Introduced Easier Living line for Statton Furniture Company, Hagerstown, Maryland; designed folding metal chairs and tables for Samsonite; designed showroom of Statton Furniture Company, Grand Rapids, Michigan

1951 Introduced Highlight dinnerware/glassware line, manufactured by Paden City Pottery, Paden City, West Virginia; introduced White Clover dinnerware, manufactured by Harker Pottery Company, East Liverpool, Ohio; designed American Modern flatware

1953 Introduced Residential plastic dinnerware, manufactured by Northern Industrial Chemical, Boston; designed Highlight flatware

1955 Designed Idealware polyethylene toys for Ideal Toy Company; designed school furniture for Samsonite; designed folding metal furniture for Featherweight Aluminum Products, Montreal

1955–61 Designed packaging for Calvert Distilling, Proctor and Gamble, Hunt Foods, and Cresca

1956 Introduced Esquire Collection dinnerware, which was distributed through chain stores until 1962, manufactured by Edwin M. Knowles Pottery Company, East Liverpool, Ohio

1959 Introduced Flair plastic dinnerware line, manufactured by Northern Industrial Chemical, Boston

1962 Designed self-service restaurant, Brass Rail Restaurants, New York

1963 Designed porcelain dinnerware line for Schmidt International, manufactured by Yamato Porcelain Company, Tajmi, Japan

1966 Designed Shun Lee Dynasty restaurant interior, New York

1967 Began work as a consultant at Bear Mountain State Park, New York State

1968 Launched "Summer in the Parks" program

1976 Died of cancer, December

C1. Designs by alumni of Cranbrook Academy, who went on to become the core of the postwar movement. Clockwise from the left: fabric by Ray Eames, c. 1955; storage unit by Charles Eames for Herman Miller, c. 1950; ceramic vase by Maija Grotell, c. 1948; Eero Saarinen's Grasshopper chair for Knoll International, c. 1948; Charles Eames's folding birch screen for Herman Miller, c. 1946; ceramic vase with stopper by Leza McVey (late '40s); modular cabinet and bench by Eero Saarinen and Charles Eames for the Museum of Modern Art's Organic Design in Home Furnishings Competition, 1940; stool by Florence Knoll, c. 1952; Harry Bertoia's Diamond chair for Knoll International, c. 1951. (Courtesy of Fifty/50, New York; photographer: Stan Ries)

C2. Eero Saarinen's Pedestal group of 1957 consisted of an armchair, two stools, a side chair, and several tables. This design was conceived as an alternative to what Saarinen called "the slum of legs" in modern furniture that had become "a sort of metal plumbing." His training had led him to believe that great furniture should be a structural whole, and his dedication to designing furniture in which the body and base were a unified structure resulted in the Pedestal group. (Photograph: Knoll International)

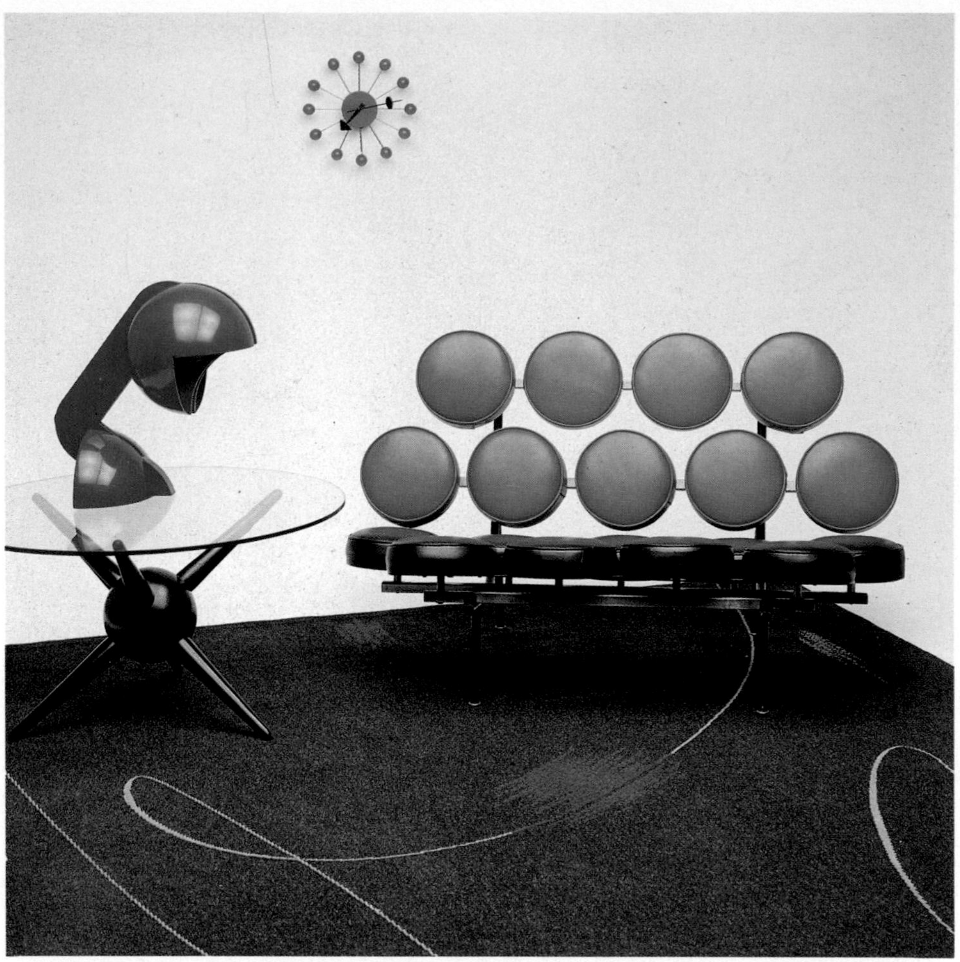

C3. Clockwise from the top: George Nelson's atom clock; Nelson's Marshmallow sofa; a German carpet labeled Westdeutscher/Kugel; Gio Ponti's "jack" table; and an Italian table lamp in metal, Martinelli Luce (designer unknown). (Courtesy of Boomerang Gallery, Chicago; photographer: Steven Miller)

C4. George Nelson's Kangaroo chair. (Courtesy of Fifty/50, New York; photographer: Michael Norgart)

C5. A Florence Knoll design for the residence of Dr. Detlev W. Bronk of the Rockefeller Institute, 1957. (Photograph: Knoll International)

C6. The Knoll Planning Unit had its first opportunity to perform on a large scale with the interior design of a major new project, the Connecticut General Life Insurance Company in Bloomfield, Connecticut. This reception area from the project illustrates Knoll's attention to detail. Sleek lines and surfaces remain uninterrupted, even down to fuse-box covers being finished in the same surfacing material as walls. (Photograph: Knoll International)

C7. This office from the Connecticut General Life Insurance Company gave Knoll an opportunity to implement space planning by running an individual analysis of the client's requirements for space, furniture, equipment, color, fabrics, art, graphics, and accessory items. Today this is a standard industry practice, but Florence Knoll introduced the idea during the postwar period. (Photograph: Knoll International)

C8. This reception area from the Connecticut General Life Insurance Company building includes the designs of Eero Saarinen and Florence Knoll. (Photograph: Knoll International)

C9. The dining room of the home of Dr. Detlev Bronk, incorporating designs by Eero Saarinen and Florence Knoll as well as textiles from Knoll Textiles Division. (Photograph: Knoll International)

C10. The Connecticut General employee cafeteria shows the unmistakable imprint of the Knoll touch in its space planning, simplicity, and attention to detail. (Photograph: Knoll International)

C11. This grouping of postwar designs includes the Noguchi table, a sofa by Vladimir Kagan, and folding screens by Charles Eames. (Courtesy of Fifty/50, New York; photographer: Michael Norgart)

C12. A collection of postwar ceramics. Clockwise from the center: mint green platter, Poppytrails by Metlox; Russel Wright American Modern relish dish in Coral; Russel Wright American Modern bowl in Chartreuse Curry, illustrating the molded organic form he preferred; a heart-shaped candle holder by Red Wing, glazed in deep peach with an ivory interior (the candle fits into a rim inside); a low bowl in Seafoam Blue from Russel Wright's American Modern collection; a fluted bowl by Bauer in a satiny black glaze; American Modern water pitcher, cream jug, and sugar bowl in Granite Grey; and finally, rare examples of Russel Wright's first foray into patterned dinnerware—a cup, saucer, and plate from his White Clover collection, introduced in 1951 by the Harker Pottery Company. (Photographer: Andrew McKinney, San Francisco)

C13. The T chair, designed by the team of Katavolos/Littell/Kelley, won the A.I.D. award for best furniture design in the United States (1952). (Courtesy of Fifty/50, New York; photographer: Watanabe Studios)

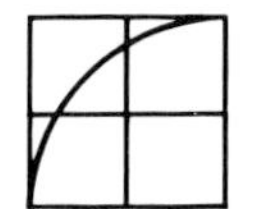

The Italians

In *The Hot House: Italian New Wave Design,* Andrea Branzi states:

> In reality the fifties should be measured from 1948 to 1962, i.e. from the defeat of the Popular Front to the explosion of a new era of social conflict with the events in Turin's Piazza Cadorna. . . . Industrial design was seen as a great opportunity to give a direction to culture, combining the restoration of the country with the opening up of a new market for quality consumer goods and secular culture, and the aim of progress with the interest of a resurgent Italian industry.[1]

During the postwar period, Italian style was not just a status symbol but more a genuine desire on the part of the Italian people to raise their society to a less provincial level of international life and culture.

Modern architecture came to Italy in 1926 with the international movement's influence on a group of recent architectural graduates—Luigi Figini, Guido Frette, Sebastiano Larco, Adalberto Libera, Gino Pollini, Carlo Enrico Rava, and Giuseppe Terragini—who founded Group 7 and collectively came to public attention. Group 7's first presentations were large-scale architectural projects—including a gasworks and a garage for five hundred cars—exhibited in Stuttgart and Monza (1927), in Essen, Milan, and Rome (1928), in Breslau (1929), and in New York (1931).

The first important example of modern Italian design is considered to be the Electric House designed by Figini, Pollini, Libera, and Bottoni, which was built for the Edison Company at the IV Monza Triennale of Decorative and Industrial Arts, an exhibit held in Monza in the summer of 1930. It was a small residence consisting of a split-level living room, two bedrooms, a bathroom, a kitchen, a dining area that was separated from the living area by curtains, and a small servant's room. The Electric House was equipped with every imaginable electrical device conceived at that time to show how electric gadgets could make life easier—footwarmers and electrically heated carpets, fans that blew hot or cold scented or unscented air, stoves, hair curlers and dryers, an electric iron, and a portable kettle.

The bathroom must have seemed a miracle of efficiency for its day, its walls faced with a new type of rubber and its interior filled with electrical appliances, including lights built into the small cabinet above the washbasin, a stove, an immersion heater for instant hot water, an electric hand dryer, and a toilet with an automatic deodorizer. The kitchen boasted an electric coffee grinder, kitchen cabinets with celluloid rolling shutters and sliding doors, and an early version of the food processor able to mince meat, knead dough, crush ice, and liquidize.

The interior and furnishings were specifically designed to complement the mechanical equipment, to harmonize with it rather than stand out, so that the visitor's focus would be on the entire setting rather than on any single item. Since nothing like this had ever before been done in Italy, the Electric House was the first project to broach many previously unexplored concepts. For the first time in Italian design, careful consideration was being given to the size of rooms in relation to their function. While the furniture of Libera and Frette might be considered somewhat crude in comparison to the work of contemporaries such as Breuer, on the whole a well-integrated display was presented. Thus, the principle of architecture as total environment was put into practice.

The influential Italian design magazine, *Domus*, edited by Gio Ponti, reviewed the Electric House, on the whole praising it for its technical innovations but stating, ". . . criteria of this sort lead to results completely remote from traditional lines, so that it is quite premature to state whether this can be regarded as Italian art."

At that time in Italy, the survival of modern architecture and industrial design depended totally on public authorities. If modern architecture and design were to become established, they would have to evolve beyond the model stage into the actual building of government-subsidized housing developments and public buildings. Within this context, it was necessary for designers to branch out into furniture and equipment for schools and offices as well as homes. The question was, could the modern designers make the grade?

Time makes prophets of us all, and we now know that the goal of creating new environments by blending architecture and decoration was, in fact, realized. In 1933, Francesco Monotti wrote in the Italian design magazine *Quadrante:*

> Little by little the whole of Italy must become an exhibition, that is, a model for all other countries, in every form of life, and thus in creation and action. The trend which has just begun promises to become even more far-reaching. Already, in many cases, the exhibition has gone beyond the walls of a building or pavilion, has come out into the garden, has abolished doors, and made use of the airy transparency of glass. Now it must enter into the actualities of everyday life, and it is up to men of goodwill to make its path easier.[2]

Italian design at this time was split into two main factions: rationalist and modernist. The rationalist movement in interior design first appeared in Italy in 1925, when Ivo Pannaggi displayed his interior designs for the Casa Zampini. Other designers soon followed the rationalist approach, which was viewed not so much as a new aesthetic but as a new approach toward analysis and design solutions. The rationalists, rooted in the Fascist viewpoint, proposed a new kind of international culture based on reason and technology. They sought to modify human physical and mental behavior by designing a new architecture for a new society.

The modernists adhered to the philosophy born in Europe that sought to transform the world through a model of social austerity. Production, not consumption, was the modernist credo. Modernists focused on the kind of human who could adopt the machine as the basis for the reorganization of society, the working class in particular. This approach was largely rejected by the working class whom it sought to reach, but as the modern movement slowly emigrated to America, it evolved into the international style.

The struggle between modernist and rationalist design raged in Italy. From 1933 to 1936 there was intense conflict between the two factions. At that point, the rationalists had the upper hand, but the modernists were anxious to show what they could do if given the chance. Between 1935 and 1940, the first Italian industrial designs produced on an international level arrived: chairs by Albini, an Olivetti typewriter designed by Nizzoli, and the Phonola plastic radio of 1938, designed by Caccia-Cominioni and the Castiglioni brothers.

Prior to 1945, Italian design had been closely linked to architecture—strongly traditional and centered in Milan. During the years 1945 to 1948, Italian industry went through a difficult period of reconstruction and modernization, but even before 1950 new ideas began to spread. Studies were being done for bath and kitchen equipment; there was experimentation in mass-produced kitchen units designed by Magnani and produced by Saffa; experimental bath units designed by Giulio Minoletti were underway; and unitized metal-tube bookshelving had arrived. Such developments were new to Italian design, although in some cases they had been developed in other countries decades earlier.

In 1947 the work of Charles Eames was published in *Domus,* and this stimulated younger architects to try out new ideas and materials. Castiglioni and Vigano tried using bent plywood. Cristiano and Frattini experimented with sheet-metal seats and rubber joints; Chessa and Zanuso worked on small armchairs in metal; and Carlo Mollino and a group of his pupils in Turin split from the Milanese traditionalist approach by designing furniture based on complex curves in plywood.

Understanding Mollino and his work is crucial to arriving at an understanding of Italian design in the postwar years. Carlo Mollino came from a wealthy Turinese family and spent much of his early years flirting with various hobbies that had no ostensible connection to his career. He dabbled in stunt flying and airplane design; he was a racing driver and designer of a rocket car; he excelled at downhill skiing, was a photographer, inventor, window dresser, women's shoe designer, and stage designer. While this may make him seem fragmented, his varied interests all coalesced in his furniture designs where he freely used fashion magazines, film, sexual fantasies, and dreams as inspiration.

Mollino received his degree in architecture from the University of Turin in 1931. Influenced by Eames, he developed a series of glass-topped tables with plywood bases of one-piece construction, pierced and bent into fantastically imaginative shapes and curves. His sculptured organic-form chairs and outrageously innovative upholstered pieces (Plates 137–139) followed his philosophy that "everything is permissible as long as it is fantastic."[3] Mollino was also an active architect, interior designer, and urban planner, as well as being noted for his writings on art and architecture.

While Mollino represented the fanciful, free-spirited aspect of Italian design, Gio Ponti was the bridge between the prewar middle-class traditionalist culture and the new wave of modernism. His Chiavari chair, which was first designed for Cassina in 1949 and underwent various modifications up to 1957, best exemplifies this. The Chiavari chair was based on traditional fishermen's chairs found in the town of Chiavari near Genoa. Ponti adapted this traditional chair design into what has become a modern classic. The chair went into production by Cassina in 1957 under the name of the Superleggera chair.

Ponti was the founder of *Domus,* which he edited until his death in 1979 (with the exception of one six-year hiatus), and the editor of the industrial design magazine *Stile* from 1941 to 1947. An architect who designed numerous buildings throughout Europe, Ponti also left his mark on furniture and industrial design and cut a wide swath through design circles by his participation in organizing the Biennale of Monza (later renamed the Milan Triennale) and by his contributions toward the institution of the Compasso d'Oro (Golden Compass) Award and the ADI (Association for Industrial Design).

Perhaps his most memorable structure is the Pirelli Tower in Milan. This skyscraper, constructed between 1956 and 1960, points up the distinct similarity between Ponti's architecture and furniture designs in his use of slim, seemingly two-dimensional lines reminiscent of the elongation found in Modigliani's paintings and Giacometti's sculpture. Designed with his partners Alberto Rosselli and Antonio Fornaroli, the Pirelli Tower is considered one of his finest postwar buildings.

Like his architecture, Ponti's furniture designs followed unexpected shapes. For example, a cabinet designed by Ponti in 1950 and decorated by Piero Fornasetti, incorporates a renaissance architectural perspective in trompe l'oeil. The upper part of the cabinet is in the form of a building front, the drop-front secretary is a view of a courtyard surrounded by a colonnade, and the base represents an interior view complete with Gothic fan vaulting. This unlikely combination rests on typically postwar conical legs. Another of Ponti's unexpected shapes can be seen in his Jack table (Plate 141), where the glass top rests on a jack-shaped base taken directly from the children's game.

Ponti's postwar furniture was produced by several manufacturers including Cassina, Arflex, Singer, and Norkiska Kompaniet. While his furniture is noteworthy, he also produced a design classic in his toilet of 1954 for Ideal Standard. His aim was to simplify the form of bathroom fixtures by eliminating all visible structural elements that detracted from the purity of line and form. Ideal Standard, an Italian company, had been producing traditional toilets since the '30s. When Ponti approached them in 1952 with his idea for a new line of modern fixtures for a project he was preparing for the Italian Institute of Stockholm, Ideal Standard was quick to agree.

Ponti's design called for stripping away all visible plumbing structures, thus requiring a complete rethinking of toilet design. The toilet design evolved between February and August of 1953 and was ready to be shown at the Milan Triennale of 1954. Ponti's bathroom fixtures utilize the biomorphic forms and organic curves associated with the postwar era, resulting in a toilet that is not only utilitarian but can stand as sculpture. It is considered a classic in its field and won the Gold Medal at the 1954 Triennale.

In addition to his furniture designs, Ponti was a prolific designer in other areas, including ceramics for Richard Ginori, enamels for Paolo di Poli, mosaics for Gabbianelli, printed textiles, and even set designs for La Scala in Milan, as well as being an active Professor of Architecture at the Milan Politecnico, and the author of nine books and over three hundred articles.

The years 1951 to 1954 were critical in the growth and organization of Italian design. During this time, new ideas were becoming more accepted, and experimental furniture was even sought after in some circles. Albini designed a unitized storage system of cut and bent plywood that reduced the walls to extremely thin panels. The design of Albini's Adriana armchair was based on the contrast between the elasticity of plywood over a framework of heavy wood, and his Margherita rush armchair (1951) incorporated both a traditional and modern approach, perhaps in an attempt to appease the two dissenting factors so prevalent in Italian design.

Noted as an architect, planner, and industrial designer, Marco Zanuso also taught at the Milan Politecnico and was editor of *Casabella*. He received his degree in architecture from the Milan Politecnico in 1939 and opened his own office in Milan in 1945.

Zanuso submitted a chair design to the New York Museum of Modern Art's 1948 International Competition for Low-cost Furniture that introduced a new mechanical joining device in which the fabric seat was suspended from the tubular-steel frame. His Lady armchair of 1951 (Plate 142) pioneered the innovative use of foam-rubber upholstery and nylon cord. It was inspired by automobile production methods and so encouraged contact between the designer and industrial processes. Manufactured by Arflex, it won the Gold Medal at the 1951 Triennale. His Lambda chair of 1962 is entirely of sheet metal construction, and his child's stacking chairs of 1964 for Kartell were the first structural application of polyethylene in furniture. In collaboration with Richard Sapper, Zanuso produced many industrial designs between 1958 and 1977, including the Grillo telephone (1965) and the Doney (1962) and Black (1969) televisions.

During the early 1950s, Zanuso's experiments with foam rubber used as upholstery resulted in small-scale production of his designs by Arflex, associated with the Pirelli company, which tried to incorporate industrial methods into furniture production. During this same period, Kartell was founded—a firm that was to become noted for their outstanding leadership in the field of design with plastics.

The American influence was felt on Italian design not only by exposure to the works of Eames, Saarinen, et al. but also by the importation of the American desire for creature comforts. Suddenly, mechanization was a major goal; the middleclass wanted refrigerators and other electric appliances. Prosperity became associated with the acquisition of industrial products, and the traditional approach of preserving and handing down treasured possessions dissipated in the rush to acquire the social status of newly designed and manufactured goods.

Between 1952 and 1954, Italian design began to mature, spurred on by a new public awareness and consumerism. This period was marked by three major events: (1) the X Triennale; (2) the founding of *Stile industria* magazine, an authoritative voice in Italian design until it ceased publication in 1963; and (3) the establishment of the Compasso d'Oro Award, which recognized "outstanding aesthetic qualities and the technical perfection of . . . production" in industrial design. (From 1959 to 1965 the Compasso d'Oro competition was held in collaboration with ADI, at the time the only unifying agent for design-related pursuits. The Compasso d'Oro soon became the most coveted award for recognition in the field of Italian industrial design.)

Due primarily to the efforts of Zanuso, the X Triennale had a more unified approach than ever before, with its theme of "The Production of Art." Prior Triennals had been focused on architecture and trade, but the X Triennale centered around the industrial design pavilion organized by the Castiglioni brothers, Roberto Mehgi, Alberto Rosselli, and Marcello Mizzoli.

The catalog of the X Triennale stated its purpose as follows:

> The subject of this key section of the X Triennale is industrial aesthetics, which in accordance with the American term that has now come into general use may be designated as "industrial design" and interpreted as the interpolation of the concept of "form" into the industrial process, or into the formal aspect of technology, the essential meeting-point between art and industry.[4]

The years 1955 to 1960 brought crisis to Italian design. The conflict between the two leading centers of Rome and Milan as the respective proponents of organic and traditional design intensified. In Rome, cultural circles totally rejected design as a serious subject for consideration and continued in their prejudice against the "minor" or applied arts. Things became particularly nasty when architects from the MSA (Movement for the Study of Architecture), a Rationalist group, refused to participate in the XI Triennale, which had again been organized around the theme of design. They cited the inadequacy of the organizing body and their philosophical opposition to design as the domain of capitalist power as the reasons for their refusal to participate. But despite these conflicts, the Triennale opened, its intention being to raise Italy's standards for production and consumption to European levels.

The schism in Italian design continued into the next decade. At the exhibition of "New Designs for Italian Furniture" held in Milan in March 1960, it was stated:

> An interior put together as a collection of individual pieces manages nowadays to look like a cross between a furniture display room and a temporary film set; the ensemble always seems to give the impression that the objects within it are interchangeable, and hence lacking all character. . . . But while there are some who believe that a synthesis can be attained only through unity of style, others, even if they are more revivalist in their approach, find that we are far from that taste for compatibility and tactful harmony of the Wiener Werkstätte's middle-class family.[5]

Ettore Sottsass, Jr. has come to be considered synonymous with avant-garde Italian design from the '60s on. Thoroughly disillusioned with the state of architecture, he attempted to make his statement through design by constantly seeking and redefining meanings. Though considered an Italian designer, Sottsass was born in Austria. The son of an architect, he received his degree in architecture from the Turin Politecnico in 1939. In 1947 he opened an office in Milan through which he was involved in the postwar reconstruction as well as exhibition design and interior design. He spent a year in the United States in 1956 working with George Nelson (Nelson had recently designed a ten-piece collection of clocks for Howard Miller "as a joke based on the Memphis foolishness."[6])

Sottsass's career appears to have taken two diverse paths, one being the simple, functional designs originated for such corporate clients as Olivetti, for whom he has been a design consultant since 1957, the other being playfully innovative furniture designs for Knoll, Abet, Memphis, Studio Alcymia, and Poltronova, plastics and lighting for Arredoluce, metalware for Alessi, as well as ceramics, painting, and sculpture. Sottsass was a part of the "antidesign" movement of the 1960s and a founder of the Memphis Group, which is currently making itself felt with its concept of "art" furniture and totally new forms in industrial design.

Sottsass's designs for Olivetti include the Elea computer series of 1959, adding machines, and typewriters such as the Praxis of 1963 and the Valentine of 1969. Such work won him the Compasso d'Oro Award in 1959 and again in 1970. In 1980 he opened a design firm in conjunction with several young architects under the name of Sottsass Associati.

Although a vital force in postwar Italian design, Ettore Sottsass is just now beginning to come into his own as the founder of Memphis, and as such symbolizes the entire postwar Italian design movement. In the period following World War II, Italian design moved from infancy to adolescence, but it was not until the 1960s and 1970s that the power, grace, and brilliance of Italian design became widely known and not until the 1980s that the Memphis movement heralded a new era in Italian design.

THE ITALIANS

1927–31	First presentations of Group 7 architectural collective of modern Italian design
1928	Gio Ponti founded *Domus* magazine, dedicated to art, architecture, and interior design
1930	Electric House, Edison Company Exhibit at IV Monza Triennale of Decorative and Industrial Arts
1948	Marco Zanuso introduced new mechanical joining device at New York Museum of Modern Art International Competition for Low-cost Furniture Design
1949	Gio Ponti's Chiavari chair introduced
1951	Marco Zanuso introduced furniture of foam rubber and nylon cord at IX Triennale; Zanuso introduced Lady chair, manufactured by Arflex, which won Gold Medal at Triennale
1954	Gio Ponti won Gold Medal at Milan Triennale for his Ideal Standard toilet design
1956	Gio Ponti's Pirelli Tower constructed in Milan
1956 & 1958	Major exhibitions of Italian design held in London
1957	Ettore Sottsass, Jr. joined Olivetti as design consultant
1959	Italian design exhibit held at Illinois Institute of Technology in Chicago; Ettore Sottsass, Jr. designed Olivetti Elea computer series and won Compasso d'Oro Award
1960	"New Designs for Italian Furniture" exhibit held in Milan
1962	Zanuso introduced Lambda chair entirely of sheet metal construction; Zanuso and Richard Sapper designed Doney television
1963	Sottsass designed Praxis typewriter for Olivetti
1964	Zanuso introduced child's stacking chairs, manufactured by Kartell, as the first structural application of polyethylene in furniture
1965	Zanuso and Sapper designed Grillo telephone
1969	Sottsass designed Valentine typewriter for Olivetti; Zanuso and Sapper designed Black television
1970	Sottsass again won Compasso d'Oro Award
1981	Memphis avant-garde exhibit in Milan (founded by Ettore Sottsass, Jr. and Barbara Radice)

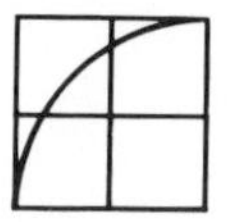

Supplemental Designers

LIS AHLMANN (1894–1979) Danish

Lis Ahlmann was a handweaver who set the standards of quality and craftsmanship for the Danish textile industry. She began designing for commercial production during the 1950s and, in 1953, became artistic consultant for the firm of C. Oleson in Copenhagen. In this capacity, she collaborated with Børge Mogensen on upholstery fabrics for his furniture designs, utilizing coordinated colors and interchangeable patterns. Mogensen encouraged her to extend her muted, subtle palette into bold patterns and colors, and these large plaids and bright stripes rapidly became the standard upholstery fabrics used on much of Mogensen's furniture.

ANNI ALBERS (1899–) American

Anni Albers is one of the most influential of twentieth-century weavers, perhaps best known for her handwoven and production textiles for Knoll (for whom she has designed since 1959), and for Sunar (for whom she has designed since 1978). Wife of the painter Josef Albers, she was born in Germany and schooled in Berlin and Hamburg, studying at the Bauhaus from 1922 to 1930 with Wassily Kandinsky and Paul Klee.

At the Bauhaus, she specialized in textile design and eventually became acting head of the Bauhaus textile department. The outbreak of World War II brought her to the United States where she taught at Black Mountain College in North Carolina from 1933 to 1949. She is noted for her precise, geometric designs, which bear a strong resemblance to the paintings of Josef Albers.

FRANCO ALBINI (1905–1977) Italian

Franco Albini was born near Como, north of Milan. He was trained as an architect, receiving his degree from the Milan Politecnico in 1919. For a time, Albini worked as an architect, city planner, and interior designer, as well as preparing designs for exhibitions and museum installations. During the early 1930s he was exhibiting his furniture at the Monza Biennale under the rationalist banner.

Albini was one of the first Italian rationalist architects to apply his skills to product design. He is known for his Mobile radio of 1941, which incorporated the components between glass, and for his "tensistructure bookcase" which consisted of taut wires. Albini also designed furniture in tubular metal and wood; these designs were produced by Poggi, Bonacina, Arflex, Pirelli, Siemens, and Fontana Arte.

As editor of *Casabella* design magazine from 1945–46, he had an opportunity to make known his views on design. These included the search for novelty for novelty's sake, unique pieces, simple and neat technical solutions to design problems, the promotion of mass-produced objects, and a proclivity for working with commonplace materials.

Albini's major architectural works were the La Rinascente department store in Rome (1957) and the interior of the Milan underground (1962). He was professor of architectural design at Milan Politecnico from 1963 to 1975. A noted Italian designer, Albini was awarded the coveted Compasso d'Oro Award in 1955, 1958, and 1964.

WINSLOW ANDERSON (1917–) American

Anderson attended Alfred University (New York State College of Ceramics), the same institution that helped Russel Wright develop his experimental dinnerware glazes. After graduating from Alfred University in 1946, Anderson joined the Blanko glass company as its first designer. He stayed with Blanko until 1953. From 1953 to 1979, he worked for the Lenox China Company, first as designer, later becoming its design director.

OLOF BÄCKSTRÖM (1922–) Finnish

Bäckström is best known for designing scissors. As cutlery designer for Fiskars from 1958 to 1980, he conceived the now famous orange-handled scissors in 1963. Bäckström did not have the technical training one might expect of the designer of such an ergonomically sound product as the Fiskars scissors. He was a self-taught woodcarver who began by designing wooden household objects, for which he won a Silver Medal at the Milan Triennale of 1957. He soon turned his considerable sculpting talents to product design, primarily designing cutlery. He won a second Silver Medal at Milan in 1960 for his camping eating utensils.

HANS THEO BAUMANN (1924–) German

Although born in Switzerland, Baumann is considered Germany's leading ceramics and glass designer. Following his studies in Dresden and Basel, he opened an independent studio in 1955. While his greatest output has been in ceramic designs for Rosenthal, Thomas, Schönwald, and Arzberg, as well as in glassware for Gral, Rheinkristall, Rosenthal, Thomas, Daum, and Süssmuth, he has also designed furniture, lighting fixtures, and textiles, all with his unmistakable stamp of rounded geometric shapes. One of his most recognizable ceramic designs is his Brasilia coffee and tea service, dating from 1975 and manufactured by Arzberg. Although produced nearly fifty years later, it strongly resembles the Arzberg china of 1931 designed by Hermann Gretsch.

SIGVARD BERNADOTTE (1907–) Swedish

Bernadotte was well known as a designer of flatware for Georg Jensen from 1930–47. What might not have been so well known is that Bernadotte is the son of King Gustav VI of Sweden. While designing for Jensen, Bernadotte's preference for pure, geometric forms influenced the designs of Jensen's silver and helped establish Jensen's reputation for contemporary international style pieces.

In 1949 Bernadotte opened an office in Copenhagen in partnership with the Danish architect Acton Bjørn. Later, they expanded to offices in Stockholm and New York. The team of Bernadotte and Bjørn patterned themselves after industrial design firms in the United States, diversifying to produce designs in silver, furniture, textiles, bookbindings, plastics, camping equipment, and industrial machinery. In 1964 Bernadotte established an independent design firm that has become one of Scandinavia's largest.

MAX BILL (1908–) Swiss

In 1955 Max Bill stated:

> Examining critically the shapes of objects in daily use, we invariably take as criterion the form of such an object, as a "harmonious expression of the sum of its functions." This does not mean an artificial simplification or an anti-functional streamlining. What we specifically perceive as form, and therefore as beauty, is the natural, self-evident, and functional appearance.[1]

Bill has always been a proponent of pure form. Although he received training as a silversmith at the Kunstgewerbeschule in Zurich and later at the Bauhaus, he has worked as an architect, sculptor, painter, designer, and design philosopher. Bill was a cofounder of the "new Bauhaus" in West Germany, where he directed the departments of architecture and product design from 1950 to 1956. In this capacity he reinstated the Bauhaus ideal of designing industrial products to follow their function while maintaining aesthetic standards.

In 1957 Bill returned to Zurich where he established a studio primarily for his painting and sculpting, but in this 1978 statement his Bauhaus ideals are still evident:

> In the ideal case I should like to build a town with everything that goes with it, or on a smaller scale a civic center including a museum presenting the development of culture—not only of art—and to design it thematically, that is to say, to create by design measures an environment which would be attractive, refreshing and socially constructive."[2]

ARTUR BRAUN (1925–) German

With his brother, Erwin, Artur Braun took control of the family radio manufacturing firm after the death of his father in 1951. The firm had begun to diversify in 1945 with the addition of household appliances, flashlights, and electric shavers, but it was not until the Braun brothers took over and put their Bauhaus approach to work that the firm of Braun really took off. With designers Fritz Eichler, Hans Gugelot, Otl Aicher, and Dieter Rams, they developed a cerebral approach to their products based on the Bauhaus ideals of functionalism, simplicity, and no extraneous ornamentation. The Brauns set out to create a cohesive corporate image, extending their philosophy to their corporate logo, packaging, and advertising image.

The first Braun product to make a statement concerning the new image was a table radio exhibited in Dusseldorf in 1955, designed by Fritz Eichler in conjunction with Artur Braun. To date, the firm of Braun continues to manufacture products in keeping with its philosophy: logical form, minimalism, simplicity.

THE CASTIGLIONI BROTHERS Italian

Achille Castiglioni (1918–)
Livio Castiglioni (1911–79)
Piergiacomo Castiglioni (1913–68)

The Castiglioni brothers were champions of Italian industrial design. They participated in the founding of the Milan Triennale exhibitions, founded the Associazione per il Disegno Industriale, and contributed to the organization of the Compasso d'Oro Awards. Both separately and together, they also taught architecture at Milan and Turin.

The brothers often worked together but sometimes collaborated with other designers. In 1945 Achille and Piergiacomo began working together on exhibition design and product designs, an association that was to last for over twenty-five years. Livio worked primarily as a lighting designer, utilizing industrial materials and experimental types of lamps, but Achille and Piergiacomo were also noted for their lighting designs—the Turbino desk lamp of 1949 manufactured by Arredoluce; the Taraxacum hanging fixtures of 1950, manufactured by Flos; and the Arco, Taccia, and Toio fixtures of the '60s, all distributed through Atelier International, Ltd., New York. Piergiacomo was responsible for creating a landmark in appliance design—the first Italian plastic radio (1939) in collaboration with brother Livio and Luigi Caccia Dominioni.

The Castiglioni brothers designed radios, televisions, and record players for Brionvega and Nova Radio; appliances; flatware for Alessi; furniture for Kartell, Bernini, Beylerian, Zanotta, Gavina; plastics; ceramics; and glassware.

FEDE CHETI (1905–78) Italian

During the 1950s Fede Cheti's large, flower-patterned chintzes, silks, and velvets were extremely popular as upholstery and drapery fabrics. Cheti opened her Milan showroom in 1930, and before long the cream of Milanese society was furnishing its homes with her fabrics. It was not until the 1950s, however, that her designs spread beyond Italy. Encouraged by Gio Ponti, she first introduced her fabrics to America in 1938, but once she won the first prize at the Venice Biennale in 1950 for her "art fabrics," she was an "overnight" success.

Cheti is also known for producing fabrics based on the designs of prominent artists such as Raoul Dufy and Giorgio de Chirico, as well as Gio Ponti. With the exception of French designer Rene Gruau's designs, all other fabrics issuing from the Cheti showroom bore her name.

GINO COLOMBINI (1915–) Italian

Gino Colombini played an important role in the development of the Italian plastics industry. As head of the technical department of Kartell from its beginnings in 1949, he was responsible for the high quality and design concepts from which Italian plastics became noted. Colombini's plastics were awarded the Compasso d'Oro in 1955, 1957, 1959, and 1960. Colombini can be cited for numerous innovations in the use of plastics: experiments in the aesthetics of plastic and in the application of design principles that created functional, beautiful designs in a medium that had formerly been regarded only for its utility.

LUCIENNE DAY (1917–) British
ROBIN DAY (1915–) British

Designers Robin and Lucienne Day have received international recognition both together and separately. Lucienne's Calyx fabric pattern of 1951 was noted as the best textile design on the American market in 1952. She received the First Award from the American Institute of Decorators, a gold medal at the Milan Triennale of 1951, and a grand prize in 1954. During the late '50s and '60s she was given three Council of Industrial Design awards.

Lucienne Day is noted for the strength and boldness of her textile patterns, particularly those for Heal Fabrics, Edinburgh Weavers, and Cavendish. She also designed wallpapers, table linens, carpets, and some porcelain pieces for Rosenthal during the years 1957–69.

Lucienne's husband, Robin, won a first prize in collaboration with Clive Latimer at the International Competition for Low-cost Furniture Design at the New York Museum of Modern Art in 1948 for storage pieces designed in London and manufactured by Johnson-Carper Furniture Company of Roanoke, Virginia. The catalog complimented the design on "the peaceful, uniform horizontal lines of the drawer faces, accented but not interrupted by finger recesses backed with brushed brass-finished plates . . . and the tubular metal supports from which the cabinets hang at a height which makes for easy access and cleaning."[3]

Following this award, Robin Day began manufacturing through the British company Hille, working in wood, plywood, plastic, and upholstered pieces. His Polyprop chair of 1963, of injection-molded polypropylene on a tubular steel frame, has become one of the most successful chairs ever produced, being inexpensive and quick to make. It won the Design Centre award of 1965. He has also designed for many public buildings in Britain, including the Royal Festival Hall in 1951 and the Barbican Arts Centre in 1968. His furniture designs for Hille won him the Gold Medal at the 1951 Milan Triennale. His varied design career—which has included aircraft interiors, exhibits, appliances, carpets, and flatware—in conjunction with his furniture designs, reaped him the reward of being named a Royal Designer for Industry in 1959. Lucienne was not far behind him: she received her Royal Designer for Industry award in 1963.

FREDA DIAMOND (1905–) American

Freda Diamond brought "good taste" to the American public of the 1950s. Diamond was a designer but is primarily noted for her work as a consultant to industry, in which capacity she set styles and trends and spoke out against the gaudy and trashy aspects of the postwar period. In 1942 Diamond was hired by Libbey glass to do a market research survey for their glassware lines, upon which they planned to base their strategy for postwar domestic production. Diamond's recommendations—theme glassware in boxed sets hyped by national advertising—were perfect for the decade in which Libbey turned to automated production. It could now sell good-quality glassware at reasonable prices. In 1950, Diamond's design for Classic Crystal tumblers was included in the "Good Design" exhibition at the New York Museum of Modern Art. She did succumb to ornamentation in later designs and recommendations but continued to speak out against unnecessary decoration of products.

PAUL FRANKL (b.?–1958) American

Frankl was born in Austria but became a major contributor to the design movement in the United States from the 1920s until his death in 1958. His early designs relied heavily on geometric forms, but his postwar furniture was typical of the curvilinear, biomorphic forms of the period. (See Plate 169, showing an unusual low table by Frankl with a cork top, manufactured by the Johnson Furniture Company in 1949. The table also came in a mahogany and pine version.)

ALEXANDER GIRARD (1907–) American

Alexander Girard has been designing textiles for Herman Miller since 1952 (Plates 144–148). He was trained as an architect in London and Rome and practiced architecture in Florence prior to opening his own office in New York in 1932. Following some successful interior design commissions for such auto companies as Ford (1943) and Lincoln (1946), he served as designer of the "Design for Living" exhibit at the Detroit Institute of Arts (1949) and worked as a color consultant to the General Motors Research Center during 1951 and 1952. Since 1953 he has directed the fabric division of Herman Miller in Santa Fe.

Girard said he began designing fabrics because what he needed was not available:

> We were doing a lot of interior work then and never could find the primary colors we wanted to use; there just were no primary colors available in this field. So we always had them made or dyed or found them in Macy's basement. . . . In those days a brilliant pink or magenta carried a connotation of double-barreled horror.[4]

The Herman Miller Textile Division produced not only all of the company's upholstery fabrics but a full line of drapery fabrics and a large selection of Girard prints available as custom orders.

Girard's work also included wallpapers, a corporate design program for Braniff airlines that included brightly painted airplanes, and interiors such as La Fonda del Sol, New York (1959–60) and a furniture group for L'Etoile restaurant in Manhattan. L'Etoile closed abruptly, and the space was taken over by an American Airlines ticket office, which retained Girard's chairs (they happened to be colored in red, white, and blue).

HANS GUGELOT (1920–65) Swiss

Hans Gugelot was one of the great influences on the forms adopted by Western postwar manufacturers. With his pupil and colleague Dieter Rams, he was an ardent exponent of the functionalist style, which is based on the "form follows function" philosophy. Throughout his career, Gugelot applied his functionalist architectural principles to his industrial design work.

Gugelot was born in Indonesia and studied at the Eidgenossischen Technische Hochschule in Zurich. He worked with Max Bill from 1948 to 1950, designing furniture for the Horgen-Glarus stores. From 1955 until his death, Gugelot was director of the production and development department of the "new Bauhaus," the Hochschule für Gestaltung in Ulm, West Germany. This position, in conjunction with his design work for Braun, Pfaff, Kodak, and other companies, contributed to the widespread influence of his functional approach to design during the postwar years. In 1956 he designed the Phonosuper phonograph/radio in collaboration with Dieter Rams, which incorporated a metal and wood housing manufactured by Braun. The Phonosuper can be considered the prototype of the new Braun designs that were to follow. Gugelot also designed the Kodak Carousel slide projector (1962), which has proved to be a timeless design.

ESZTER HARASZTY (ca. 1910–) American

Hungarian-born Haraszty was director of Knoll textiles from 1949 to 1955, a period during which she revolutionized the colors and fabrics of commercial upholstery goods. She had a nearly infallible eye that enabled her to assemble textile designers and weavers to produce fabrics that would be suitable for machine production while remaining innovative.

Marianne Strengell and Evelyn Hill supplied handwoven designs; prints came from Angelo Testa, Stig Lindberg, Astrid Sampe, and Sven Markelius. Haraszty also designed fabrics herself. Her Knoll stripe of 1951 and Fibra of 1953 were exhibited in the New York Museum of Modern Art's "Good Design" show, and in 1956 she won an A.I.D. International Design award for her fabric design, Triad. Haraszty is also responsible for Transportation Cloth.

With her remarkable eye for color, Haraszty introduced the color combination of orange and pink, which not only broke all the rules but opened up the eyes and minds of many who had previously considered such clashing combinations color heresy.

For that, if for nothing else, she has deservedly earned a place in design history. In 1958 she opened an independent design studio in New York.

FINN JUHL (1912–) Danish

In 1951 the Baker Company introduced Juhl's furniture designs to America, where they were subsequently shown at the "Good Design" exhibits in New York and Chicago. It was through Juhl's work in the 1940s that Danish design rose to international heights.

Like his famous countrymen, Hans Wegner and Arne Jacobsen, Juhl preferred simple forms and natural materials. He had studied architecture under Kaare Klint at the Royal Danish Academy of Fine Arts in Copenhagen. In 1937 he began collaborating with cabinetmaker Niels Vodder, who initially handcrafted Juhl's designs. By the time Baker picked up his work, Juhl's designs were being mass-produced, but they still adhered to the designer's rigid specifications for quality.

Juhl is noted for his "floating seats," which are suspended on crossbars rather than on the chair frame. In addition to furniture, Juhl designed interiors, including the Trusteeship Council Chamber at the United Nations in New York. His design work also extends to appliances, porcelain, lighting, carpets, and woodenware.

KATAVOLOS/LITTELL/KELLEY (1949–55) American

William Katavolos, Ross Littell, and Douglas Kelley were all graduates of the Pratt Institute in New York. During their six-year partnership they designed furniture, textiles, and dinnerware for Laverne Originals, a company that had been founded by Erwine and Estelle Laverne in 1938. (The Lavernes were originators of the "invisible" furniture group of 1957, constructed of transparent plastic to give a sense of expansive space by being unobtrusive. The Champagne chair, as the "invisible" chair was called, is a plexiglass shell on an aluminum pedestal base with an upholstered seat cushion, resembling Saarinen's Pedestal group in form.)

The team of Katavolos/Littell/Kelley designed their New Furniture group of chairs and tables in leather, glass, chrome, and marble for Lavern Originals, and they were exhibited at the "Good Design" show of the Museum of Modern Art in New York in 1953 and 1955. Their T chair (see C13) won the A.I.D. award in 1952 for the best furniture design in the United States.

POUL KJAERHOLM (1929–80) Danish

Kjaerholm's furniture designs are associated with the austere functionalist forms that were the frequent outcome of Bauhaus-based concepts.

In spite of his traditional training as a cabinetmaker at the School of Arts and Crafts in Copenhagen, Kjaerholm's personal style led him to amalgamations of materials that bore his own stamp. Kjaerholm designed exclusively for industry and had a preference for mixing the coldness of steel with the relative warmth of natural materials such as woven cane, canvas, leather, wood, and rope (Plates 149–158). His 1956 chair of chromed steel and leather, manufactured by Fritz Hansen, won the Grand Prize in the Milan Triennale of 1957. A wickerwork version of the chair design was produced, but Kjaerholm's attention to detail extended to his padding the steel rails at the back and seat edge to provide comfort.

EBSEN KLINT (1915–69) Danish

Ebsen Klint was the son of Kaare Klint. His training included studies at the Royal Danish Academy of Architecture in Copenhagen as well as apprenticeships in architectural firms and a stint as an industrial designer for Philips in the Netherlands. His best-known works are his collaborative effort with Børge Mogensen on school furniture (1962) and his folded-paper hanging light of 1947, manufactured by Le Klint (Plate 159).

Klint began working with Mogensen beginning about 1959 on a series of chairs that were to be designed specifically for schools where students had to sit for long periods. Working in conjunction with physiotherapist Eigil Snorrason, they produced chairs in four different sizes, the smallest being used in kindergarten classes, the two middle sizes suitable for elementary school use, and the largest for high schools and colleges. (For further information, see the section on Børge Mogensen.)

Klint's hanging lamp of 1947 was similar to many others being produced by the firm of Le Klint at that time. It consisted of a globe of pleated, plastic-coated paper suspended from a slim electrical cord, the overall design being reminiscent of Japanese origami.

RAY KOMAI (1918–) American

Komai studied at the Art Center College of Los Angeles, taking courses in interior, industrial, and graphic design. In 1944 he worked in advertising in New York, and in 1948 he opened his own design office in partnership with Carter Winter. His molded plywood chair of 1949, with slit seat and chromed tubular steel legs, is in the collection of the New York Museum of Modern Art. It was manufactured by the J.G. Furniture Company, which produced his other furniture designs, including tables and upholstered seating. He has also designed wallpaper and textiles.

JACK LENOR LARSEN (1927–) American

Just say "textile designer" to most interior designers and the name of Jack Lenor Larsen immediately springs to mind. He is one of the most distinguished names in the contemporary textile industry, being not only a designer but a writer and teacher—a highly creative and innovative artist (Plates 161–164).

Some of Larsen's innovations in textiles include: the first printed velvet upholstery fabrics; the first stretch upholstery fabric (1961); and Interplay, a saran monofilament developed in 1960 as warp-knit casements.

Larsen also adheres to the "form follows function" principle, believing that the inherent characteristics of fiber should dictate the outcome of the fabric. This philosophy has led him to develop upholstery fabric for Pan American and Braniff Airlines; theater curtains for the Center for Performing Arts at Wolf Trap; quilted silk banners for the Sears Tower in Chicago; and upholstery collections for Cassina and Vescom.

After training at the University of Washington and the Cranbrook Academy of Art, Larsen opened a studio in New York in 1952. It was at this time that he adopted the "handwoven" look in fabrics manufactured on power looms, a look that has been widely imitated. In 1958 he organized the Larsen Design Studio to experiment with and develop new materials and processes for the textile industry. This allowed the firm to expand into consulting and design for large-scale architectural projects.

Larsen has written *Elements of Weaving* with Azalea Thorpe; *Beyond Craft: The Art Fabric* with Mildred Constantine; *Fabrics for Interiors* with Jeanne Weeks; *The Dyer's Art: Ikat, Batik, Plangi;* and *The Art Fabric: Mainstream* with Mildred Constantine.

His numerous awards include a Compasso d'Oro at the Milan Triennale of 1964 and nomination as a Royal Designer for Industry in 1982.

RAYMOND LOEWY (1893–) American

Although Loewy is an industrial designer, his massive impact on the field of design in general claims him a place in any discussion of interior design. Loewy opened his own design studio in New York in 1930 after training in France as an engineer. His first major achievement was the Sears Coldspot refrigerator of 1934, which became a design classic.

It is estimated that during the postwar period Loewy's influence in the field of design was so immense that three out of every four Americans came into contact with a Loewy design at least once a day. He designed the Coca-Cola dispenser, the Schick razor, Pepsodent toothpaste tube packaging, the Lucky Strike cigarette pack, and the can for Carling Black Label beer, as well as the Electrolux vacuum cleaner.

During the 1940s and 1950s, Loewy set the standards for automobile design with the 1947 Studebaker Champion, the 1953 Starline, and the 1962 Avanti. He also designed the color scheme for John F. Kennedy's Air Force One personal Boeing 707 airplane and worked with NASA on habitability systems for the Skylab series of space vehicles. Involved with transportation, graphic design, packaging, interior design, and product design, Loewy was the first designer to make the cover of *Life* magazine.

ENID MARX (1902–) British

Enid Marx was a member of the Utility Furniture Design Panel of the 1940s and as such was responsible for designing most of the utility furnishings and fabrics sold in Britain from the late war years through the postwar period. The Utility Panel was established in 1943 and continued in operation through 1952. Strict quotas rationing supplies available for furnishings were overseen by the panel, whose duty it was "to produce specifications for furniture of good, sound construction in simple but agreeable designs for sale at reasonable prices, and ensuring the maximum economy of raw materials and labor."

The resultant furniture line consisted of sturdy pieces constructed of oak or mahogany, of very simple form. The prototype group introduced in 1943 became the manufacturing standard. Even after wartime austerities were over, the utility look survived, manufactured by several firms who saw it as a way to raise the design consciousness of the masses.

Enid Marx was forced to work with extremely limited raw materials. For example, until 1946 only four colors were available in two types of cotton yarn. Also, it was essential to maintain small-scale patterns in order to minimize fabric loss in piecing patterns for upholstery. Marx designed muted textiles in abstract geometrics that became the standard of the utility period.

She was among the designers chosen to participate in the Royal Pavilion at the Festival of Britain in 1951.

PAUL McCOBB (1917–69) American

For a time, Paul McCobb was the golden boy of furniture design in the United States. During most of the 1950s, his designs were constantly published in the press, and his work appeared repeatedly in the "Good Design" exhibits of the Museum of Modern Art in New York. At Bloomingdale's, New York, the

Paul McCobb Shop was showing fifteen room settings with 348 of his items on display in 1957.

McCobb is considered the founder of a new look in American interiors, promoting low lines, natural woods, and slim foam pillows (Plate 166). He popularized modular furniture and advocated the use of room dividers and wall storage systems, which he referred to as "living walls." Like many of his contemporaries, his goal was to design a timeless look, suitable to modern lifestyles, that was well made and economical.

McCobb opened an independent office in 1945 after working for a time as a painter, interior designer, and display designer. In 1950 he launched his first low-cost furniture designs, in collaboration with B.G. Mesberg as furniture distributor, named the Planner group. Later, more expensive furniture was produced along similar design concepts—the Directional, Predictor, Linear, and Perimeter furniture groups. McCobb's furniture was manufactured by the Winchendon Furniture Company of Massachusetts.

McCobb's Planner group was similar in concept to the early Eames/Saarinen designs, consisting of single, double, and multiple drawer chests that could be combined with cabinets and bookcases by standing alone or stacking on benches. The benches themselves could also be used as tables.

As quickly as he had risen to design stardom, McCobb disappeared from the scene. While his work continued to be of high quality and maintained the initial design concepts, the fickle public clamored for something new. The furniture market's insatiable need for new designs soon pushed Paul McCobb far into the background and eventually out of production altogether.

GRETHE MEYER (1918–) Danish

Grethe Meyer was trained as an architect. She frequently worked with Børge Mogensen and was instrumental in his research into the size standardization of consumer products. (See "Børge Mogensen" section for further details.) With Mogensen, she codesigned the Boligens Byggeskabe (BB) and Øresund storage systems. She is also known for her stacking glassware for Kastrup glassworks and her Blue Line ceramic tableware (awarded the Danish ID prize in 1965), as well as the "Firepot" series of oven-to-table ware, designed for Royal Copenhagen.

ORLA MØLGAARD-NIELSEN (1907–) Danish

Mølgaard-Nielsen introduced laminate gluing and plywood to the Danish furniture industry. He also advanced the principle of knockdown furniture with the Ax series (1950) of chairs and tables, manufactured by Fritz Hansen. The Ax chair is of knockdown construction with a laminated beech frame and a teak seat and back. Although the chair is no longer in production, it received a Diploma of Honor at the Milan Triennale of 1951 and again in 1954. It also was awarded the "Good Design" stamp of approval in the United States. The Ax series was the result of a collaboration by Mølgaard-Nielsen and Peter Hvidt, also an architect and cabinetmaker, who had formed a partnership in 1944 and had begun producing a line of sectional furniture based on the earlier concepts of Kaare Klint.

Both Mølgaard-Nielsen and Hvidt were trained at the School of Arts and Crafts in Copenhagen. It was there that Mølgaard-Nielsen met the young student Hans Wegner and introduced him to Arne Jacobsen, giving Wegner his first real break in the industry.

VERNER PANTON (1926–) Danish

Panton is a Dane living in Switzerland who is noted for his chair designs, which might be termed "futuristic." It is easy to imagine Panton chairs on the set of a science fiction film. He describes his penchant for working with new materials in the following statement:

> I try to forget existing examples even though they may be good and concern myself above all with the material. The result then rarely has four legs, not because I do not wish to make such a chair, but because the processing of materials like wire or polyester calls for new shapes. The mere question of four legs I find rather unimportant.[5]

Panton worked as an associate of Arne Jacobsen from 1950 to 1952 before opening his own offices in Binningen, Switzerland in 1955. He was trained as an architect and designer at the Royal Academy of Fine Arts in Copenhagen.

Panton has concentrated on chair design, from his 1956 knockdown nickel-rod chair, manufactured by Fritz Hansen, through his wire cone chair of 1959, his S-chair of 1965, to his jigsaw plywood models of the 1980s. Panton's fiberglass-reinforced polyester stacking chair of 1960 is a one-piece continuum of molded plastic, the culmination of his search for a chair that could be designed entirely of a single material. The chair was produced by Herman Miller beginning in 1967.

In addition to chairs, Panton has also designed lighting, carpets, and textiles. He won the Interior Design Award in the United States in 1963 and 1968, the Rosenthal Studio Prize in 1967, and the Diploma of Honor at the International Furniture Exhibition in Vienna, 1969.

ERNEST RACE (1913–63) British

Race was trained at the Bartlett School of Architecture of the University of London. Ernest Race Ltd. (later renamed Race Furniture) was formed in 1945. It was an amalgamation of Race's designs with that of a tool-and-die manufacturer who wanted to apply engineering techniques to furniture production. Because of wartime shortages, Race was not permitted to use wood or fabric in his furniture designs. He turned instead to aluminum alloy reclaimed from aircraft salvage. His BA chair, of cast aluminum with a padded plywood seat and back, was exhibited at the "Britain Can Make It" show in 1946. The chair was made without arms and was suitable for dining or public use in commercial applications. The frame was coated with enamel, and the seat and back covering was vinyl or hide. The BA chair won a Gold Medal at the Milan Triennale of 1951.

His other designs include a metal-framed wing chair (1947) and storage units that won an honorable mention in the Museum of Modern Art's International Competition for Low-cost Furniture Design of 1948. The museum catalog states:

> Ernest Race's simple scheme for a wardrobe impressed the jury because of its neat structure and good looks. The fact that it did not present a solution to the storage problem that would be widely acceptable in this country [United States] did not make it suitable material for a prize. But the jury was unanimous in its desire to call attention to its virtues.[6]

Race also designed the Antelope chair, intended as outdoor furniture for the Festival of Britain held in 1951. The Antelope chair was constructed of a steel-rod frame and a plywood seat. The frame was rustproofed and enameled in white. The seats were available in a choice of six colors. The Antelope chair won a Silver Medal in the Milan Triennale of 1954.

EDWARD WORMLEY (1907–) American

In both 1951 and 1952, six of Wormley's designs were included in the "Good Design" exhibits of the Museum of Modern Art in New York. He worked in both the modern and traditional styles, designing mass-market furniture for Dunbar of Indiana from 1931 to 1941.

After training at the Art Institute of Chicago, Wormley worked in the design studio of Marshall Field, Chicago from 1928 to 1931, then accepted the position with Dunbar. In 1945 he opened his own design studio in New York but continued to supply furniture, carpet, and textile designs to Dunbar.

Wormley was remarkably adept at translating the latest trend into designs that were palatable to the public taste, and much of his postwar work reflects the Scandinavian and Italian influences so prevalent at the time. One of his most elegant designs is the Listen to Me chaise, designed for Dunbar in 1947, constructed of white maple, American cherry, woolen upholstery, and copper-wire supports.

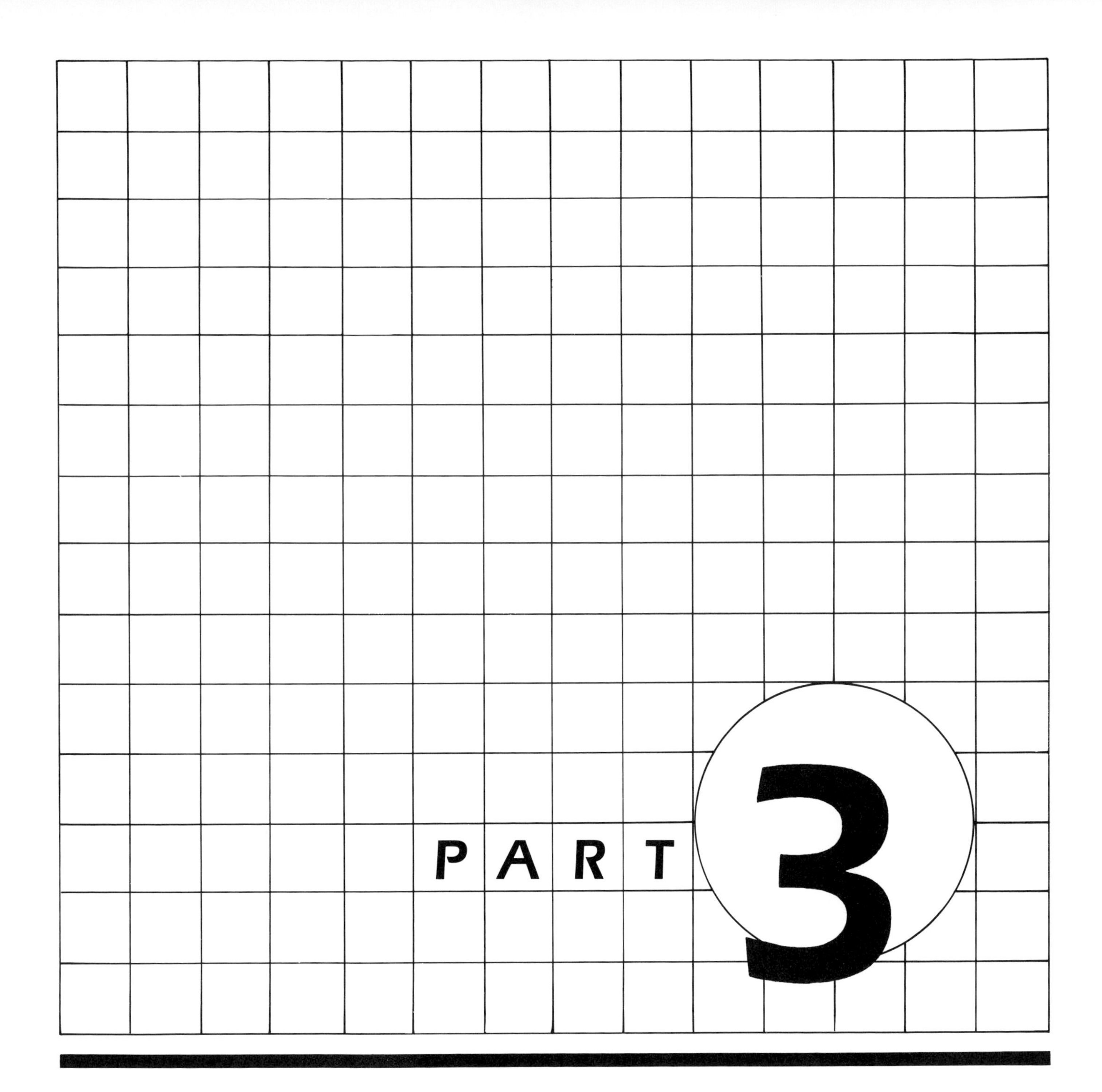

Materials and Methods of Construction

Construction Materials and Methods

In the development of furniture, first came handcrafts, then came the Industrial Revolution, then came turmoil. A simplistic statement, perhaps, but a realistic description of the history of furniture design.

Once the machine age arrived in full force, there was a grinding clash between handcrafts and machine-made products. There was confusion. There was debate. "Is the machine capable of producing art?" asked William Morris. He decided it was not and called for a return to handcrafts. But he was wrong. The machine is capable of producing art *if* it is properly used. This was the key to early-twentieth-century furniture design—experimentation to find the optimal materials and methods of construction.

In spite of Morris's rejection of the machine, his contributions were many, perhaps his greatest being his insistence that art and design must be an integral part of everyday life. Morris, like the originators of the Bauhaus and the Organic designers, was rooted in the belief that harmony was of major concern in any art or design project. Rooms of one spirit, one viewpoint, united by a single theme, became the cornerstone of the Arts and Crafts movement. Similarly, Eero Saarinen's goal of ridding a room of the "slum of legs" came from the basic concept of relating an individual piece to the larger whole. Saarinen believed that:

> Confusion comes from trying to amalgamate several conflicting ideas in one room. A room is like a piece of art: it is just one idea. . . . Perhaps the most important thing I learned from my father was that in any design problem one should seek the solution in terms of the next largest thing. If the problem is an ashtray, then the way it relates to the table will influence its designs. If the problem is a chair, then its solution must be found in the way it relates to the room.[1]

Gradually, this same philosophy extended into the use of materials.

From the Industrial Revolution to the present day, two main streams have existed: those who work with the machine and those who seem disinclined to acknowledge its invention. While art nouveau, art deco, and subsequent styles, right up to the current Memphis movement, strive to use ornamentation as a means of striking back at machine technology, some designers have chosen to accept the machine and its potential and to work with it in developing new techniques, new technologies, and new concepts. In this category are such designers as Belter and Thonet, who worked with machines to find fresh ways of bending wood. Going even beyond this class are the likes of Breuer, Le Corbusier, and Aalto, whose visionary approaches mated design and industry to form entirely new products. Breuer's invention of tubular metal chairs and Aalto's utilization of bent plywood introduced new structural forms. They laid the groundwork for Eames and Saarinen and a host of postwar designers who were able to build on these ideas, to use war-developed technologies in revolutionizing the furniture industry.

WOOD

Historically, wood has been the primary source of construction material for furniture since ancient times. Even in contemporary furniture, wood still plays a dominant role. Woods can be divided into two main families: hardwood and softwood. Softwoods are evergreens such as pine, spruce, fir, hemlock, cedar, and redwood. Hardwoods come from the deciduous tree group. They include birch, maple, oak, and walnut, as well as such "exotic" woods from tropical climates as rosewood, zebrawood (Macassar ebony), mahogany, and teak. Softwoods are generally used for building construction or inexpensive furniture, while hardwoods are preferred for furniture because of their higher strength and durability.

The technique of gluing woods together was known in antiquity, but it was not until the twentieth century that laminated woods were truly exploited in the construction of new furniture forms. By 1840, Michael Thonet was making chairs from narrow strips of wood veneer bent and glued together under pressure in a wood mold. To appreciate fully the technological innovations of molded plywood during the postwar period, we cannot overlook the work of this nineteenth-century designer whose bentwood designs were the forerunner of so many things to come. While Thonet's curves were based on those of the traditional Windsor chair, his furniture was immediately recognizable as a design original. It also employed the inventive notion of using knockdown parts, which made it inexpensive to produce and easy to transport. Thonet designs were the inspiration for Le Corbusier, Breuer, Aalto, and others, and still sell well today.

Lamination, another technique used frequently in postwar furniture, was well known as far back as 1856. In that year, furniture maker Henry Belter applied for a patent on a technique he had developed for gluing layers of wood veneer with their grains at right angles to each other. This technique is essentially the same as that used in the construction of modern plywood. Plywood consists of layers of wood veneer laminated together with the grain direction running the opposite way in each successive layer for balance and strength. Lamination takes place when the layers are glued together under pressure. The resulting plywood is extremely resistant to problems of warping and splitting.

The main benefit of lamination is that it enables wood to be worked in ways impossible with sawed lumber. It is sometimes mistakenly believed that plywood is a cheap substitute for expensive hardwoods because of its association with the veneer process, in which thin layers of rare or ornamental woods are used to cover woods of lesser quality. In fact, plywood should actually be considered as a completely different material with separate properties. This erroneous assumption might be a factor in the similarly erroneous notion that furniture of the '40s and '50s was cheap, throwaway, or a passing fad.

The belief that plywood is cheap dates to the Paris exhibition of 1878 where American chairs were displayed with seats and backs of bent, perforated plywood, then termed "wood veneer." These chairs were considered inexpensive substitutes for "real" wood furniture. Plywood soon began appearing as a cheap substitute for wood in the backings for mirrors, cheap chests, and cupboards. It was not until the intervention of World War I that demands were made that brought about notable changes and improvements in plywood structure. Around 1918, the name "plywood" was coined in an attempt to dispel the negative associations that were becoming attached to the term "veneered wood." It was hoped that the new name, plywood, would help this material to be viewed favorably as a new construction material.

The production of reliable woods in the period between the two world wars revolutionized the furniture industry. Since the fifteenth century, furniture had relied on paneled framing; now, the plywood alternative provided a simpler, less expensive construction material that was well suited to mass production. Another benefit of plywood is that the lamination process eliminates wood's natural tendency to warp with humidity changes.

Several steps were involved in the manufacturing process of wood lamination. First, logs were cut to the desired length, the bark removed, and the logs then soaked to make them pliable. Next, the rough outer layers were removed with veneer lathes and the veneer stripped off in a continuous ribbon. The thin sheets of wood were then trimmed to size and fed into drying machines through a roller system. As the sheets passed between the rollers, they were covered with adhesive. The sheets were then pressed together with a hydraulic press and left to dry for a few days prior to scraping and trimming.

Another innovation came via molded plywood, which was developed during World War II for the aviation industry. This was the technology employed by Eames and Saarinen in their molded plywood chair designed for the Organic Design in Home Furnishings competition of 1940. Compared to ordinary wood, plywood is an extremely stable material, lending itself well to broad, simple surfaces. The invention of molded plywood and its subsequent use in furniture permitted an entirely new way of looking at furniture design. For the first time we had the technology to produce light furniture—both visually light and light in weight.

In the Museum of Modern Art catalog of 1953, *What Is Modern Interior Design?*, Edgar Kaufmann, Jr., wrote:

> Today, lightness seems a natural trait in a room. . . . Lightness in modern interiors is sometimes said to originate in practical or functional considerations. . . . Lightweight furniture can make housekeeping less burdensome . . . [it] has tended to reinforce the modern designer's interest in open structures, free spaces and light lines which can be traced back to the Japanism of the [18]70s and 80s.[2]

This sense of lightness that is equated with postwar design depended largely on the availability of new construction methods and materials. Only when considered in the context of their bulky, overstuffed predecessors can the postwar shell chairs be truly appreciated for their amazing sense of lightness. The typical prewar overstuffed chair was constructed of as many as thirty or more separate pieces of wood of different shapes, screwed or glued together into a rigid, heavy construction. Thick burlap was stretched to accommodate the seat springs. Then, two helical springs with a large piece of baling wire were needed to support the center section under the seat springs. The chair back contained additional springs braced by heavy webbing, all of which were tied and braced against each other and the frame. On top of all this, a fiber pad was applied, then a mass of hair or cotton padding set in place before the piece was finally covered with upholstery fabric—quite a procedure. The typical overstuffed frame alone, without legs or covering, weighed about forty-five pounds. When compared to the lightness of Eames's and Saarinen's shell chairs, the difference is astonishing.

METAL

Historically, furniture was not "designed" per se. It was fashioned by the hands of the craftsman—the carpenter or the coffin maker. Only after the Industrial Revolution did it become economically prudent to devise production methods suitable to the machine that discouraged handwork. When modern designers came into being, they were concerned with conceiving designs that could both be adapted easily to machine production and actually exemplify, rather than camouflage, their industrial origins. Designers labored to produce "machine art" that would testify to the machine's coming of age—they promoted sleek, smooth surfaces, rounded corners, and gleaming polished finishes that emphasized the furniture's machine-produced origins.

Together with molded plywood and plastic, tubular metal became a favorite construction material of postwar designers. Although metal furniture was common in the nineteenth century, it was rarely found in commercial use until the early twentieth century. The rising costs of fine furniture woods prompted experimentation with metal in furniture design, first as decorative hardware and eventually as the prime construction material. By the nineteenth century, metal furniture had become commonplace. Cast iron or brass were often used in those days, but steel became the trademark of twentieth-century furniture. In lesser use were bronze and aluminum.

The obvious advantages of metal furniture are its inherent nonflammability and the ease with which it adapts to industrial production methods. In furniture, metal usually takes the form of tubing, sheets, bars, or small structural elements. Furniture frames are connected by cutting metal tubes into sections, bending the cut lengths, and assembling them by welding or mechanical connectors. After the piece is welded, it is polished and finished to minimize the joins.

Today, sheet metal is commonly used in kitchen and office furniture in the form of shelving, doors, drawers, filing cabinets, and the like. One drawback of steel is that it rusts quickly, even from such small amounts of moisture as indoor humidity. Aluminum does not rust, but it does develop an unattractive dull gray surface that can detract from its appearance. To prevent the oxidizing process, metal is often finished with paint, plastic coating, or plating—most often in chrome or brass for furniture. Anodizing is a special finish reserved for aluminum, in which the metal is coated with a transparent or sometimes colored finish to preserve the metallic appearance. Brass, bronze, dark blues, and black are available. During the 1930s, Russel Wright produced a line of spun aluminum tableware in which the aluminum was treated with emery cloth to produce a brushed effect.

Unfortunately, most early designers who used metal used it as a substitute for wood without considering its individual properties. It was not until 1903 that Frank Lloyd Wright "expressed the true nature of metal as well as the nature of the structure" in the Larkin building. Wright took into account the inherent properties of metal when designing the office furniture for the Larkin building, and in so doing, he created a harmonious design that integrated the structure, the interior decoration, and the furniture. In 1936, Wright again expressed this understanding of materials in his furniture for the S.C. Johnson Administration building where, in keeping with organic design principles, he conceived the furniture in harmony with the structure by blending the color of floors and walls with the painted finishes and upholstery of the chairs.

Napoleon used folding metal campaign furniture. The Victorians were very fond of cast-iron tables and chairs. But it is Marcel Breuer who is credited with the innovation of using metal tubing as the primary structural material for furniture, although his designs were but an extension of the tubing used in Victorian brass beds. The major difference between Breuer's designs and those of the Victorian era were the thought processes behind the use of materials. Breuer, as a modern designer, was responding to a series of questions related to function: How will this piece be used? How will this piece relate to both the interior and the architecture? These questions were considered *before* the design was begun as opposed to the traditional method, whereby the same forms were used over and over again, the ornamentation being the only differentiating factor.

Breuer credited his bicycle with giving him the idea of designing steel furniture: he found its simple, functional lines and its gleaming metal surfaces so attractive that he wanted to reproduce them in furniture designs. His first tubular-steel chair, the Wassily chair (1925), was constructed of nickel-plated cold-drawn tubing with welded joints and glide runners.

Of his early designs Breuer wrote:

> Already back then I was thinking about replacing the thick upholstery used on chair seats with stretched fabric. I also wanted a flexible, springy frame. The combination of stretched fabric and flexible frame I hoped would make the chair more

comfortable to sit on and keep it from looking clumsy. I also tried to achieve a certain transparency of form and along with it an optical as well as physical lightness. In the course of my work on series manufacture and standardization I had come across polished metal surfaces—reflecting, pure lines in space—as new components of our home furnishings. In these shimmering curving lines I saw not only symbols of modern technology but technology itself.[3]

The concept embodied in these words of Breuer is vital to the motivations of postwar design—the technology of war merged with the needs of the people to create a new era in furniture design.

As progress became our most important product, many designers approached the machine aesthetic with the dedication of novitiates. They felt duty-bound to explore all the possibilities of which machine technology was capable in their pursuit of both economy and speed (to keep up with growing demand).

PLASTIC

In the catalog for the International Competition for Low-cost Furniture Design of 1948, Edgar Kaufmann, Jr., wrote:

> At the end of World War II American families found themselves faced with a tremendous housing problem. In part they had to make the best of existing accommodations by crowding them with far greater numbers than had been intended originally, or else they had to try to secure one of the new dwellings which were erected, though too slowly to satisfy the need. In either case families found themselves in smaller homes than had been usual. If these homes were to be in any sense livable or comfortable, these furnishings had to be efficiently planned and trimly scaled. Deeper than this lay the important question of cost. The market supplied furniture at many price levels, but serviceability and efficiency were not always directly related to these prices and it was hard to find desirable furniture at low cost. American ingenuity and American technology had provided this country with an admirable standard of living, but seemingly in regard to the home and its furnishings these forces were not yet fully mobilized. In the hope that new ideas and better results could be found, a competition was launched under the auspices of the Museum of Modern Art and an enterprising group of American retailers and manufacturers. . . .[4]

This competition encouraged the use of new materials and new methods that became the hallmark of postwar furniture design.

It was no longer enough to produce a fine, carefully crafted product. Designers now had to progress, constantly pursuing the latest technology, the newest material. They had to be innovative, original—even futuristic. Bent and molded plywood made possible new shapes. Metal tubing and wire were used in new configurations. But the true technological innovation of twentieth-century furniture was plastic.

As an adjective, "plastic" can be variously defined as formative, flexible, synthetic, or capable of continuous and permanent change. What more could a machine-age designer ask from a construction material? Plastics can assume nearly any form. They were born into an industrially advanced technology and seemed the perfect medium for experimentation with new forms.

At first, plastics often imitated natural materials—synthetic leather for upholstery applications, woodgrained laminates as surfaces, and so on. But when designers began to think of plastic in a new light, when they began experimenting with it without trying to copy any other known material, breakthroughs really began. Plastics made possible structural forms in furniture that previously we had only been able to imagine. Without the development of plastics, most postwar furniture designs would simply not exist.

Each plastic has a generic and a chemical name. It may also have one or more trade names, making a perfect climate for utter confusion. However, it becomes a little simpler when we realize that all plastics fall into one of two categories: thermoplastics or thermosetting plastics. Thermoplastics harden when cooled and soften when heated. This process can be repeated indefinitely with the same results. Thermosetting plastics are formed from a chemical process in the presence of heat and pressure. Reheating will not soften thermosetting plastics.

Thermoplastics are formed primarily by the injection-molding process by which the plastic is heated to the soft stage, then forced into a closed mold where it is allowed to cool. The mold is then opened and the part forced out by ejection pins.

The first commercial plastic was invented in the United States in 1868 as a substitute for the ivory in billiard balls. It was called celluloid. Celluloid belongs in the cellulose group, which can be further categorized into cellulose acetate (developed in 1927) and cellulose nitrate. Cellulose acetate has been used in the manufacture of artificial silks and photographic film. Cellulose nitrate has been used in explosives, rayon, and varnishes.

Cellulose is the primary substance in the cell

walls of plants. The derivative "cellophane" is a thin, transparent film made from cellulose, most often used as food wrapping or packaging material.

Over forty years passed before the second plastic, known as Bakelite, came into being. Developed by Dr. Leo Henrik Baekeland in 1909, it was formed from phenol-formaldehyde resins. The phenolic group was tough and hard but brittle. The naturally dark brown color dictated its color range of dark brown or black. Bakelite was used extensively in early radios and costume jewelry, where it often passed for amber.

Between 1909 and 1926, two additional plastics were introduced—cold-molded plastic and milk-based casein. After these breakthroughs, production speeded up considerably with the introduction, in 1927, of cellulose acetate, which became the first injection-molded plastic in 1929. Then, in 1936, came acrylic, also known as polymethyl methacrylate. Acrylic is composed of a group of olefin acids often used for furniture, of which Plexiglas and Lucite are well-known trade names. It is available in colored or transparent sheets, rods, or tubes. It can be cast, cut, heat bent, and assembled with either cement or mechanical connectors.

Both polyethylene and polyesters were introduced commercially in 1942. Polyethylene is a resin made by the polymerization of ethylene. It is most often used in kitchen products, bottles, and toys, being translucent, lightweight, and tough. Polyesters are strong and hard and are used widely as the base for fiberglass furniture, automobile body parts or boat hulls, and as textile fibers.

In 1957 came the birth of polypropylene, which finally made possible extensive use of injection-molding. Previously, this process had been nearly useless in furniture design because of the lack of a really tough material. Polypropylene allows strong, rigid industrial moldings without any need for reinforcement and is far less expensive than fiberglass. Polypropylene is also shiny and clear and can be colored to stainproof, chip-resistant finishes. As a furniture material, polypropylene came into its own during the 1960s and ensuing years.

In addition to the use of plastic as a structural material for postwar furniture, the process of foam molding also permitted innovations in upholstery. Urethane, styrene, and polypropylene can be processed to form air bubbles, causing the material to become a foam that can be produced in sheets or slabs and then used in a variety of ways, most commonly as upholstery cushions or, beginning in the 1960s, as the basic structural unit for furniture.

Even while some were touting plastics as the miracle materials of the '50s, problems were beginning to surface. Sometimes we tend to glorify new discoveries beyond reason. The "wonder drugs" that were to cure all ills fell short of our expectations. So did plastics. Sunlight attacked some; air pollution caused others to deteriorate; flexing caused breakdown; extreme flammability and the production of toxic fumes during combustion were unexpected hazards. What's more, modern life is hard on furniture. We lovingly crate antiques for shipping; they are cared for and protected. Not so with modern furniture, which is subjected to all manner of abuse—from rough handling during transport to being put to uses for which it was never intended (for example, the habit of standing on chairs to reach distant objects)—and generally expected to be virtually indestructible. Indeed, in spite of defects in materials, it sometimes surprises us by complying.

ENGINEERING

The best postwar furniture was engineered with the same precision given to an aircraft. Stability and strength were considered. Would the object remain in place without tipping over? Would it resist forces that would cause it to sag or vibrate or come apart at the seams? Whether or not furniture satisfied these criteria depended to a large extent on the proper choice of materials to limit stress on joints and elemental parts.

Just as the architectural engineer must consider static loads and dynamic loads, so must the furniture designer. Static loads are those inherent in motionless objects and are caused by gravitational force pulling downward on the object. Dynamic loads occur as a result of changing forces, such as the weight of people occupying chairs or the weight of objects placed on or in case goods. For example, while a sofa might appear to support three people, collapse could occur if the three people were excessively overweight and that factor had not been taken into consideration in the sofa's design. Along similar lines, shelving may collapse under the weight of books or objects if it is not properly designed.

The postwar designer was concerned with both intended and unintended uses for furniture—children using beds as trampolines; tabletops and chairs being used as ladders, for example. This type of thinking required a built-in safety factor in order to avoid problems.

Another consideration was the object's center of gravity. Although gravitational pull must be taken into account, it is possible to design an object around a point at which it will balance in any position. Because most furniture is symmetrical, it is usually possible to locate a center of gravity at the center line. In the case of objects that are not symmetrical, two or more centers of gravity might be considered, one for each separate element.

Other problems confronting furniture designers of this era were stresses: compression, tension, bending, shear, and torsion. Compression occurs where materials are squeezed by gravitational loads. This can occur in the legs of chairs or tables or any support elements. Tension occurs where materials are pulled or stretched. Hanging objects are subjected to a high degree of tensile stress. Bending stress is a combination of compression and tension. Any object designed to carry a load can be subject to bending. The most obvious example is shelving slung between two end supports, where the center of the shelf can sag. Shear is fairly rare in furniture construction but can occur when heavy loads on short spans cause the supporting member to snap off. Torsion is a twisting stress that often results when furniture is used improperly, such as when a table is dragged along the floor, causing stress in the joints.

In the postwar period, with the disappearance of the craftsman and the simultaneous ascendance of technology, the professional designer first assumed a major role in determining the appearance of the physical environment. Today, the designer must be not only an artist with a thorough knowledge of technology, he or she must be an adventurer willing to explore and fail and try again, a person able to take the smallest germ of an idea and follow it through the lengthy process to its conclusion—sometimes against great odds.

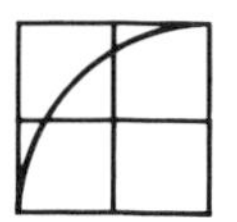

Designers and Their Designs

The successful postwar designers were individuals who rose to such challenges. Eames, Saarinen, Nelson, Bertoia, Noguchi, Russel Wright, and the dozens of others working at their sides had that special combination of daring, determination, and creativity necessary to draw from the old, utilize diverse technologies, and produce totally new and exciting designs.

CHARLES EAMES

One of the most outstanding designers of the postwar period was Charles Eames. Whatever Charles Eames designed, Herman Miller manufactured. Today, this seems a fairytale situation; indeed, Eames has said, "Well, I had a constraint, a feeling that I didn't want to do anything that would get those nice people in trouble. Whatever happened with the Herman Miller Company and us came from taking the kind of risks no one would, or could take today."[1]

Eames was always in the forefront of technology. When he was unable to find available technology to suit his purposes, he was flexible enough to adapt. For example, when Eames began the design of the molded plastic shell chair, the technology to manufacture the chair simply did not exist. Eames compromised and chose sheet metal because of the highly developed mass-production techniques associated with stamped metal parts. Also, Neoprene coating, which permitted heat transfer, had already been developed. Eames took advantage of these two developments in the construction of his shell chair, which was later produced in molded plastic when the technology became available.

Charles and Ray Eames began experimenting with glass-reinforced plastics in their Venice, California workshop. This material was then being used for making lightweight radar domes by such companies as Zenith Plastics, a firm known to Eames because of its association with Eames's architectural projects. Zenith Plastics also manufactured plastic gas-tank linings, which Eames used for the Japanese-inspired *shōji* screens in his own home.

When Eames approached Zenith in the mid-1940s about producing molded plastic furniture, the prototype was made by a slow, costly, hand process. Woven cloth embedded with fibers was immersed in a series of quick-catalyzing resins, laid by hand, and then sandpapered. Desperate for an economical model to show at an upcoming Chicago furniture market, a representative from the Herman Miller Company, who was selling the chairs, went to the Zenith plant with the idea that Eames's original concept of sheet metal chairs could be made up in less costly plastic. In 1950 Zenith showed Eames a Christmas-tree base made of fiberglass-reinforced plastic, which he recognized as the way to mold the shell for his chair. Since the process required only a single set of dies, it was considerably less expensive than the stamped-steel shell model. The fiberglass chair was introduced in 1951, twelve years after Eames and Saarinen had conceived it. This design represents the first successful application of fiberglass-reinforced plastic for consumer use.

Since Zenith Plastics was seeking an entry into the consumer market, they suggested that the chairs be mass produced using hydraulic presses. Engineer Sol Fingerhut was called upon to devise a method of using a matched metal mold. Cost was figured entirely in terms of tonnage of resin, and an initial cost of $6.25 per chair based on a run of 10,000 was suggested. In an effort to cut costs, the initial run was reduced to 2,000. Zenith Plastics agreed to this relatively small order because they were so anxious to break into a new market. Thus, the Eames plastic shell chair came into being.

Product development of the plastic model was plagued by what Eames termed "really miserable problems," ranging from hazards created by glass particles flying in the air at the plant to the challenge of devising a technique for letting the fibers show through the surface without roughness. During a nine-month period of intensive work, Eames, with the help of Sol Fingerhut and members of Zenith Plastics, finally found solutions to these problems. Even so, each of the early shell chairs was practically handcrafted, and the entire surface was finished by hand rubbing with emery cloth.

Eames and Saarinen's first joint attempts at chair design (1940–41) involved the use of a thin laminated shell of wood veneers shaped to take the thrust of the springs on seat and back, which was braced with wooden strips at the points where the springs were attached. This process immediately eliminated the need for the built-up wood frame. What is more, instead of bulky stuffing, Eames and Saarinen used foam rubber. In further experimentation, they achieved what had never before been done in chair design—continuous contact with and support of the body. The ordinary chair had a seat and back that supported the body at two or three points. In the case of the typical overstuffed chair, the body sank into a general softness hoping to find support somewhere along the way.

The shell of the original Eames/Saarinen chair was formed from strips of veneer and glue laminated in a cast-iron form by a process developed by the

Haskelite Corporation. In this way, more comfortable support could be secured with a minimum of material, and the finished chair weighed only twenty pounds, compared with its forty-five pound overstuffed predecessor. The first Eames/Saarinen chair sported a rubber pad, covered with upholstery fabric, to provide softness at all points. Later models were to utilize the same principle with other materials.

The original drawing of the armchair submitted to the Organic Design in Home Furnishings exhibit by Eames and Saarinen shows aluminum legs that were to be attached to the plywood shell by a new rubber-weld joint capable of taking a stress of at least nine hundred pounds per square inch. In actual production, however, wooden legs had to be substituted for the metal ones because wartime shortages made it difficult to obtain aluminum legs.

The chair was first made of plaster on wire mesh reinforcing so that it could be carefully molded to the body to provide maximum support and comfort. Adjustments were made by fracturing the plaster shell and resetting it correctly. In order to record the concave form obtained, a light crate of strips of masonite was made. These strips followed the contours of the plaster model and recorded the modulations of form inside the chair—in essence the masonite structure served as the armature from which a cast-iron mold was made. The wooden shell of the finished version of the chair was glued up in this mold by the Haskelite Corporation. When completed, the shells were then trimmed, fitted with rubber, finished, and upholstered by the Heywood-Wakefield Company. A special, patented joint held the wooden legs firmly to the shell even in the case of expansion or contraction of the wood. The completed armchair was shown covered in a textured solid upholstery fabric by Marli Ehrman, whose experimental textile work also appeared in the Organic Design in Home Furnishings exhibit.

In addition to the shell chairs submitted to the Organic Design in Home Furnishings exhibit, Eames and Saarinen also submitted case goods. The case furniture they designed was veneered in Honduras mahogany. It carried the principle of standardization farther than any other group produced in the United States up to that time.

An 18-inch module was adopted, the units being 18 inches square or 36 inches in length for dining-room case goods. The bases on which these units rested were 13-inches high and available in lengths to hold two, three, or four units. They could also be combined to form larger groupings. The units were totally flexible—they could be combined in various configurations on accompanying benches. Independent pieces of furniture of almost any size and scale could be assembled by grouping the units horizontally or vertically or both, in conjunction with the benches. The units were fitted with small rubber grips underneath to keep them from slipping on top of each other. One particularly innovative configuration was a group of a tabletop with two legs fit on a 15½-inch-high unit to form a desk. It became the prototype for many similarly designed desks of the 1950s and later.

These Eames/Saarinen designs for the first time exploited the base for itself. The advantages of this system were many: units that rest directly on the floor provide difficulties in rooms where a baseboard prevents their fitting snugly against a wall. The base system designed by Eames and Saarinen not only avoided such difficulties by raising the units off the floor but also added many new possibilities by extending the utility of the bases for seating or display.

The drawers in the units were completely interchangeable. Two of the shallow drawers were exactly equal in depth to one larger drawer, and the units were originally constructed with sufficient runners so that eight small drawers, or four large drawers, or any corresponding combination of small and large drawers could be grouped. Eventually, production models had to be modified because of the extremely complicated merchandising problem of ordering drawers and cases separately and allowing customers to mix and match at random. Finally, five standard arrangements were decided upon that still gave a large range of possibilities in any one unit.

Eames continued to design chairs based on the principle of occupant comfort. Strange as it may seem, very few chairs have ever been designed with comfort as the primary objective. In fact, this concept is hardly more than a hundred years old. The vast majority of chairs permit the occupant reasonable comfort for less than an hour before tension spots and a feeling of strain set in. Charles Eames took a rather radical approach. Rather than adopting the methods of a physiologist in trying to design a chair for the way people *should* sit, he instead observed how people actually *did* sit and accommodated his design to them.

From this premise, Eames designed his famous lounge chair (introduced in 1957)—one of the most comfortable chairs ever produced. In the Eames tradition, the appearance of the lounge chair is also unique, its look being inherited from its construction materials and the concept on which it was based rather than on some preconceived idea. Eames had experimented with lounge chairs before in segmented shell form, but they had not been upholstered. Now he wanted to try something new. He wanted a chair that welcomed the occupant, a chair that "looked like a well-used baseball glove."

In order to achieve a wrinkled, broken-in appearance, he used buttons in the black leather to hold surface creases. The plywood shell components were of rosewood, which contributed to the feeling of richness and warmth that he intended. The seat, back, and ottoman pads were constructed of foam centers overlaid with down, which reversed to offset settling at pressure points.

Originally, both chair and ottoman swiveled on pivot bases, but since this caused the rosewood edges of the two pieces to rub against each other and scar, the ottoman was produced in a stationary model. Eames said he only introduced the swivel in the first place "because it would be more fun."

Perhaps the most difficult design problem he faced in the lounge chair was the connections. In fact, Eames has estimated that 80 percent of his time spent on the design was in trying to make the connections adhere to the body of the chair. With the help of Don Albinson, he constructed ten full-sized working models of the arm, which was finally linked to the chair body by a steel plate on a rubber mount. The shells were joined together by rubber buttons for a certain amount of flexibility and, although Eames intended to mount the chair on a four-legged base like the ottoman, he found that five legs were necessary for the required strength and balance. He later stated that the five-star base looked quiet and centered and that the chair belonged in a room where quiet was desirable.

People who own the Eames lounge chair sometimes think it too comfortable—it is so restful that it is hard to stay awake and virtually impossible to concentrate on complex texts while sitting in it.

Eames has said that the chair's development was very casual. It was originally built for Billy Wilder as a gift. Eames later showed the design to the Herman Miller management who thought they might be able to sell "a few." The chair and ottoman were introduced in 1957 at a retail price of $634.00. They met with extraordinary success and have been in full production ever since.

Though trained as an architect, Charles Eames often referred to himself as an artist. But beyond that, he was also an inventor and technologist—a true Renaissance man. He created films and exhibition designs for such diverse clients as the Moscow Fair and IBM. His achievements merited him many awards, among them an Emmy for his film *The Fabulous Fifties*. In 1961 he was accorded the highest distinction in the field of design, the Kaufmann International Design Award.

EAMES MOLDED PLYWOOD CHAIRS

The Eames plywood line of chairs (Plates 38, 39, 41, 42, and figure 1) was available in a multitude of options that varied over the years: mahogany (1946–48); rosewood (1946–48 and briefly in the 1960s); oak (1953); avodire (1946–48); slunkskin (1948–53); yellow (1946–48); red (1946–58); black (1946–1960s); birch (1946–58); calico ash (1946–66); zebrawood (1958–59); teak (1958–61); leather (1948–53); fabric (1948–53); walnut (1946–58 and 1962–present). The molded plywood screens were available in standard finishes of birch, calico ash, black, red, or oak.

DCM—dining and desk height; chrome-plated or black rod legs
Height: 29¼ in. (74 cm)
Width: 19½ in. (49 cm)
Depth: 21¼ in. (54 cm)
Seat height: 18 in. (46 cm)

LCM—low chair for reading or lounging; metal legs
Height: 28⅜ in. (72 cm)
Width: 22¼ in. (57 cm)
Depth: 25⅜ in. (65 cm)
Seat height: 15¼ in. (39 cm)

LCW—low chair; molded plywood legs
Height: 28⅜ in. (72 cm)
Width: 22¼ in. (57 cm)
Depth: 25⅜ in. (65 cm)
Seat height: 15¼ in. (39 cm)

EAMES MOLDED PLASTIC ARMCHAIRS

The Eames molded plastic line (1952–68) consisted of shells constructed of thermosetting resin reinforced with glass fibers (Plate 44 and figures 2, 3). Metal bases were made of rod wire finished in Bright Zinc or Black Oxide, a chip-resistant finish, or in chromium-plated steel.

Eames Molded Plastic Shell Colors
Integral colors: Elephant Hide Gray, Greige, Parchment, Lemon Yellow, Seafoam Green, Red
Applied finishes: Dark Blue, Mustard, Light Gray

DAX—dining and desk height; plated or black rod legs
Height: 31 in. (79 cm)
Width: 24⅞ in. (64 cm)
Depth: 24 in. (61 cm)
Seat height: 17⅝ in. (44 cm)

DCM

LCM

LCW

Molded Plywood Chairs (Charles Eames)
Manufactured by Herman Miller, Inc.

DAR—dining and desk height; wire strut base
Height: 31½ in. (80 cm)
Width: 24⅞ in. (64 cm)
Depth: 24 in. (61 cm)
Seat height: 17⅞ in. (45 cm)

DAT—office desk chair, tilting unit; star base with casters
Height: 34 in. (86 cm)
Width: 27⅞ in. (64 cm)
Depth: 23 in. (58 cm)
Seat height: 16½ to 20 in. (42 to 50 cm)

PAC—dining and desk chair; pivot base of cast aluminum and steel
Height: 32¼ in. (82 cm)
Width: 24⅞ in. (64 cm)
Depth: 24 in. (61 cm)
Seat height: 18½ in. (47 cm)

MAX—lower than DAX; plated or black rod legs
Height: 27½ in. (70 cm)
Width: 24⅞ in. (64 cm)
Depth: 24 in. (61 cm)
Seat height: 15¾ in. (40 cm)

RAR—wire and birch; rocker base
Height: 26⅞ in. (69 cm)
Width: 24⅞ in. (64 cm)
Depth: 27 in. (68 cm)
Seat height: 16 in. (41 cm)

LAR—lounge height; wire cage base
Height: 24¼ in. (62 cm)
Width: 24⅞ in. (64 cm)
Depth: 24½ in. (63 cm)
Seat height: 12¼ in. (31 cm)

SAX—standard height for conversation or reading; plated or black rod legs
Height: 29½ in. (75 cm)
Width: 24⅞ in. (64 cm)
Depth: 24½ in. (70 cm)
Seat height: 16¾ in. (43 cm)

DAW—dining and desk chair; legs of turned birch or walnut with metal cross-bracings
Height: 31¼ in. (79 cm)
Width: 24⅞ in. (64 cm)
Depth: 24 in. (61 cm)
Seat height: 17⅞ in. (45 cm)

PAW—same as DAW but with swivel base
Height: 31¼ in. (79 cm)
Width: 24⅞ in. (64 cm)
Depth: 24 in. (61 cm)
Seat height: 17⅞ in. (45 cm)

DAX DAR DAT PAC

MAX RAR LAR DAG—Wall Guard Base

Molded Plastic Armchairs (Charles Eames)
Manufactured by Herman Miller, Inc.

DAX-1 DAR-1 DAT-1 PAC-1

MAX-1 RAR-1 LAR-1

Upholstered Plastic Armchairs (Charles Eames)
Manufactured by Herman Miller, Inc.

DSX

DSR

MSX

PSC

Molded Plastic Side Chairs (Charles Eames)
Manufactured by Herman Miller, Inc.

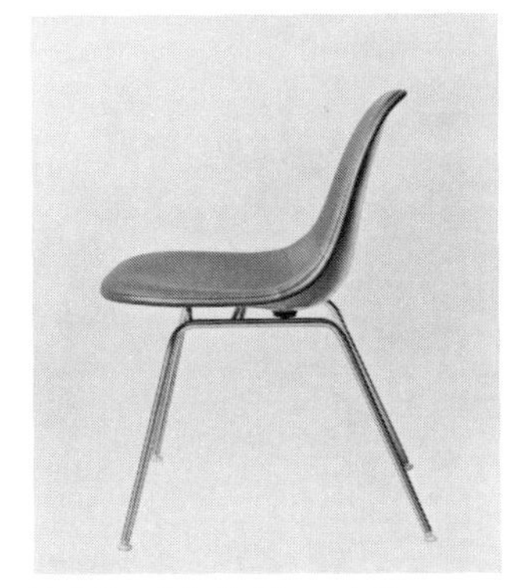

DSG—Wall Guard Base

LAX—lounge chair; lower than DAX and angled for restful support
Height: 26⅛ in. (66 cm)
Width: 24⅞ in. (64 cm)
Depth: 25⅜ in. (65 cm)
Seat height: 14⅞ in. (38 cm)

MOLDED PLASTIC SIDE CHAIRS (ARMLESS)

DSX—dining and desk chair; plated or black rod legs
Height: 31¼ in. (79 cm)
Width: 18½ in. (47 cm)
Depth: 22 in. (55 cm)
Seat height: 18 in. (46 cm)

DSR—dining and desk chair; wire strut base with self-leveling glides
Height: 31⅛ in. (78 cm)
Width: 18½ in. (47 cm)
Depth: 22 in. (55 cm)
Seat height: 17½ in. (44 cm)

MSX—lower version for occasional seating; plated or black rod legs
Height: 28¾ in. (73 cm)
Width: 18½ in. (47 cm)
Depth: 23 in. (58 cm)
Seat height: 15¾ in. (40 cm)

PSC—dining or desk chair on pivoting, cast aluminum and steel base
Height: 32¼ in. (81 cm)
Width: 18½ in. (47 cm)
Depth: 22 in. (55 cm)
Seat height: 18½ in. (47 cm)

The *DAG* is a wall-guard base for areas where the chair will be used against a wall. The rear legs extend to prevent the chair back from damaging the wall. It is available with any color shell chair or upholstered armchair.

Upholstered versions of the plastic armchairs and side chairs came with an applied finish on the back of the shell. Chairs upholstered in blue, black, ultramarine, dark gray, charcoal, or navy came with a black applied finish on the back; the backs of chairs upholstered in other colors had an applied beige finish.

EAMES UPHOLSTERED WIRE CHAIRS

Eames upholstered wire chairs (figure 4) were available in varying dining and desk heights as well as a lounge height. Bases were black tube legs, wire frame, pivot base, or black wire cage base. Upholstery was available in a variety of materials and colors including: black leather; raw umber, charcoal, red, or blue Naugahyde; tweed, raw umber light, black, dark grey, crimson, yellow, ultramarine, raw

DKX-1 DKR-1 PKC-1

MKX-1 LKR-1

DKX-2 DKR-2 PKC-2

MKX-2 LKR-2

Upholstered Wire Chairs (Charles Eames)
Manufactured by Herman Miller, Inc.

umber dark, ochre, or navy fabric. Shells were of black or white wire frames.

DKX-1—dining or desk height; wire frame, black tube legs
Height: 32⅜ in. (83 cm)
Width: 19 in. (48 cm)
Depth: 21 in. (53 cm)
Seat height: 19 in (48 cm)

DKR-1—dining and desk height; black wire base, wire frame
Height: 32 in. (81 cm)
Width: 19 in. (48 cm)
Depth: 21 in. (53 cm)
Seat height: 18¾ in. (47 cm)

PKC-1—pivot base of black baked enamel and polished aluminum
Height: 32¼ in. (82 cm)
Width: 19 in. (48 cm)
Depth: 21 in. (53 cm)
Seat height: 18¾ in. (48 cm)

MKX-1—middle-height chair for reading; black metal legs
Height: 28¾ in. (73 cm)
Width: 19 in. (48 cm)
Depth: 22 in. (56 cm)
Seat Height: 16⅞ in. (43 cm)

LKR-1—lounge height; black wire cage base
Height: 26 in. (66 cm)
Width: 19 in. (48 cm)
Depth: 21¾ in. (55 cm)
Seat Height: 13½ in. (34 cm)

The removable one-piece upholstery pads also came in a Harlequin version in varying configurations of red, yellow, blue, black, tan, and gray panels. A partially upholstered model that revealed sections of the basic wire shell was available in the bases mentioned above under the names DKX-2, DKR-2, PKC-2, MKX-2, and LKR-2.

EAMES LOUNGE CHAIR AND OTTOMAN

The Eames 679 and 671 lounge chair and ottoman (1956) have molded plywood frames, rosewood veneer, swiveling cast aluminum bases, leather-covered latex foam, and down upholstery (Plate 46).

Lounge chair
Height: 33⅜ in. (85 cm)
Width: 34 in. (86 cm)
Depth: 32¾ in. (83 cm)

Ottoman
Height: 15 in. (38 cm)
Width: 34 in. (86 cm)
Depth: 21 in. (53 cm)

EAMES ALUMINUM GROUP

The Eames Aluminum group (1958) consisted of several models: the 680 dining chair, the 681 lounge chair, the 682 lounge chair with arms, the 683 reclining chair, the 684 reclining chair with arms, and the 685 ottoman. Their frames were of polished aluminum and the base finish was black and polished aluminum. The pieces were upholstered in Naugahyde in charcoal, raw umber, terra verte dark, ultramarine blue, and tan dark, or in Saranylon Stripe in blue or grey (Plate 47).

EERO SAARINEN

Eero Saarinen's first piece for Knoll in the 1940s was the Grasshopper chair of laminated wood. According to Florence Knoll, "It was a perfectly nice chair, but it wasn't one of the great successes."[3] Saarinen's breakthrough came when he began working in molded fiberglass, which resulted in his famous Womb chair.

Florence Knoll encouraged Saarinen to tackle the biggest of a series of fiberglass chairs first because she wanted something she could curl up in. There were great difficulties with materials and construction methods, but finally Saarinen found a boat builder in New Jersey who, after some persuasion, reluctantly agreed to work with them in fiberglass. Florence Knoll said:

> He was skeptical. We just begged him. I guess we were so young and so enthusiastic that he finally gave in and worked with us. We had lots of problems and failures until they finally got a chair that would work. We were worried about its strength, but no one has ever broken one to my knowledge. . . . It's one of the few chairs I know of that has a patent. It was based on the hole of a truncated cone, believe it or not.[4]

THE WOMB CHAIR (NO. 70 CHAIR)

The Womb chair, also known as the No. 70 chair, used the pattern for the No. 71 chair and was introduced by Knoll International during the years 1945 to 1948 (Plate 49). Its construction was of a molded plastic shell and fabric-covered latex foam upholstery on a chromium-plated tubular steel frame with nylon swivel glides. There was also an accompanying ottoman, the No. 74.

Saarinen said of the Womb chair:

> In arriving at the design, many problems had to be recognized. People sit differently today than in the Victorian era. They want to sit lower and they like to slouch. In my first postwar chair, I attempted to shape the slouch in an organized way by giving support for the back as well as the seat, shoulders and head. The "womb" chair also has three planes of support.[5]

No. 70 Womb chair
Height: 35½ in. (90 cm)
Width: 40 in. 101 (cm)
Depth: 34 in. (86 cm)
Seat height: 16 in. (40 cm)

No. 74 Womb ottoman
Height: 16 in. (40 cm)
Width: 25½ in. (67 cm)
Depth: 20 in. (50 cm)

THE NO. 71 CHAIR

Saarinen had previously designed the No. 71 chair (Plates 50, 51) of molded fiberglass for General Motors Technical Center in Warren, Michigan. The No. 71 chair grew out of Saarinen's belief that the building for the General Motors plant (the design of which he was working on) needed furniture to harmonize with the architecture. Of this design Florence Knoll said, "It was scary for them [General Motors] to have a piece adopted on so large a scale. . . . [It was] the first real event in using one of Eero's designs in a big commercial establishment."[6]

Knoll introduced the No. 71 office chair in 1951. It was available as an open back-swivel/tilt armchair with casters or as an open-back fixed arm chair with glides. The frame was a molded reinforced plastic shell with a contour plywood seat form on a leg base of tubular steel either in a polished chrome finish on nylon glides or on a four- and five-star base of polished stainless steel topcap over a steel armature. The swivel/tilt mechanism had adjustable tension with a 2¾-inch height adjustment.

No. 71 chair—swivel/tilt model
Height: 31¾–34½ in. (81–87 cm)
Width: 26 in. (66 cm)
Depth: 24 in. (61 cm)
Seat height: 17¼–20 in. (44–50 cm)

No. 71 chair—fixed model
Height 31½ in. (80 cm)
Width: 26 in. (66 cm)
Depth: 24 in. (61 cm)
Seat height: 18 in (45 cm)

THE NO. 72 CHAIR

An armless variation, known as the No. 72 chair (Plates 52, 53), was also constructed of a molded reinforced plastic shell with contour plywood seat form. The leg base was of tubular steel in a polished chrome finish on nylon glides or on the same four- or five-star bases.

No. 72 chair—swivel/tilt model
Height: 30½–33¼ in. (77–84 cm)
Width: 22¼ in. (56 cm)
Depth: 20¼ in. (51 cm)
Seat height: 16¼–19 in. (41–48 cm)

No. 72 chair—fixed model
Height: 32 in. (81 cm)
Width: 22¼ in. (56 cm)
Depth: 20¼ in. (51 cm)
Seat height: 18¾ in. (47 cm)

THE PEDESTAL GROUP

Saarinen's Pedestal group was introduced by Knoll during 1956–57 (see C2). The chairs came in arm and armless versions, constructed of fiberglass shells on an aluminum base with a wool-covered seat pad. The pedestal tables came in a wide variety of sizes, in both oval and round shapes. The tabletops also came in a variety of options: oak veneer or walnut veneer with an oil finish; white plastic laminate; Italian cremo marble or colored marble in Madera (gray beige), Rosso colomendino (brown rose), or St. Laurent (dark brown) on a metal pedestal base with a white fused finish.

Pedestal armchair (also known as the Tulip chair)
Height: 32 in. (81 cm)
Width: 26 in. (66 cm)
Depth: 23½ in. (59 cm)
Seat height: 18½ in. (64 cm)

Pedestal side chair
Height: 32½ in. (82 cm)
Width: 19½ in. (49 cm)
Depth: 22 in. (56 cm)
Seat height: 18½ in. (47 cm)

Pedestal stool
Available with optional swivel mechanisms and two height options.

Diameter: 15 in. (38 cm)
Height: 17⅝ in. (45 cm)
16 in. (40 cm)

Pedestal tables

No. 160 (small round)
Diameter: 16 in. (40 cm)
Height: 20½ in. (52 cm)

No. 162 (small round)
Diameter: 36 in. (91 cm)
Height: 15 in. (38 cm)

No. 163 (small round)
Diameter: 20 in. (50 cm)
Height: 20½ in. (52 cm)

No. 164 (large round)
Diameter: 54 in. (137 cm)
Height: 28½ in. (73 cm)

No. 172 (small round)
Diameter: 36 in. (91 cm)
Height: 28½ in. (72 cm)

No. 173 (medium round)
Diameter: 42 in. (106 cm)
Height: 28½ in. (72 cm)

No. 174 (oval)
Width: 78 in. (198 cm)
Depth: 48 in. (122 cm)
Height: 28½ in. (72 cm)

No. 176 (medium round)
Diameter: 48 in. (122 cm)
Height: 28½ in. (72 cm)

The Pedestal group finishes changed throughout the years. In 1957, standard finishes were white, charcoal, and gray beige, with black available as a custom order. In 1962, standard finishes were white and beige (the gray beige renamed). During 1973–74 the only standard finish was white with black and beige available as custom orders.

GEORGE NELSON

George Nelson was not only the guiding light behind the Herman Miller Furniture Company for over twenty years, he was noted for his "grass-on-Main-Street" approach advocating shopping malls, his furniture designs (which include a daybed, a slat bench, a residential desk, a line of miniature cabinets, the Thin Edge case group, steel-frame cases, modular seating, the Marshmallow sofa, the Coconut chair, the Comprehensive Storage System (CSS), the Sling sofa, and the Catenary chair), and certainly for his innovative approach to organizing storage space in his design for the Storagewall.

Early on, Nelson sought alternatives to traditional furniture, which he found unsuitable for modern needs. Of the conventional bureau, he wrote:

> The bureau is one of the silliest storage compartments ever created by man. It contains three to five drawers, which are twice as wide and as deep as they need be. The bottom drawer is close to the floor, and one generally has to squat to open it. A bureau has four surfaces which are exposed to the room, which means that they must be dusted or polished periodically. It juts out into the room, wasting not only the space where it stands, but a considerable area around it. And it is expensive. . . . This inconvenience and waste of time and space is entirely unnecessary. More and more people are discovering that chests of drawers can be built into a bedroom wall just as the closet is built in.[7]

STORAGE SYSTEMS

In May 1945, *Life* magazine featured the Storagewall system designed by George Nelson and architect Henry Wright. D.J. De Pree of the Herman Miller company was impressed by the concept and invited Nelson to design a line of furniture for the company. In 1949, Miller presented Nelson's Basic Storage Components (BSC) system, which was an adaptation of the Storagewall designed for mass production and economical pricing. The BSC consisted of unitized modules—drawers, sliding doors, desk unit, radio, phonograph, and speaker panels—and offered a variety of hardware and lighting fixtures. The units were designed to be installed in a frame that could either be purchased from Herman Miller or constructed by a carpenter at the customer's discretion. The BSC system was one of the first examples of modular furniture in the United States. Later, Nelson produced the Omni system for the Aluminum Extrusion Company along similar lines, but this turned out to be in violation of his agreement with the Miller company, so he then designed a similar system for Herman Miller called the Comprehensive Storage System (CSS).

Nelson's CSS is a brilliant example of multipurpose furniture, based on the original Storagewall concept. The Storagewall was Nelson's answer to the growing problem of more accumulated possessions with less space in which to store them. Nelson reasoned, as the Scandinavians had done, that most household goods could be stored in spaces ten inches or less in depth with connecting storage components of shelves, writing surfaces, or cupboards, erected against unused wall space. The CSS had twenty-two basic component units, including drawers, space for files and books, and a desk.

The system was designed to expand both vertically and horizontally, the user having the freedom to mount the units against walls or to employ them as freestanding dividers. Shelving and storage units were slung between adjustable aluminum poles that were pressure-fitted between ceiling and floor and incorporated a continuous track, giving the CSS great flexibility—any of its component storage units could be placed at will at any height or in any configuration.

CSS was an example of knockdown furniture at its best, rendering it far less expensive than carpenter-constructed cabinetry, yet serving the same function while retaining an aesthetically pleasing visual image. The CSS was manufactured by Herman Miller from 1959 to 1973, but it spawned hundreds of imitations that are still being marketed.

THE MARSHMALLOW SOFA

In addition to case goods, Nelson also designed seating ranging from the whimsical to the elegant. His Marshmallow sofa of 1956 (Plate 63 and C3) was perhaps his most fanciful piece, belying the reputation of modern design as dull and utilitarian. The Marshmallow sofa was composed of upholstered foam-padded discs attached to metal rods fastened to cross-stretchers, two rows for the back and two rows for the seat. These rods attach to two curved side rails supported by four legs of square metal tubing in black or satinchrome. It was manufactured from 1956 to 1963, but only a few hundred were made, making it fairly rare today.

Marshmallow sofa
Height: 32½ in. (82 cm)
Width: 52 in. (132 cm)
Depth: 33 in. (83 cm)
Seat height: 16 in. (40 cm)

THE COCONUT CHAIR

Nelson's Coconut chair (Plate 64), also introduced in 1955, was designed to be constructed of polished chrome with a steel shell. The shell was formed from sheet steel with a multicolored fleck baked-on finish. The legs were of polished chrome-steel rod. Upholstery material was available in Naugahyde, leather, and certain fabrics. The Coconut chair also had a matching ottoman, an upholstered pad with polished chrome-steel rod legs, which was also designed to be used as a vanity bench in conjunction with the vanity unit of the Thin Edge case group. The Coconut chair was described in the Miller catalog as:

> . . . a lounge chair of low, brake-formed and welded sheet steel [later the shells were of molded fiberglass], padded and upholstered, supported on three thin cast polished chrome steel rod legs with connecting struts. Of interest is the fastening of the metal legs to the shell. This is one Nelson contribution to the design of a modern lounge chair. Known as the "coconut" chair because of its wedge-like form, the chair provides padded seating comfort without bulkiness. The shell itself seems suspended in space because of the design of the thin legs.[8]

Coconut chair
Height: 32½ in. (82 cm)
Width: 40 in. (101 cm)
Depth: 33¾ in. (85 cm)
Seat height: 13¾ in. (35 cm)

Coconut ottoman
Height: 16¼ in. (41 cm)
Width: 23¼ in. (59 cm)
Depth: 18⅜ in. (46 cm)

THE KANGAROO CHAIR

Another of Nelson's 1956 designs was the Kangaroo chair (Plate 65 and C4), a highback lounge chair constructed from a molded plywood shell upholstered on both sides, with an attached seat and back cushion supported by a polished chrome-steel base.

Kangaroo chair
Height: 39 in. (99 cm)
Width: 36 in. (91 cm)
Depth: 36 in. (91 cm)
Seat height: 15 in. (38 cm)

THE SWAGGED-LEG CHAIR

By 1958, Nelson had branched out to the Swagged-leg chair (Plate 67), which came in four versions: DAA (flexible black, 18-inch seat height); MAA (flexible back, 16¼-inch seat height); DAF (fixed back, 17½-inch seat height); MAF (fixed back, 15-inch seat height). The chair consisted of two padded, molded plastic shells that formed the contoured seat and back, connected by curved metal rods attached with shock mounts. The base was formed of four thin polished chrome tubes splayed out from a center column to four points on the floor, ending in self-adjusting rubber tips. Various color options were available for the seat and back; initially white, gray, or black and later an olive green. Any combination of colors could be ordered. The legs could be specified in black, white, or polished chrome.

DAA—flexible back
Height: 34 in. (86 cm)
Width: 27⅝ in. (70 cm)
Depth: 25 in. (64 cm)
Seat height: 18 in. (46 cm)

MAA—flexible back
Height: 30 in. (76 cm)
Width: 27⅝ in. (70 cm)
Depth: 26 in. (66 cm)
Seat height: 16¼ in. (42 cm)

DAF—fixed back
Height: 31¼ in. (87 cm)
Width: 28½ in. (72 cm)
Depth: 22 in. (56 cm)
Seat height: 17½ in. (44 cm)

MAF—fixed back
Height: 28¾ in. (73 cm)

Width: 28½ in. (72 cm)
Depth: 22 in. (56 cm)
Seat height: 15 in. (38 cm)

THE ATOM CLOCK

Another of Nelson's major contributions to postwar design was his atom clock (Plate 65 and C3). Designed in 1949 for the Howard Miller Clock Company of Zeeland, Michigan, it has become one of the major visual symbols of postwar industrial design. In designing the atom clock, Nelson specifically sought out a select market of consumers ready to accept innovation and willing to pay for it. Nelson's clock is based on the absolute basics of time measurement—six lines intersecting each other at a midpoint. The design makes use of the idea that a wall clock is mostly an accessory item—that while it must serve a function, it is primarily decorative. It also assumes that adults do not need numbers by which to tell time, so instead of the traditional numbering, the atom clock substituted birch knobs on the ends of brass or steel spokes. Because of the open design, the wall becomes the background, and the clock naturally seems a part of the architecture rather than an appendage added as an afterthought.

HARRY BERTOIA

THE DIAMOND CHAIR

While Eames, Saarinen, and Nelson divided their time between plywood and plastic, Harry Bertoia was experimenting with wire as a medium for furniture. A plastic-coated wire dish rack was the inspiration for Bertoia's Diamond chair of 1952 (Plates 72–74). The Diamond chair, manufactured by Knoll International, has earned the right to be considered a modern classic. This chair and its various incarnations have become such commonplace sights in our lives that it is easy to forget that just thirty years ago they were nothing more than a vague idea in one man's mind.

While wire-mesh furniture construction dated back at least a hundred years prior to Bertoia's work, Bertoia revolutionized the concept by making the mesh its own supporting element. This was made possible by advances in metallurgy and metalworking that resulted from the production of military hardware during World War II.

Bertoia relied on intuition and his own body in designing the Diamond chair. Feeling totally at home with wire, it seemed logical to experiment with the medium in chair design. During the experimentation process, Bertoia worked with Dick Schultz and Don Pettit on adapting bent wire to mass-production techniques. But after trying several methods of bending the wire by machine, it wound up being more practical and cheaper to do it by hand in wooden jigs. That way the wire snapped back into the desired shape. The Diamond chair is still produced using this method.

The Diamond chair consists of a steel shell of welded wires crisscrossed in diamond-shaped sections from which the chair derives its name. The diamond-shaped grids flare outward, forming the armrests, while the chair back arches concavely to cradle the spine and shoulders so that the entire shell has a graceful fluidity of line reminiscent of Eames's work. Side braces support the shell and also serve as legs. A detachable foam-rubber seat pad is available in a variety of upholstery materials, and an armless version was also produced.

In spite of his experiences in furniture design, Bertoia remained deeply rooted in sculpture. Referring to the Diamond chair he said, "The chairs are studies in space, form and metal too. If you will look at them you will find that they are mostly made of air, just like a sculpture. Space passes right through them."[9]

Diamond chair—with arms
Height: 30½ in. (77.5 cm)
Width: 33¾ in. (85.7 cm)
Depth: 28 in. (71.1 cm)
Seat height: 15¾ in. (40 cm)

Diamond chair—armless
Height: 30 in. (76 cm)
Width: 21¼ in. (54 cm)
Depth: 20¾ in. (53 cm)
Seat height: 15¾ in. (40 cm)

FLORENCE KNOLL

Florence Knoll, or "Shu," as she was nicknamed, readily admitted that she did not consider herself a furniture designer but a person who filled in the gaps when a particular design was needed. Still, her "fill-ins" (Plates 77–86) include tables, chairs, sofas, desks, stools, divisional wall elements for residential and commercial spaces, night tables, chests of drawers, room dividers, files, and display cases—not a bad showing for someone who just "filled in."

Florence Knoll moved away from the Danish direction of design that Knoll had initially undertaken, moving, as she said, "toward the Bauhaus approach." Her furniture is pure of line, some of her chairs and tables bearing a remarkable resemblance to Nelson's less whimsical works. In her furniture designs, as with her influential presence at Knoll International, she insisted on "no compromise, ever." Typical construction materials for her furniture echoed the high quality of her work: teak, rosewood, marble, and polished steel.

One of her simplest works is a light, portable stacking stool. This stool, which she designed in 1948, was based on a wooden version by Alvar Aalto, but Knoll's version was of steel rod legs with a plywood-filled top covered with plastic laminate. The design was in production until 1966 but was later reproduced by Knoll International for the Innovative Furniture in America exhibition of 1980.

While both Hans and Florence Knoll certainly contributed much to the field of design through encouraging the use of new materials, perhaps their most vital contribution was their introduction of a new way of thinking about space. The Knolls were instrumental in promoting the idea that the interior designer should become the coordinator of space, furniture, mechanical equipment, choice of color and fabrics, and selection of art, graphics, and finishing details. With Knoll, nothing was left to chance. Disparate elements were transformed into designs that can be likened to symphonies in which an astonishing balance and harmony is achieved. Like music, a Knoll interior can remain in the background or can be totally involving. The balance, the harmony, the unity are indisputably present in Knoll designs.

Dick Schultz and Bob Longwell were part of the early design team at Knoll. Their recollections of how Florence tackled a project are particularly revealing. After working for dozens of hours to make up a prototype in the workshop:

> . . . all of a sudden Shu would say, "I want to see it." She was always very nice and very cordial. Made you feel at ease, and then she'd start picking it apart. She'd say, "Well, I think we should change that radius a little bit. It just doesn't fit in with this aspect of the unit. There's just—something's not right about it." Sometimes she would tape on pieces of cardboard so you'd get back and you'd see what she was talking about as far as line and perspective and balance and so on.[10]

The team would then build another prototype and bring it back for Shu's approval:

> . . . and she'd pull that one apart, saying, "Well, I think that radius, instead of being a quarter of an inch, ought to be a three-eighth-inch radius." The team would reply, "Well, Shu, it was a three-eighth radius last time . . . then her ire would come forth. "Don't tell me . . . that wasn't three-eighths . . . I would never have tolerated. . . ." So we'd say, okay, all right. We'd go back and we'd do it over again and we'd cuss and carry on about her. But you know, after all was said and done and she finally agreed on it, it was letter perfect. It was absolutely perfect.[11]

GILBERT ROHDE

Gilbert Rohde's influential designs of the 1930s provided the foundations for many postwar designs. Rohde was often copied—so much so that unless a piece is signed by him, there is always a doubt as to its authenticity. Not all of Rohde's furniture was signed, but some pieces from Herman Miller bear a metallic silver label affixed with small tacks inside drawers or on the back or underside of case goods. The label is approximately two inches long and one inch wide and reads: *Herman Miller Furniture Company, Zeeland, Mich., Original Rohde Design.* Then follows a line with Gilbert Rohde's signature, after which comes the word, *Designer.*

Rohde is credited with introducing the idea of modern storage pieces to the American public and with developing the sectional sofa. In commercial design, Rohde's Executive Office Group (EOG) (Plates 102, 103), officially introduced in 1942, was, like many of his other concepts, years ahead of its time in relation to public taste. The EOG comprised 15 modular units that could be grouped into over 400 different configurations. In retrospect, it can be viewed as the forerunner of the Eames/Saarinen systems that were publicly presented during the next decade.

Rohde favored simple but unusual construction materials. His bedroom suite 3323 (Plate 94, dated 1934, was of white holly inlaid with Paroba in a very light natural finish. The legs and other structural parts were of polished chromium-plated steel tubing with considerably more metal than was used on any other modern commercial furniture of the time.

The 4100 series of 1941 (Plates 98, 99), also known as the Paldao group, demonstrates economical, functional use of space through storage cabinets with pull-out leaves that become tables and, when not in use, can completely slip away out of sight.

The 4200 series, the Blueprint group of 1942 (Plate 101), is a fine indicator of things to come. It provides ample storage in modular sections that can be assembled in endless combinations to suit the user.

Perhaps Rohde's most radical designs for their time were his sectional seating units of 1939 (Plate 96), which still look remarkably contemporary today, and his Paldao group of 1941 (Plate 100), which heralds the biomorphic forms that were to become so prevalent in the following decade.

ISAMU NOGUCHI

Isamu Noguchi, sculptor, made only brief forays into the world of furniture design, yet his images have made a strong and lasting impression. The Noguchi table, manufactured by Herman Miller, remains unique. His rocking stool for Knoll is well known. But while his lunar and akari lighting have both been frequently imitated, they have never been copied without losing much of the grace and purity of the originals.

THE NOGUCHI TABLE

It is perhaps poetic justice that the Noguchi table (Plate 105, C11) came about as a response to rampant plagiarism of his work. Its forerunner was his design of 1939 for A. Conger Goodyear—a glass-topped table with a free-form sculptural base in rosewood, 30 inches high and 84 inches long.

When Noguchi felt he had been wronged by Robsjohn-Gibbings' having stolen one of his designs, he retaliated by making a variation of his own design of the Goodyear table to illustrate George Nelson's article, "How to Make a Table." It was this table, stripped to the bare bones of construction, that Herman Miller began producing and that became known as the Noguchi table. Like the Goodyear table, it too is constructed of a simple sculptural base with a glass top. The Noguchi table was in production from 1947 to 1973. A special limited edition of 400 was made in 1980, but the demand was so great that the table was reintroduced into the market by Herman Miller in 1984.

THE ROCKING STOOL

Noguchi's rocking stool of 1954 (Plates 106, 107) was influenced by one of his trips to Japan. Initially, he wanted to produce the stool in plastic, based on the polyurethane washing basins being used in Japan. He felt that plastic, like the marble in which he was fond of working:

> . . . must be approached in terms of absolutes; it [could] be broken, but not otherwise changed. Unlike working with wood or metals, there could be no temptation to weld or glue. The very limitations of the medium imposed a kind of honesty; to find the minimum means for construction and expression rather than the myriad possibilities that metal welding soon came to involve.[12]

Unfortunately, as had happened so often throughout his career, Noguchi was thwarted once again, this time by Hans Knoll, who insisted that the stool be made of wire along the lines of Harry Bertoia's work. Noguchi eventually gave in, and his initial concept of a plastic stool was translated into wire and wood.

AKARI LIGHTING

Noguchi's akari lighting was developed from a desire to explore less encumbered perceptions—"the less thingness of things." To this end, he chose paper, plastic, and bamboo, all of which adapted well to his feeling for the quality and sensibility of light. In 1948 he designed for Knoll the akari table lamp of plastic and wood, which stood 15¾ inches (40 cm) high. Variations were produced, including the akari hanging lamp (1966) for George Kovacs of mulberry-bark paper and wire, 20 inches (50.8 cm) high. Noguchi's akari lighting concepts have been unabashedly copied to such an extent that their originator is often overlooked.

ARNE JACOBSEN

Arne Jacobsen is as well known for his architectural creations, which include innovative educational facilities, as he is for his furniture designs. He had a great impact on postwar design with his three-legged plywood 3100 Ant chair of 1952, his Egg and Swan chairs of 1958, and the Series 7 group, manufactured by Fritz Hansen.

THE ANT CHAIR

The Ant chair comes in two versions—the 3100 with three legs (Plates 110, 111) and the 3101 with four legs. Both Ant chairs are available in natural beech plus seven lacquer finishes: white, gray, black, yellow, orange, gala red, and green. The shells are of molded plywood, the bases of chromed steel tubing 14 mm in diameter. The 3101 four-legged model can be supplied with various accessories including a linking device, ashtray, seat and row numbers, and a transport trolley.

Ant chairs, 3100 and 3101
Height: 30 in. (77 cm)
Width: 19 in. (48 cm)
Depth: 19 in. (48 cm)
Seat height: 17 in. (44 cm)

THE SWAN CHAIR

The Swan chair (Plate 117) is also available in two versions—a low model, 3320 and a high model, 3322—upholstered in fabric, leather, or vinyl. The shell is of molded polyurethane reinforced with fiberglass over which molded latex is glued. The starbase is of polished cast aluminum on a column of chromed steel. Both the 3320 and 3322 models swivel, and the 3322 is equipped with a pneumatic height adjustment. The Swan chair won Jacobsen a Silver Medal at the Second International Furniture Exhibit in Vienna.

Swan chair, 3320 (low model)
Height: 29½ in. (75 cm)
Width: 29 in. (74 cm)
Depth: 27 in. (68 cm)
Seat height: 15 in. (38 cm)

Swan chair, 3322 (high model)
Height: 31–34 in. (80–87 cm)
Width: 29 in. (74 cm)
Depth: 27 in. (68 cm)
Seat height: 16½–19 in. (42–49 cm)

THE EGG CHAIR

Jacobsen's Egg chair (also known as No. 3316) is available in fabric, leather, or vinyl and is equipped with a loose seat cushion (Plate 118). Like the Swan chair, the shell is of fiberglass-reinforced molded polyurethane on which molded latex is glued. The Egg chair also has a five-star base of polished cast aluminum and a chromed steel column. The Egg chair swivels and has an adjustable tilting mechanism plus a nonswiveling matching ottoman, 3127.

Egg chair, 3316
Height: 42 in. (107 cm)
Width: 34 in. (86 cm)
Depth: 31 in. (79 cm)
Seat height: 14½ in. (37 cm)

Egg ottoman, 3127
Height: 15 in. (37 cm)
Width: 22 in. (56 cm)
Depth: 16 in. (41 cm)

THE SERIES 7 GROUP

Jacobsen's Series 7 (Plates 112–114) group includes the 3107 chair, which was displayed at the 1957 Triennale Exhibition in Milan, where it won the Grand Prize. It was also awarded the Gold Medal at the Second International Furniture Exhibition in Vienna. The 3107 chair is part of the Series 7 group of five models, all with identical seat and back shells of molded plywood consisting of nine layers of wood laminated with two layers of textile. The bases of the 3107 and 3207 are made of chromium-plated steel tubing 14 mm in diameter with a wall thickness of 2 mm. The sections exposed to particularly rigorous use are extremely solid. The Series 7 group features patented two-part ferrules made of Desmopan, a synthetic rubber. Both the 3117 and 3127 are equipped with pneumatic height-adjustment devices and twin casters. The pedestal chair 3137 may be affixed to the floor with concealed screws or, on special order, can be delivered on a swivel base with automatic return. The 3107 and 3137 are available with optional writing tablets for left or right sides, covered with a white plastic laminate. Both the 3107 and 3207 can also be delivered with a ganging device that can be pushed under the seat completely out of sight when the chairs are not used in row arrangements.

The Series 7 group is available in a wide variety of finishes and options. Lacquer finishes include white, gray, black, yellow, orange, gala red, or green. Stained finishes include whitewashed, gray, orange, brown, or black. Veneer finishes are availabe in beech, oak, or teak. The chairs are also availabe with or without upholstery, and there are three versions of upholstery padding: seat padding only, seat and back padding with an exposed outer shell, or complete padding.

3107—basic chair model
Height: 31 in. (78 cm)
Width: 20 in. (50 cm)
Depth: 20½ in. (52 cm)
Seat height: 17 in. (44 cm)

3207—armchair
Height: 31 in. (78 cm)
Width: 20 in. (50 cm)
Depth: 20½ in. (50 cm)
Seat height: 17 in. (44 cm)

3117—armless chair with pedestal base and pneumatic height adjustment
Height: 17–29 in. (44–52 cm)
Width: 20 in. (50 cm)
Depth: 20½ in. (52 cm)

3217—armchair with pedestal base and pneumatic height adjustment
Height: 26–30 in. (66–74 cm)
Width: 20 in. (50 cm)
Depth: 20½ in. (52 cm)

3137—armless floorfixed chair
Height: 31 in. (78 cm)
Width: 20 in. (50 cm)
Depth: 20½ in. (52 cm)
Seat height: 17 in. (44 cm)

THE OXFORD CHAIRS

Jacobsen's Oxford chairs (Plates 119, 120) were not marketed by Fritz Hansen until 1962, but since they were conceived earlier it is appropriate to mention them within the context of this book. The Oxford chairs were originally designed to coordinate with Jacobsen's architectural project at St. Catherine's College in Oxford in the early '60s. Like most other Jacobsen designs, there are several versions available, with high or low backs, with or without arms.

As standard models, the Oxford chairs are available in several different underframes, all with a swiveling five-star base of cast aluminum: (1) with round, black nylon toes; (2) with double casters and pneumatic height adjustment; (3) with tilt mechanism, pneumatic height adjustment, and double-casters. The Oxford chairs can be special ordered with a starbase that has nylon glides with tops in chromed steel; it is also available as a floorfixed model with the column in chromed steel and a fixture for bolting them directly to the floor, whereby the screws are covered by a disc of stainless steel.

Upholstery for the Oxford series is available in two versions: the Medium, with 22–40 mm molded foam, or the Deluxe, with 22–55 mm molded foam glued directly to the seat/back and the laminated wooden armrests. the arm bracket is of cast aluminum.

3171—armless low-back model, nylon toe
Height: 35½ in. (90 cm)
Width: 18½ in. (47 cm)
Depth: 21¼ in. (54 cm)
Seat height: 17⅜ in. (44 cm)

3271—armrest low-back model, nylon toe
Height: 35½ in. (90 cm)
Width: 25¼ in. (64 cm)
Depth: 21¼ in. (54 cm)
Seat height: 17⅜ in. (44 cm)

3181—armless low-back model with pneumatic height adjustment, double casters

3191—same with tilting mechanism
Height: 35½–38½ in. (90–98 cm)
Width: 18½ in. (47 cm)
Depth: 21¼ in. (54 cm)
Seat height: 17⅜–20½ in. (44–52 cm)

3281—armrest low-back model with pneumatic height adjustment, double casters

3291—same with tilting mechanism
Height: 35½–38½ in. (90–98 cm)
Width: 24¼ in. (64 cm)
Depth: 21¼ in. (54 cm)
Seat height: 17⅜–21¼ in. (44–54 cm)

3172—armless high-back model, nylon toe
Height: 50¼ in (128 cm)
Width: 18½ in. (47 cm)
Depth: 21¼ in. (54 cm)
Seat height: 17⅜ in. (44 cm)

3272—armrest high-back model, nylon toe
Height: 50¼ in. (128 cm)
Width: 24¼ in (64 cm)
Depth: 21¼ in. (54 cm)
Seat height: 17⅜ in. (44 cm)

3182—armless high-back model with pneumatic height adjustment, double casters

3192—same with tilting mechanism
Height: 50¼–53½ in. (128–136 cm)
Width: 18½ in. (47 cm)
Depth: 21¼ in. (54 cm)
Seat height: 17⅜–20½ in. (44–52 cm)

3192—armrest high-back model with pneumatic height adjustment, double casters

3292—same with tilting mechanism
Height: 50¼–53½ in. (128–136 cm)
Width: 25¼ in. (64 cm)
Depth: 21¼ in. (54 cm)
Seat height: 17⅜–20½ in. (44–52 cm)

Jacobsen's chairs are still in production and are available from Fritz Hansen.

BØRGE MOGENSEN

Børge Mogensen, like Arne Jacobsen, relied heavily on wood as a construction medium. He dabbled a little in steel but preferred wood and avoided plastics at all costs. Because of his training as a cabinetmaker, it is likely that Mogensen felt more comfortable with such organic materials as the wood, leather, and natural fibers that he used extensively throughout his career. Even though he was not trained with the eye of an architect, he was concerned with function. His work included many multipurpose pieces based on the concepts of standardization promoted by Kaare Klint.

THE BOLIGENS BYGGESKABE (BB) SYSTEM

Mogensen often collaborated with other designers including Aage Windeleff, Steen Eiler Rasmussen, and Hans J. Wegner, but one of his most important collaborations took place in the company of Grethe Meyer. Together they developed the Boligens Byggeskabe (BB) storage system (Plates 123–126), introduced in 1954, which utilized a floor-to-ceiling, wall-to-wall approach of permanently installed shelving and cupboard systems over stackable modular units. The BB system was the forerunner of the Øresund system, which he developed between 1955 and 1967. Both the BB and Øresund units were designed to be used separately or in combinations to form modular storage covering an entire wall. In this way, they became dominant architectural features.

The BB system's frame was of solid Oregon pine with rabbeted doors of plywood veneered with Oregon pine or Bangkok teak. The sides, tops, and shelves were of gray-painted masonite on frames with brass mounts. Bases had self-leveling screws to allow for sloping floors.

Cabinets with hinged doors
Width: 14¼ in. (36.3 cm)
20½ in. (52.8 cm)
27¼ in. (85.8 cm)
33½ in. (85.8 cm)
40¼ in. (102.3 cm)

46½ in. (118.8 cm)
53½ in. (135.3 cm)
Depth: 13¼ in. (33.6 cm)
26¼ in. (66.6 cm)

Cabinets with sliding doors
Width: 53½ in. (135.3 cm)
64¼ in. (168.3 cm)
79¼ in. (201.3 cm)
Depth: 27¼ in. (69.4 cm)

HANS J. WEGNER

Like his fellow Scandinavians, Jacobsen and Mogensen, Hans Wegner also had a proclivity for working with natural materials. His Chinese chair of 1944 paid homage to the simplicity of line and form often found in Oriental furniture designs. With his Peacock chair of 1947, Wegner demonstrated a flair for adapting traditional forms, such as that of the Windsor chair, on which the Peacock chair was based. Wegner's Folding chair of 1949 was a good example of his use of natural materials; 1949 was also the year in which he designed his Classic chair, sometimes referred to simply as The Chair. The Classic chair remained Wegner's personal favorite. By 1953, Wegner's dedication to simplicity and function culminated in the three-legged version of the Valet chair, which was a variation of the 1951 four-legged model.

THE CHINESE CHAIR

Wegner's interest in Oriental furniture forms led to his design of the Chinese chair (Plate 127), which is an interesting blend of Oriental and Scandinavian simplicity. Its rounded back with single splat brings to mind a mandarin chair, yet the overall feeling is one of solid Scandinavian construction. The Chinese chair was constructed of cherry wood, with a loose seat cushion of leather.

Chinese chair
Height: 32¼ in. (82 cm)
Width: 22½ in. (57 cm)
Depth: 21 in. (53.5 cm)
Seat height: 16 in. (41 cm)

THE PEACOCK CHAIR

The Peacock chair (Plate 128) consists of a large hoop with sixteen radiating spindles. Instead of bentwood, a solid piece of laminated wood is used for the back hoop; it is formed from four strips of solid ash laminated and shaped. With the exception of the arms, which are made of oil-finished teak, the chair is constructed of wax-finished oak.

Peacock chair
Height: 40⅞ in. (103 cm)
Width: 30⅞ in. (77 cm)
Depth: 30⅞ in. (77 cm)

THE CLASSIC CHAIR

Wegner's Classic chair (Plates 129, 130) was made of solid wood and designed for hand labor. The frame was either of wax-finished oak or oil-finished teak with a seat of woven string or cane.

Classic chair (also known as the Round chair or The Chair)
Height: 30 in. (76 cm)
Width: 22⅜ in. (57 cm)
Depth: 18⅛ in. (46 cm)

THE FOLDING CHAIR

The Folding chair (Plate 131) was based on the principle of triangular construction incorporating the seat surface, front leg, and front brace, with balance achieved through a flat, horizontal seat surface. The Folding chair frame was of solid oak with a woven cane seat and back.

Folding chair
Height: 29½ in. (75 cm)
Width: 24 in. (61 cm)
Depth: 18½ in. (47 cm)

THE VALET CHAIR

In the Valet chair (Plates 134, 135), Wegner used solid wood for the entire construction: solid pine for the frame with a seat of solid teak. The Valet chair was Wegner's answer to managing without a "gentleman's gentleman." It was designed so that a jacket and trousers could drape properly on it. The seat height and angle permitted easy removal of shoes, and there was ample storage space provided for jewelry and the contents of pockets.

Valet chair
Height: 37 in. (94 cm)
Width: 20 in. (51 cm)
Depth: 19½ in. (50 cm)

Another of Wegner's chairs, the Chair 24, designed in 1950 and produced by Carl Hansen and Sons, was of an oak or beech frame in a variety of finishes, including five colors of lacquer. It was first exhibited at the Furniture Fair of Denmark in 1951.

RUSSEL WRIGHT

In the area of down-home appeal to the American public, few postwar designers could rival Russel Wright. While he was certainly no stranger to failed projects, his stamp on the postwar design scene was indelible. From his spun-aluminum ware of the 1930s to his phenomenally popular American Modern dinnerware of the postwar period, Wright's contributions to the "softwares" of American interiors were considerable. He designed tea sets, flatware, and his famous "informal serving accessories" in pewter, sterling, spun aluminum, and chromium-plated brass. He modernized the radio with his table-sized models for Wurlitzer of 1932, which quickly replaced the mammoth console sets, and he invented the concept of "stove-to-tableware." In fact, we owe much of today's relaxed, informal methods of entertaining to Russel and Mary Wright.

Wright's architectural projects were often in the vanguard. Following the repeal of Prohibition, Wright designed one of New York's first legal cocktail lounges, the Restaurant de Relle on Madison Avenue, which featured aluminum stools, collapsible cork-topped tables, and indirect lighting concealed behind copper-paneled walls. In 1932 he demonstrated his fondness for natural materials by designing a chair for his own apartment that was exhibited at the Museum of Modern Art in 1939. The chair was made of primavera wood with ponyskin upholstery material and followed organic lines.

Wright's later furniture designs used boxy forms and veneered surfaces of contrasting woods (Plate 136); he also created a solid maple line produced by the Conant Ball Company. In 1935 Wright introduced his Modern Living line of furniture, constructed of solid maple, available in either a reddish stain or an unstained "blonde" finish—a term credited to Mary Wright that soon became symbolic of pale '30s furniture.

By the 1950s Wright was ready to launch his Easier Living furniture line for the Statton Furniture Company. The Easier Living line was based on many of the ideas laid down in the Wrights' book, *Easier Living.* The furniture incorporated several gimmicks such as a lounge chair, one of whose arms can be used as a writing surface, with the other opening into a magazine rack; a coffee table with a sliding top incorporating porcelain food containers; beds with tilting headboards that adjust for reading in bed and also have concealed storage compartments; slipcovers that snap on and off for easy maintenance; and nightstands with pull-out shelves for eating in bed. In his Easier Living line, Wright also promoted a coordinated grouping of rugs, draperies, and upholstery materials. While his designs were inventive in their multipurpose approach, they were aesthetically flawed, being blocky and ungraceful when compared to the work of Eames, Saarinen, or Nelson. Even his folding metal furniture of 1950, while brightly colored and practical, lacked the elegance of line characteristic of the furniture being produced by his contemporaries.

Of all Wright's works, his own home at Dragon Rock in upstate New York can be considered his masterpiece, marking the culmination of his design concepts and his preference for natural materials. Draperies, slipcovers, and area rugs were changed with the seasons to complement the altering landscape, which was visible through the large two-story windows. Blue, green, and white were favored during the summer months, while the winter found the Wright's home decorated in warm reds and browns. Even the kitchen cabinet doors were reversible from red to white, depending on the season.

Russel and Mary Wright had purchased the eighty-acre property in 1941 for use as a weekend retreat, but during the twenty-year period until its completion in 1961, it evolved into a workshop for Wright's "design for living" ideas.

Dragon Rock was built in an abandoned stone quarry, and Wright described it as a "prototype," a "designer's experiment," saying that he wanted "to prove that a house of good contemporary design could be as livable as traditional ones; that it could be romantic, sentimental, even lovable."[13]

Wright used Dragon Rock to illustrate his love of natural materials, first by following the natural contours of the land in laying out the site and landscaping, and by diverting a stream to the abandoned stone quarry to create a large artificial pond that became Dragon Rock's focal point. The house is cut into the side of the quarry and contains eleven different levels, with the living and dining areas in one wing, and a separate guest wing. He also designed private space in the form of his own studio, separate from but connected to the main house, with its own bath, concealed kitchen, and terraces.

In the interior, Wright employed a diversity of natural materials: natural slate floors; an uncut cedar tree acting as a support post for the ceiling; large natural rocks topped with pillows serving as seating; a massive corner fireplace made of boulders; a curving stone staircase; and a bath with large rocks and a miniature waterfall. Every level of the house opened onto an outdoor terrace to take full advantage of the natural vistas.

Wright drew heavily on Japanese design principles in the construction of Dragon Rock, often trying to merge Eastern aesthetics with Western technology. He experimented with leaving exposed styrofoam insulation between the wood beams of the den ceiling; he embedded wildflowers from the property into plastic panels used as partitions in the kitchen and bathroom; he even tried pressing hemlock needles into wet epoxy paint to texture the walls. Again borrowing from the Japanese, most decorative objects were displayed on a rotation basis so that visual clutter was kept to an absolute minimum.

Wright's attention to detail can be illustrated in his family menu planner system. He compiled a collection of one hundred menus for his family, each menu accompanied by a list of appropriate supplies, including specific flatware, linen, glass, and ceramic ware for the meal; he even specified the exact colors and designs that were to be used. But attention to detail soon became an obsession. He went so far as to label refrigerator shelves and arrange foods in order of use. As life at Dragon Rock became more and more systematized, the "easy living" that it was intended to promote soon dissolved into militaristic regimentation.

Furthermore, the structure of Dragon Rock itself was not without problems. It was easy to trip on the uneven slate floors; the damp of the quarry site caused rapid deterioration of wood; and the plastic partitions included for their easy care proved anything but as they began to crack and discolor. Also, the rocks in the living room needed regular vacuuming, which proved to be a tiresome chore.

In spite of Dragon Rock's problems, which made it impractical as a residence, Wright should be commended for his living experiment. Who could fault anyone trying to blend Eastern aesthetics and Western technology into a natural, beautiful, easy-care environment? By putting his ideas into practice, Wright embodied the very soul of the postwar movement.

THE ITALIANS

While much of postwar design was influenced by the mingling of East and West, the Italians took a different path. Their primary aim was to become a part of the international mainstream while displaying their individuality to an international culture. Many of the materials and methods of furniture construction in Italy echoed those occurring on the international scene. Bruno Sardella, Bruno Vallone, Gio Accolti Gil, and Alfonso Mormile used reinforced polyester in their Eameslike shell chairs (1955) produced by Ionio. Bent plywood was favored by Mario Ravegnati, Antonello Vincenzi, and Bubi Brunori for their armchair (1951) for Darbo, and Robert Mango's conical child's chair manufactured by Tecno (1954) featured tubular iron legs painted black.

The Italians readily accepted new technologies and rapidly adapted them to furniture design. Marco Zanuso's 1951 Lady armchair (Plate 142) for Arflex incorporated the new synthetic materials Nastrocord and Pirelli Sapsa. Ettore Sottsass, Jr., worked with aluminum sheet, molded brass tubing, plastic, and wood.

It is not so much the materials or methods of construction that differentiated the postwar Italian designers, however, but rather their stylistic approach. The work of many of the Italian designers is characterized by a great freedom of line and form, perhaps best illustrated by the works of Carlo Mollino (Plates 137–139). His fanciful shapes of molded plywood and glass, influenced by anatomy and aeronautics, verge on the surreal. Cabinetmakers and small workshops freely plundered the designs of Mollino and Zanuso, flooding the market with copies aimed at the middle class.

Ernesto N. Rogers, the first editor of *Domus*, summed up the philosophy of Italian design in the phrase, "from a spoon to a city," implying that all design, regardless of size, should be treated with the same importance and care. When *Domus* decreed, "Design as the result of utility plus beauty," it was repeating the Sullivan/Wright "form follows function" philosophy.

CONCLUSION

The postwar era gave us two main innovations in furniture design: wall storage systems and dynamic new ideas in chair design. Building from the basic functional designs of the 1920s and 1930s, the postwar designers engaged in ergonomic and anthropometric studies to arrive at the optimum support posture for the average human body. They incorporated the newest materials and the latest technology to create chairs of molded plywood, fiberglass, and pressed steel, trading weighty padding for the lightness of latex foam. For the first time, totally new chair forms were developed that bore little resemblance to their forebears.

Following on the heels of the successful Organic Design in Home Furnishings competition of 1940, the Museum of Modern Art sponsored another competition in 1948—the International Competition for Low-cost Furniture Design—to which over three thousand designs were submitted. Don Knorr won first prize for his chair, which the catalog described as "a piece of flat sheet metal [which] has been cut to the proper shape and bent around to meet itself in a seam in the seat of the chair." Davis Pratt, cowinner of the second prize for seating, designed one of the first examples of pneumatic chairs, which the catalog described as "an inflated ring within a fairly heavy envelope which distributed resilience over a large surface." It was not until the 1960s, however, that blow-up chairs had a well-publicized if brief popularity. Another cowinner of the second prize,

Charles Eames, adapted his winning design of 1940 to the newly developed material, fiberglass-reinforced plastic, which established new norms for the furniture industry and introduced limitless possibilities for furniture designers.

The 1950s saw the introduction of a molding technique utilizing expanded polystyrene that was used in chair shells. Much experimentation was done in this medium, resulting in a wide diversity of chair designs, but only a few were worthy of production. By the mid-'50s, the champion upholstery material, latex foam, found a challenger in ester-based urethane foam, which commonly came to be known as polyester foam. Polyester foam was more economical than, but inferior to, latex since it broke down rapidly and had poor recovery properties. The introduction of polyester foam into the lower-priced end of postwar upholstered goods contributed to an image of inferiority that was both unfortunate and unfair considering the thousands of hours, the design brilliance, and the high-quality materials that went into developing the prototypes.

Worried about the possible effects of the Industrial Revolution, William Morris asked the question: is the machine capable of producing art? In his 1967 article, "The Chair as Art," Reyner Banham spoke eloquently to this issue:

> The Chair has become so potent a symbol that a purely functional chair could now only be designed by a computer or a Martian. For any member of the human race it is too loaded with overtones of Westernization . . . of white man's justice, of corporate power . . . of godliness, of episcopacy, electrocution, elegance (as in sedan-chair) and, chiefly, of aesthetic self-expression second only to the fine arts. Almost every chair of consequence in our current environment has its designer's handwriting all over it; is signed as surely as a painting.[14]

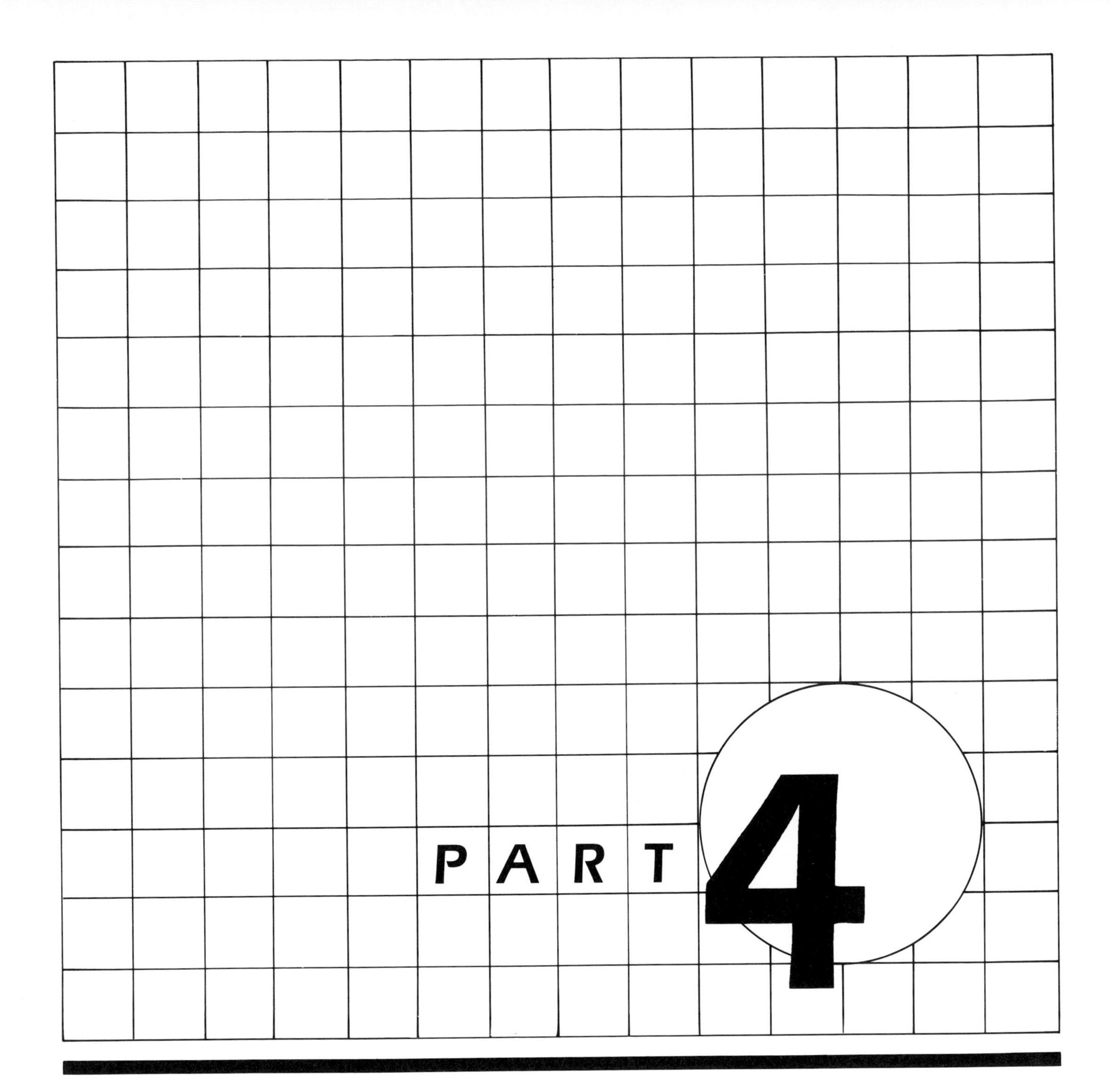

The Furniture and Designs

Note: The photographs in this section have been arranged mainly in chronological order to show the gradual influences of the earlier historical periods on postwar design. By following this progression, stylistic trends should become apparent.

1. The original version of this armchair was designed by Walter Gropius in 1910 for the vestibule of the Fagus Factory. It has since been reproduced and is available through Tecta. Its blocky wooden form is reminiscent of some of Russel Wright's postwar work and the early furniture of Frank Lloyd Wright. (Photograph: Tecta)

2. This tea service was designed by Walter Gropius (founder of the Bauhaus), Louis A. McMillen, and The Architects Collaborative (TAC), U.S.A. for Rosenthal. It was first produced in 1969, but the shapes clearly indicate Bauhaus-inspired design principles. During the Bauhaus's finest years, its Interior Design Workshop had the closest working relationship with industry. (Photograph: Rosenthal)

3. The Barcelona chair was designed by Ludwig Mies van der Rohe for the German Government Pavilion at the Barcelona International Exhibition of 1929. Philip Johnson said of this chair: *The Barcelona chair, the most beautiful piece of furniture he has ever designed, is large enough for two people to sit in. The single curve of the back crossing the reverse curve of the seat expresses "chair" better than any other contemporary model. As always, Mies's impeccable craftsmanship plays an important part in his furniture design. Everything is calculated to the last millimeter: the width and thickness of the strap metal and the radius of the curves at the joints; the width and spacing of the leather strapping, the size of the upholstery buttons, the fineness of the welting and the proportions of the leather on the cushions.* This same attention to detail was to be found in the work of the postwar designers who built on these foundations. (Photograph: Knoll International)

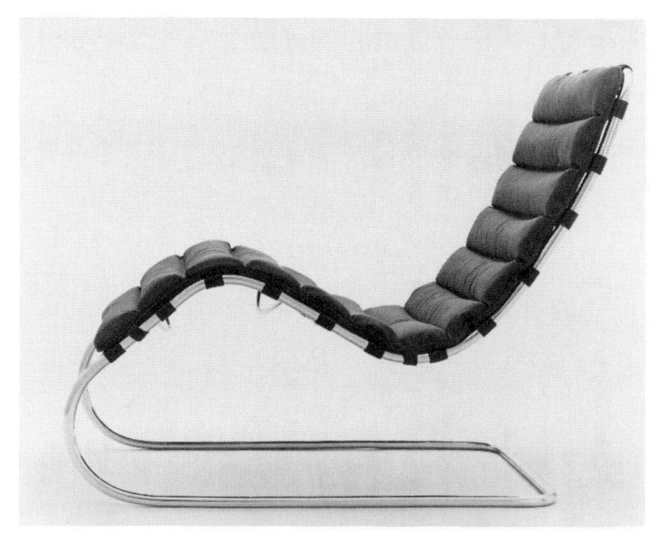

4. This chaise longue by Mies van der Rohe follows the form of the body—a concept that became increasingly important in the later organic designs of the postwar period. (Photograph: Knoll International)

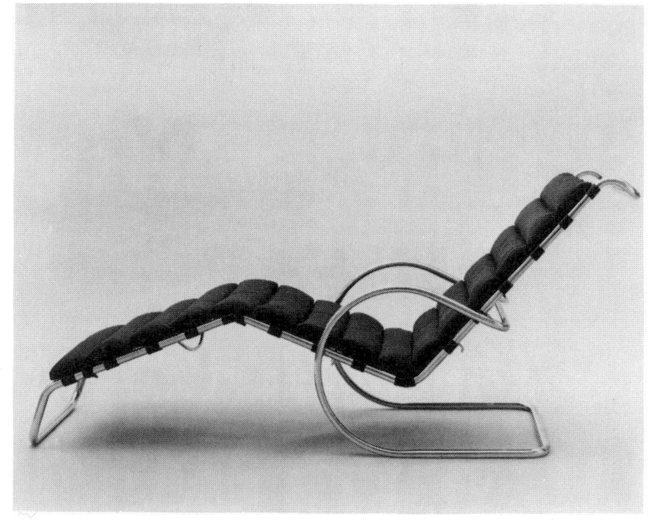

5. This adjustable chaise longue, designed by Mies van der Rohe in the '20s, heralds the outdoor aluminum furniture of the 1940s and 1950s that is still in production today. (Photograph: Knoll International)

6. The Tugendhat chair by Mies van der Rohe (1930) is shown here in one of its versions. The Mies van der Rohe Archive in The Museum of Modern Art has a set of eighteen blueprints showing the Tugendhat chair in various incarnations with different support frames, armrests, and both with and without spring connectors. The chair was designed for the Tugendhat house and consists of leather straps and leather-covered loose cushions on a frame of chrome-plated steel. It is also available in an armless version. (Photograph: Knoll International)

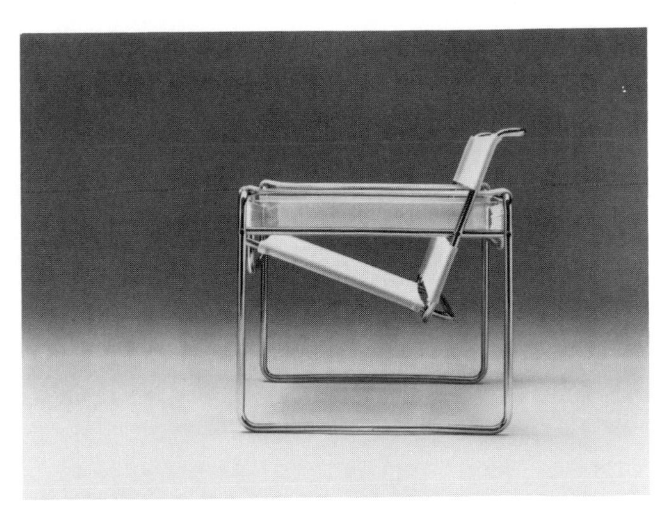

8. Marcel Breuer's Wassily chair (1925) derives its nickname from the painter Wassily Kandinsky. The chair was designed for Kandinsky's house on the Bauhaus campus at Dessau and was first shown publicly in 1927 at the Weissenhof housing development Werkbund Exhibit in Stuttgart. The original chair, constructed of tubular steel, was foldable and covered with an extra-strong fabric of woven cotton threads strengthened by paraffin, developed by Grete Reichardt of the Bauhaus. Several additional versions of the chair have been produced that include alternative arrangements of the tubular metal rods, and leather covering instead of fabric. The Wassily chair is an important transitional piece between the earlier metal rod furniture of the Victorian era and the tubular designs of the postwar period. (Photograph: Knoll International)

7. This glass and steel tube table by Mies van der Rohe comprises similar visual elements to the designs of Le Corbusier and Eileen Gray. It was shown in the Tugendhat House in Brno, Czechoslovakia, in 1930. (Photograph: Knoll International)

9. Another of Marcel Breuer's designs, this tubular steel table/stool (1925–26) is typical of his early cubistic style. Breuer began his experimentation with 20-mm steel tubes with the intention of developing a chair base by turning the stool ninety degrees. However, the material was not strong enough to support sufficient weight. (Photograph: Knoll International)

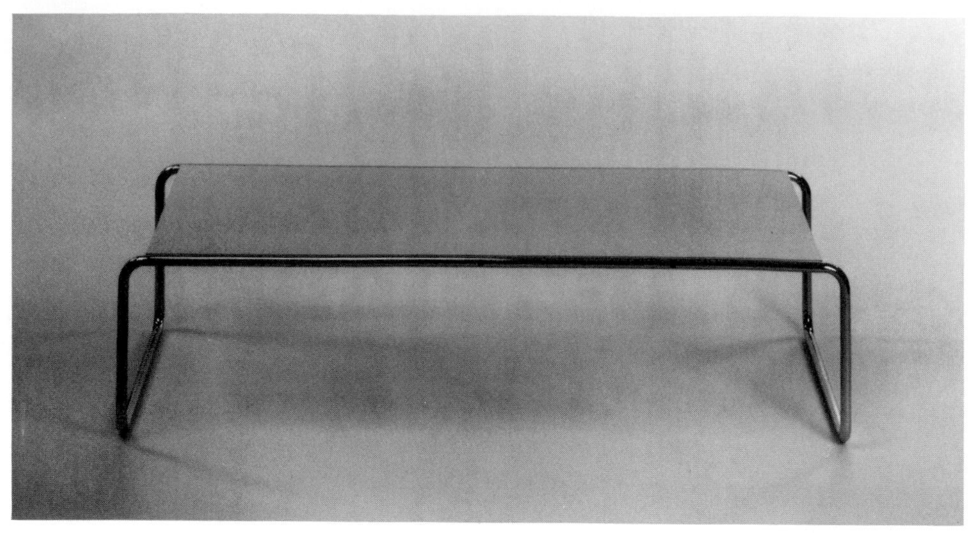

10. This Marcel Breuer design of 1925 simply elongates the cubistic stool/table into a coffee-table version, pointing up Breuer's attention to construction details. (Photograph: Knoll International)

11. Marcel Breuer's Cesca chair is a logical progression from his work on the tubular steel table/stool. In its original form it consisted of three materials in their natural colors: a bentwood frame, Viennese wickerwork, and nickel-plated steel. The Cesca chair was introduced in 1928, in both an armless version and a version with arms. Other designers of the period produced remarkably similar chairs, including Mart Stam's gas-pipe chair of 1926 and Mies van der Rohe's cantilever chair of 1927. (Photograph: Knoll International)

12. This version of the Cesca chair with arms has a chromium nickel-plated steel tube frame, cane seat and back, and a stained frame surrounding the canework. (Photograph: Knoll International)

13. Le Corbusier designed this table between 1925 and 1928. Cassina began reproducing it in 1965 and lists it as an adjustable-height conference table of elegant proportions, available with either a wood or glass top. The table height may be adjusted in place by hand adjustment of the support pads. Although this design is more than fifty years old, it still retains a timeless, contemporary quality. The use of glass and metal was highly influential on the designers of the postwar period. (Photograph: Atelier International/Cassina)

14. Le Corbusier's Casiers Standard storage cabinets were originally designed in conjunction with Pierre Jeanneret and shown at the Pavillion Esprit Nouveau in 1925. Reproduction began in 1978 by Cassina, with cabinetry available in ash-stained walnut or in a black, blue, ochre, green, gray, or bordeaux finish with solid wood edges. The Casiers Standard are modular storage units available in two depths—37.5 and 75 cm, three widths—37.5, 75, and 112.5 cm, and a single height of 75 cm.

The units can be linked by screw fixings at the sides or rear walls. When used as a freestanding unit, one placed upon the other, there is a special adjustable plinth base available. Metal legs and pedestals are also available for certain configurations.

The cabinets are available in three versions: completely closed with doors or roller shutters, open, or partially closed/partially open. Internal fittings such as shelves, filing cases, drawers, chest of drawers, internal modular units, and mirror backs are also optional. (Photograph: Atelier International/Cassina)

15. This version of Le Corbusier's Casiers Standard (1925) is shown with a pedestal base. (Photograph: Atelier International/Cassina)

16. This configuration of Le Corbusier's Casiers Standard clearly shows the influence it had on the storage units of the postwar period. (Photograph: Atelier International/Cassina)

17. The modular construction of this Casiers Standard storage system by Le Corbusier, first designed in 1925, is remarkably similar to storage systems and kitchen cabinetry that became popular in the postwar era. (Photograph: Atelier International/Cassina)

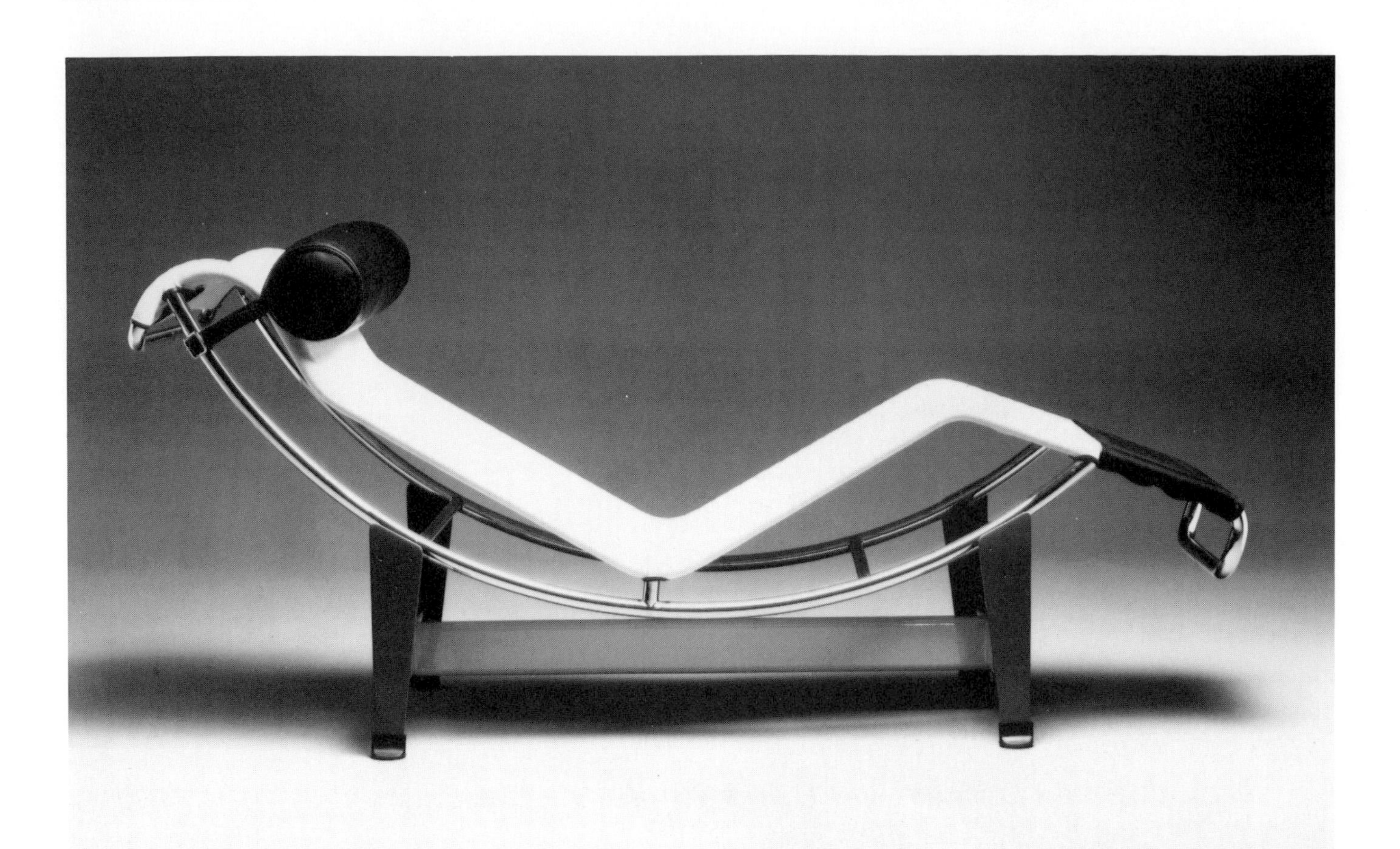

18. This fully adjustable chaise longue was designed in 1928 by Le Corbusier, Pierre Jeanneret, and Charlotte Perriand. The lower part of the fram is iron, the upper part is nickel-plated steel tubing. The original upholstery was either horsehide or fabric. The frame of steel tubing is formed to fit the human body and rests on the iron legs without being attached to them, so that its position can be changed, although the user has to get up to do so. (Photograph: Atelier International/ Cassina)

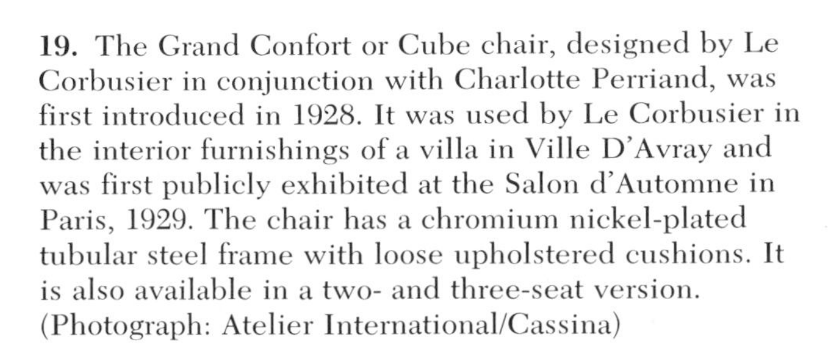

19. The Grand Confort or Cube chair, designed by Le Corbusier in conjunction with Charlotte Perriand, was first introduced in 1928. It was used by Le Corbusier in the interior furnishings of a villa in Ville D'Avray and was first publicly exhibited at the Salon d'Automne in Paris, 1929. The chair has a chromium nickel-plated tubular steel frame with loose upholstered cushions. It is also available in a two- and three-seat version. (Photograph: Atelier International/Cassina)

20. This Extended Lounge chair was designed by Le Corbusier in 1928. It is also available in a two-seat sofa. Its construction is the same as the Grand Confort chair—highly polished steel tubing hand-formed and bent with heat, applied within special jigs to ensure exact tolerance and clarity of line. The seat supports use rubber straps and coiled steel springs. A choice of fabrics, vinyls, and leathers is available in the reproduction version, which has been produced by Cassina since 1965. (Photograph: Atelier International/ Cassina)

21. This design by Le Corbusier, Pierre Jeanneret, and Charlotte Perriand is available as an armchair, a two-seat sofa (shown), or a three-seat sofa. It was first manufactured by Thonet in 1929 but was reproduced by Cassina beginning in 1965. These classic models are produced under licence from the estate of Le Corbusier, which is indicated by a stamp signature and serial number on each model. The chair frames are of highly polished hand-formed, bent-angle steel. The seat supports use specially produced rubber straps surrounding high-tensile-strength coiled steel springs. (Photograph: Atelier International/Cassina)

22. The Transat chair was designed by Eileen Gray in 1927. Its lacquer frame holds the padded leather sling with pivoting backrest. Chromed steel connectors define the joints of the frame. The prototype was made of a padded suspended canvas sling in a sycamore frame. While the prototype was actually designed in 1926, the first public showing was not until 1927 in Amsterdam and at the Galerie Jean Desert in Paris. This chair is an early example of knock-down furniture. It can be reduced to a completely flat form in moments and is essentially a variation on the deck chairs so well known on the ocean liners of the 1920s. (Photograph: Ecart International)

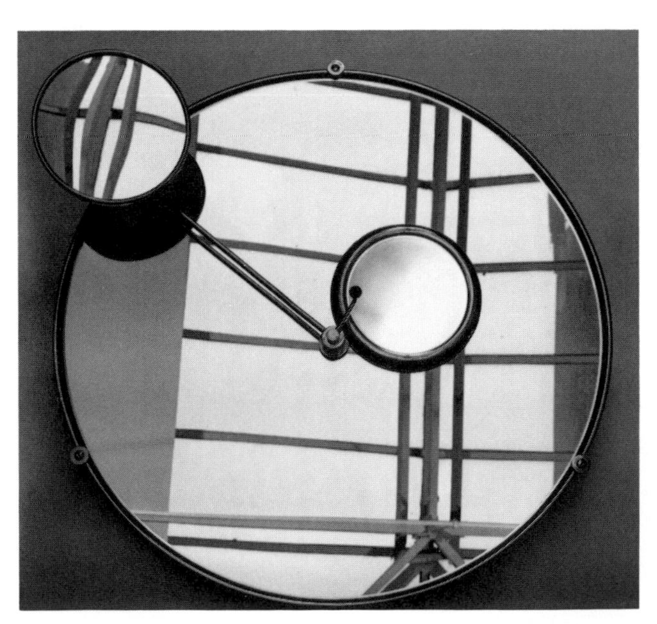

23. This highly utilitarian Satellite mirror by Eileen Gray, dating from the early '20s, repeats the circuclar form of the table in Plate 27. The Satellite mirror is in reissue by Ecart. (Photograph: Ecart International)

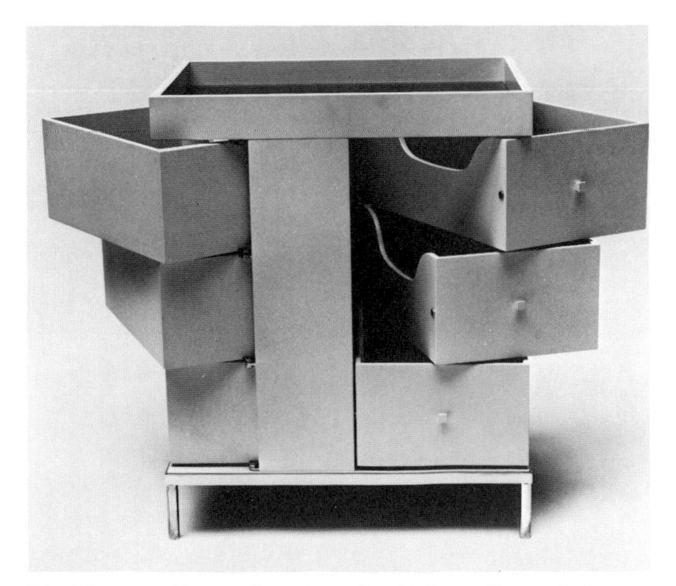

24. This small wooden chest by Eileen Gray, dating from the early '20s, is typical of her use of the pivoting drawer which, from 1923 on, was used repeatedly in her chests. The influence of her design can be seen throughout the postwar period and might have been the inspiration for Joe Colombo's Boby stand of 1968. (Photograph: Ecart International)

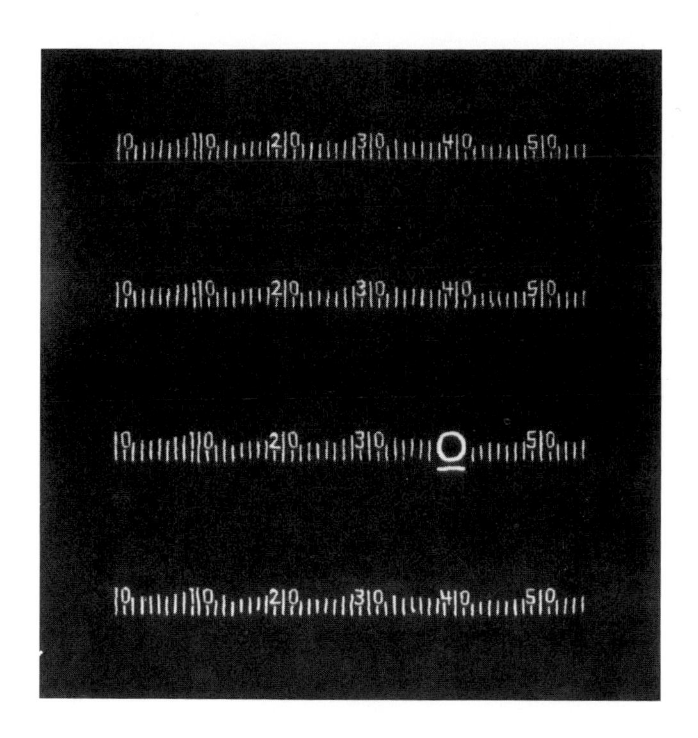

25. Eileen Gray's carpet designs of the early '20s were in great demand throughout her career. Her Blackboard rug, shown here, is one of her better-known carpet designs, currently available as a reissue. (Photograph: Ecart International)

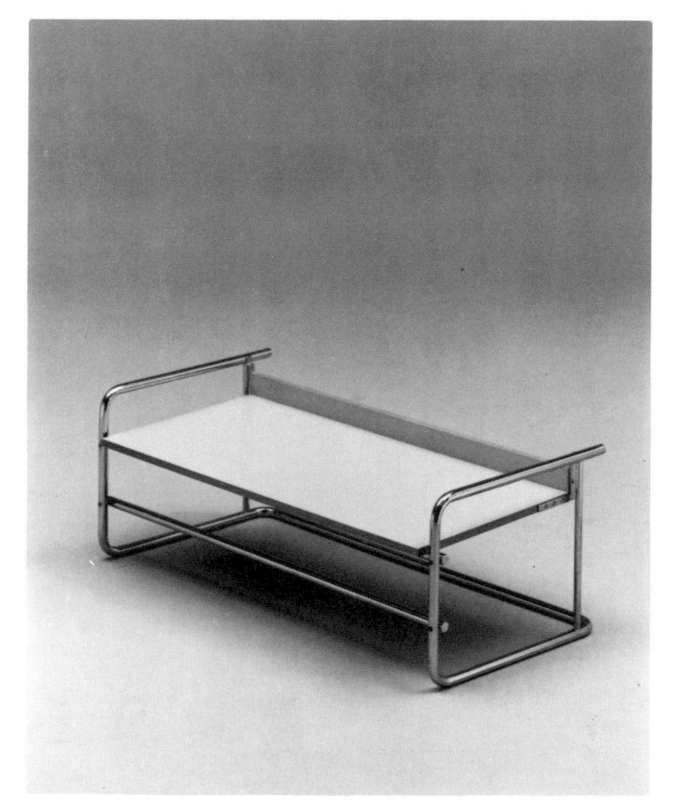

26. This tubular steel design by Eileen Gray (early '20s) is reminiscent of Marcel Breuer's work, although perhaps not as pure of line. (Photograph: Images/ Kaleidos)

27. Eileen Gray's well-known adjustable steel tube and glass table designs have been highly influential in the area of "occasional tables." This table was used in the house at Roquebrune, which she designed in conjunction with fellow-architect Jean Badovici during the mid-1920s. The table found a functional use in the guest bedroom, where it could be easily adjusted to serve breakfast in bed. (Photograph: Images/Kaleidos)

28. This Eileen Gray table design dates from 1927. It is constructed of a polished chrome-plated or white-enameled steel frame with a black lacquered base and top. Its circular form repeats the feeling of her Satellite mirror (Plate 23) and is repeated again in the glass and tubular metal tables shown in Plate 27. (Photograph: Images/Kaleidos)

29. The Eileen Gray Bibendum chair of 1929 is constructed of a chromium-plated tubular steel base with fully upholstered seat, back, and armrests. It is covered in aniline leather or fabric. (Photograph: Images/Kaleidos)

30. The Jean T table by Eileen Gray (1929) has a polished chromium tubular-steel base, with a white top. It can be extended from 64cm to 128 cm. (Photograph: Images/ Kaleidos)

31. Eileen Gray's tube floor light has been very influential in the "high tech" lighting of recent years, though it preceded "high tech" by decades. (Photographs: Images/ Kaleidos)

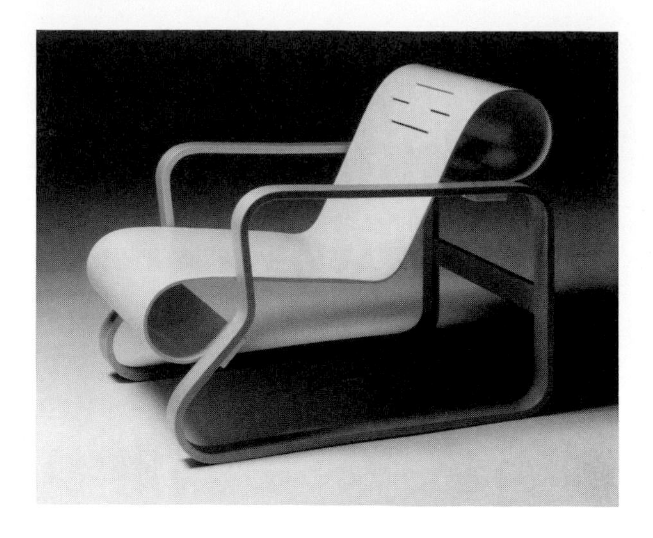

32. An early Alvar Aalto chair design (1930–33) that was developed for the Paimio Sanatorium. The armchair seat and back are of bent plywood with supporting sides laminated and bent into a closed curve. (Photograph: Artek)

33. In addition to designing furniture and lighting, Alvar Aalto was also an important designer of glassware, especially in the 1930s. Aalto's glassware is simple and functional. His plates, bowls, and glasses are designed to be used together, and the individual pieces can easily self-stack for maximum utilization of space.

The Savoy vase, pictured here, won first prize at the Paris World's Fair of 1937. It was entered in the competition under the name of "eskimoerindeus skinnbyxa," meaning "The Leather Pants of an Eskimo Woman." The entry was drawn in pencil and colored crayon on paper and cardboard and consisted of vases and bowls of varying heights. After winning first prize, it was put into production by the Iittala Glassworks under the name of the Savoy vase. (Photograph: Iittala Glassworks)

34. A taller version of the vases shown in Plate 33, designed by Alvar Aalto in 1936. (Photograph: Iittala Glassworks)

35. This Alvar Aalto armchair of laminated wood framing with webbed seat and back utilizes Aalto's Y leg, which was constructed by splitting the Aalto leg into two parts and rejoining these into one leg bent ninety degrees in two directions. The chair was introduced in 1947. (Photograph: Artek)

36. This X-leg stool, designed by Alvar Aalto, was introduced in 1954. The X leg is a variation of the Aalto leg, which was constructed of solid wood, bent ninety degrees, laminated, and assembled with screws. The Aalto leg was developed in the 1930s, but the X-leg variation of the '50s was more complex, requiring that the Aalto leg be split into five parts and joined into one fan-formed leg that was then doweled into the seat. The seat was either of solid ash or upholstered. Aalto also used the X leg in a square-shaped and hexagonal-shaped model stool and in tables with ash or oak veneer tops or removable glass tops. (Photograph: Artek)

37. Hanging lighting fixtures became very popular during the postwar period. This version, designed by Alvar Aalto, was introduced in 1955. (Photograph: Artek)

38. A rare look at a collection of prototypes from Charles Eames's Molded Plywood group (1945). (Photograph: Herman Miller, Inc.)

39. Charles Eames's LCW dining chair of 1946 was constructed of molded and bent birch plywood. A proponent of Organic Design, Eames preferred to create an all-wood chair for greater unity and integrity of design. Because the seat and back are molded in compound curves, their strength and rigidity can be maintained even with thin sheets of plywood. The chair has been criticized because of the visual discrepancy in the thickness of the carrying structure necessary for support, as it seems to contradict Eames's intent. Nevertheless, the chair remains one of Eames's most famous and instantly recognizable designs. (Photograph: Herman Miller, Inc.)

40. Eames's folding screen (1946), one of his most beautiful designs, came about as a by-product of his experiments with plywood. Each piece of plywood was pressed into a flattened U-curve in lengths of either 34 or 68 inches. The pieces were joined by a full-length canvas hinge sandwiched into the laminations. Great flexibility was possible because the sections were only 9½ inches wide, permitting the graceful undulating curves. Also, the sections nested against each other, making storage very easy in small spaces. The screen was produced in natural ash plywood and, to a lesser degree, in red or black aniline stain. In spite of its beauty and functionalism, the screen did not sell well and was soon withdrawn from production. (Photograph: Herman Miller, Inc.)

41. A dining room outfitted in Charles Eames's Plywood group furniture of 1946. The background is formed from Eames's plywood folding screens. Rubber plants and shag carpeting complete the scene. (Photograph: Herman Miller, Inc.)

42. The Charles Eames Molded Plywood group, showing the dining table with folding metal legs (1947), the DCM dining/desk chair with rod legs, the LCM low chair with rod legs, the LCW low chair with molded plywood legs, the circular coffee table on three steel rod legs, and the folding screen. (Photograph: Herman Miller, Inc.)

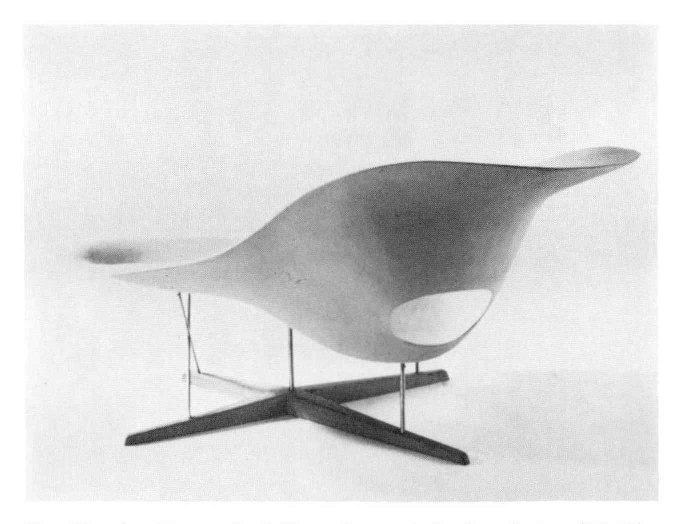

43. Charles Eames's full-scale model of a chaise (1948) of stressed-skin shell with hard rubber foam between two layers of plastic. (Photograph: Herman Miller, Inc.)

44. Variations of Charles Eames's Molded Fiberglass (Plastic) group. Included are the DAX, DAR, DAT, PAC, MAX, RAR, and LAR; the upholstered models—PAC-1, DAX-1, DAR-1, DAT-1, MAX-1, RAR-1, and LAR-1; molded plastic side chairs—DSX, DSR, MSX, and PSC; and the upholstered wire chairs—DKX-1 and 2, DKR 1 and 2, PKC 1 and 2, MKX-1 and 2, and LKR-1 and 2. For detailed construction information, refer to Part 3, "Materials and Methods of Construction." (Photograph: Herman Miller, Inc.)

45. A variety of Charles Eames's storage units from 1950 show the influence of Le Corbusier's Casiers Standard units (Plates 14–17). (Photograph: Herman Miller, Inc.)

46. Eames's lounge chair and ottoman (1956) are constructed of a molded plywood frame with rosewood veneer on a swiveling cast aluminum base, with leather-covered latex foam and down upholstery. Eames broke with the tradition of the decade in this design, which surpassed in comfort even the plump armchairs found in English men's clubs. (Photograph: Herman Miller, Inc.)

47. Eames's Aluminum group (1958). The seat and back are made as one continuous plane slung between structural ribs of die-cast aluminum. An elegant design, the structure consists of six metal components in two different styles, with more structural detail concealed within the seat pad. The most interesting technical development is the seat itself, which is constructed of front and back layers of fabric or vinyl sandwiched to an inner layer of vinyl-coated foam. This combination of materials is welded together through pressure and high-frequency current, with welds occuring at intervals that visually appear as horizontal ribs on both sides of the pad. (Photograph: Herman Miller, Inc.)

48. Eero Saarinen's first piece for Knoll in the 1940s was the Grasshopper chair. Although it was not one of his greatest commercial successes, it set trends for successive decades. (Photograph: Knoll International)

49. Eero Saarinen's Womb chair, also known as the No. 70 chair, was introduced by Knoll during 1945–48. Its construction was of a molded plastic shell and fabric-covered latex foam upholstery on a chromium-plated tubular-steel frame with nylon swivel glides. There was also an accompanying ottoman, the No. 74. (Photograph: Knoll International)

50. Eero Saarinen's No. 71 chair was originally conceived for the General Motors Technical Center in Warren, Michigan. It grew out of Saarinen's idea that the building for the plant on which he was working needed furniture to harmonize with the architecture. The No. 71 chair was Saarinen's first big break into large-scale commercial furniture design. (Photograph: Knoll International)

51. A group of Eero Saarinen's No. 71 chairs around a conference table. The chairs are comfortable enough for extended periods of sitting and double nicely as dining chairs. (Photograph: Knoll International)

52. Eero Saarinen's No. 72 chair, designed in the mid-'50s, was an armless variation of his No. 71 chair, which Knoll had introduced in 1951. The No. 72, like the No. 71, was constructed of a molded, reinforced plastic shell with contour plywood seat form. The base was available in two options, either with tubular steel legs in a polished chrome finish (Plate 53) or with the four- or five-star base shown here. (Photograph: Knoll International)

53. Eero Saarinen's No. 72 chair, showing the optional tubular-steel leg base. (Photograph: Knoll International)

54. George Nelson's side chair of 1946 consisted of foam padding on a tubular steel frame. Thousands of its clones gained fame in the "chrome sets" of postwar period dining rooms. (Photograph: Herman Miller, Inc.)

55. This photograph of George Nelson's Basic Storage Components (BSC) of 1949 shows the influence the design had on his later Comprehensive Storage System (CSS) of 1959, shown in Plate 68. (Photograph: Herman Miller, Inc.)

56. George Nelson's 1940s version of a media center consists of modules from his Basic Storage Components (BSC) System, which in turn was an adaptation of the Storagewall, designed for mass production and economical pricing. (Photograph: Herman Miller, Inc.)

57. One of the basic building blocks of his case goods, this early '50s George Nelson platform doubled as the base for modular storage units (Plate 56) and could serve as a bench or coffee table. In conjunction with the Basic Storage Components (BSC), it represented one of the first examples of modular furniture in the United States. (Photograph: Herman Miller, Inc.)

58. George Nelson's chaise longue (1954) viewed in an upright position. Plate 59 shows an elongated version with relaxation in mind. (Photograph: Herman Miller, Inc.)

59. George Nelson's chaise, with foam cushions and chrome, supports the body in total comfort. It shows some of the early influences of Mies van der Rohe (Plate 6) and Le Corbusier (Plate 18). (Photograph: Herman Miller, Inc.)

60. George Nelson's L-shaped desk (1954) offers maximum storage with minimum clutter. It is a highly functional and space-saving piece of office equipment. (Photograph: Herman Miller, Inc.)

61. A variation on George Nelson's Executive Office Group (EOG) L-shaped desk, which is also shown in Plate 60. This is an earlier version, dating from 1950, that replaces the perforated metal file drawer with more conventional cabinetry. (Photograph: Herman Miller, Inc.)

62. George Nelson branched out into sectional furniture, in keeping with his concepts of modularity in storage components. This sectional chaise longue (1955) even incorporates a clip-on table for snacking. Behind it, Charles Eames's folding plywood screen forms a beautifully undulating background. (Photograph: Herman Miller, Inc.)

63. George Nelson's whimsical design, the Marshmallow sofa (1956), is seen here covered in fabric, although vinyl was also available. (Photograph: Herman Miller, Inc.)

64. Nelson's Coconut chair, another 1956 entry into the design world. (Photograph: Herman Miller, Inc.)

65. George Nelson's Kangaroo chair was introduced by Herman Miller, Inc. in 1956. A high-back lounge chair, it was constructed from a molded plywood shell upholstered on both sides, with an attached seat and back cushion supported by a polished chrome-steel base.

Nelson's 1949 atom clock hangs on the wall. It is based on the absolute essentials of time measurement and makes use of the idea that a wall clock is mostly a decorative accessory item. Because of the clock's open design, the wall forms a natural background, and the clock becomes an integral part of the architecture. (Photograph: Herman Miller, Inc.)

66. George Nelson's Sling sofa was not introduced until 1964, but its shell form and its base show the influence of his previous work on the Kangaroo chair (Plate 65). The visual harmony lacking in the Kangaroo chair has been fully resolved in the elegance of the Sling sofa design. (Photograph: Herman Miller, Inc.)

67. A group of George Nelson's Swagged-leg chairs (1958). (Photograph: Herman Miller, Inc.)

68. The Comprehensive Storage System (CSS) designed by George Nelson is an example of knockdown furniture at its best. It was far less expensive than carpenter-constructed cabinetry yet served the same function, while retaining an aesthetically pleasing visual image. The system was designed to expand both vertically and horizontally, with the consumer having the freedom to mount the units against walls or to use them as freestanding dividers. Shelving and storage units were slung between adjustable aluminum poles pressure-fitted between ceiling and floor on a continuous track, giving the CSS great flexibility. Any of its component storage units could be placed at will at any height or in any configuration. The CSS was manufactured by Herman Miller, Inc. from 1959 to 1973, but it spawned hundreds of imitations that are still being marketed. (Photograph: Herman Miller, Inc.)

69. Another version of George Nelson's Comprehensive Storage System (CSS) that shows its flexibility by incorporating a music center. In the foreground is a fixed-back model of Nelson's Swagged-leg chair. (Photograph: Herman Miller, Inc.)

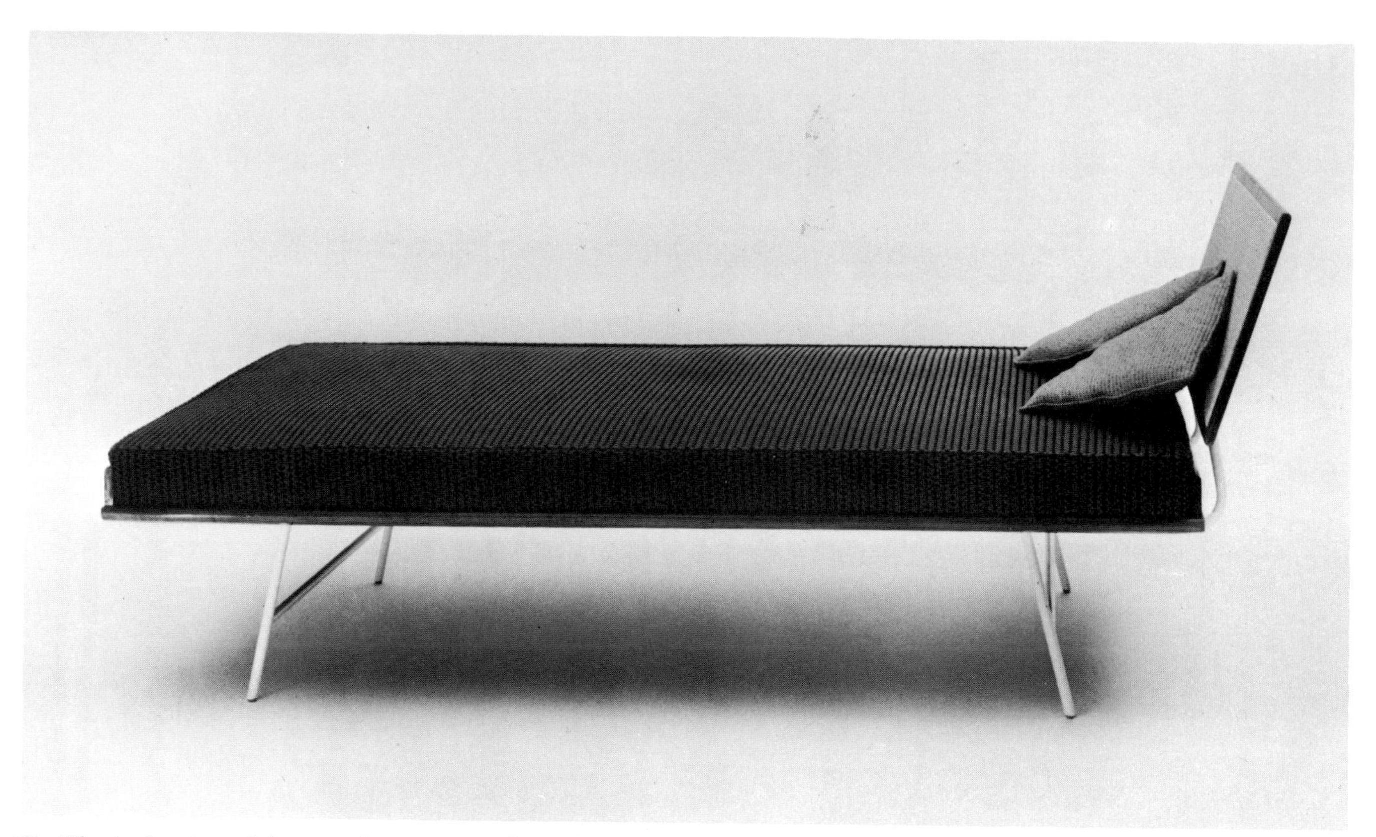

70. The bed stripped down to bare essentials as designed by George Nelson in this thin-edge foam slab bed from the 1950s. The sparse elemental form is reminiscent of a Japanese futon. (Photograph: Herman Miller, Inc.)

71. An example of George Nelson's Thin Edge Case group in rosewood. The shape of the legs has become symbolic of postwar design. (Photograph: Herman Miller, Inc.)

72. Harry Bertoia's Diamond chair (1952), manufactured by Knoll International, has earned the right to be considered a modern classic. (Photograph: Knoll International)

73. A high-back padded version of the Diamond chair with matching ottoman, designed by Harry Bertoia. (Photograph: Knoll International)

74. A pair of Harry Bertoia's wire chairs with a table designed by Isamu Noguchi. (Photograph: Knoll International)

75. Hans Knoll handled marketing in the United States for the Hardoy chair (also known as the Butterfly chair), of canvas or leather slung on a metal tube frame. The Hardoy chair has become a legendary symbol of postwar design. It is one of the most widely copied pieces of furniture on an international scale, with as many as 5,000,000 produced in the United States alone since 1950. The chair is generally considered to have been designed by Argentinian architect Jorge Ferrari Hardoy, although there is considerable conjecture as to its conceptual origins. It has been attributed in part to architects Antonio Bonet and Juan Kurchar and to an English patent filed on March 22, 1877 by civil engineer Joseph Fenby. Royalties and rights of ownership have been nearly obliterated. (Photograph: Knoll International)

76. One estimate proposes that the Hardoy chair was being turned out at the rate of 3,000 copies per week by "independent producers" in the Los Angeles area alone during the 1950s. Hans Knoll filed a lawsuit test case against one of the many copiers, but he lost, and the "butterfly" chair copies were soon being turned out again at an astonishing rate. (Photograph: Knoll International)

78.

77–80. A series of case goods designed by Florence Knoll and produced by Knoll International during the postwar period. (Photographs: Knoll International)

79.

80.

81–86. A series of furniture designs (all mid-'50s) by Florence Knoll, illustrating her "meat and potatoes" approach. (Photographs: Knoll International)

82.

83.

84.

85.

86.

87. The CBS executive offices (completed in 1964), designed by Florence Knoll with chairs by Eero Saarinen. Typical construction materials for Florence Knoll's designs included teak, rosewood, marble, and polished steel. (Photograph: Knoll International)

88. One of the offices designed for CBS at 485 Madison Avenue in New York by Florence Knoll (1954), incorporating Mies van der Rohe chairs. (Photograph: Knoll International)

89. Florence Knoll's design for the CBS offices was completed in 1964. This view incorporates furniture by Mies van der Rohe, Eero Saarinen, and Hans J. Wegner as well as Knoll's "fill-ins." (Photograph: Knoll International)

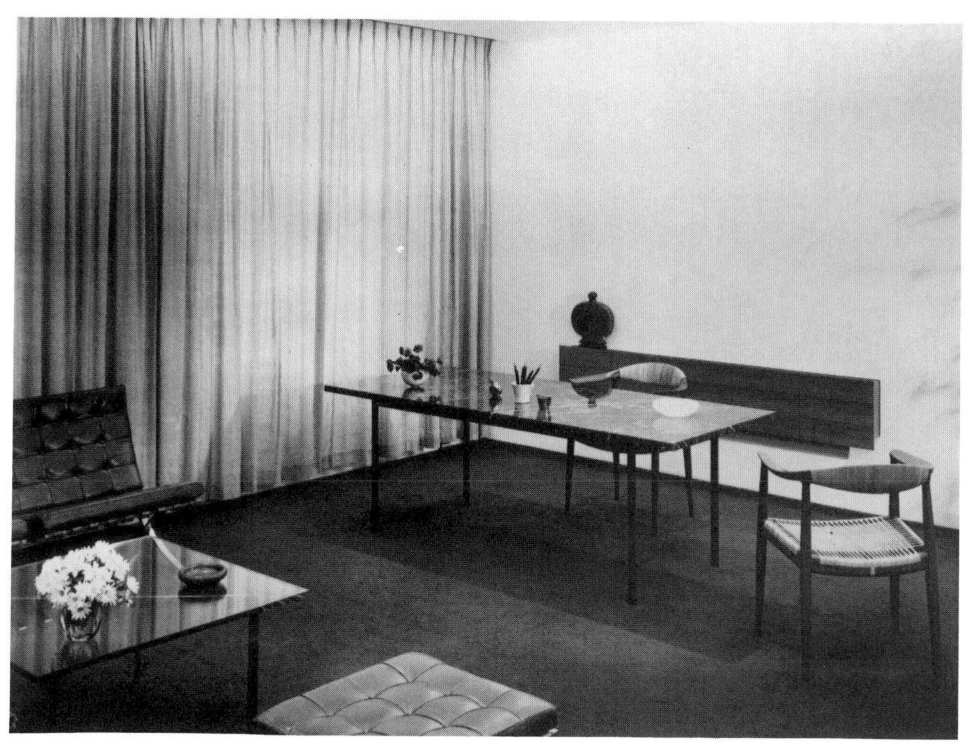

90. The CBS office project gave "Shu" Knoll the opportunity to put her ideas about space planning into operation. Unlike the typical cluttered office of the postwar period, Knoll's design provided storage space in the wall-mounted cabinets, leaving the desk a clutter-free expanse of marble, flanked by Wegner chairs. (Photograph: Knoll International)

91. This CBS office is similar to the one that "Shu" Knoll created for her husband, Hans. Hans's private office was only 12 × 12 feet, but it was so effectively planned that it enlightened many executives as to the ways of effective space utilization. (Photograph: Knoll International)

92. This view of the H.J. Heinz Company project of 1958 gives ample opportunity to observe the detail paid by the Knoll Planning Unit, which included minimizing all extraneous hardware. This passageway shows the expanse of uncluttered space so favored by the Knolls. (Photograph: Knoll International)

93. The entrance to the H.J. Heinz Company as designed by Florence Knoll in 1958. Its sparseness and reliance on architectural detailing are typical of her work. (Photograph: Knoll International)

94. The Gilbert Rohde 3323 bedroom suite (1934) is of white holly inlaid with red English elm. The legs and other structural parts are of polished chromium-plated steel tube. Considerably more metal is used on this suite than on any other commercial modern furniture of its time. (Photograph: Herman Miller, Inc.)

95. The biomorphic form of the mirror, the sectional seating, and the recessed lighting are all hallmarks of '50s design, yet this photograph was taken in 1939, when Gilbert Rohde first designed his sectional sofa, which remains remarkably contemporary looking even today. (Photograph: Herman Miller, Inc.)

96. The Gilbert Rohde 3900 series (1939) shows his sectional sofa in use at a social gathering. The upholstery fabric's distinctive texture became commonplace during the next fifteen years. (Photograph: Herman Miller, Inc.)

97. This Gilbert Rohde sofa design of 1939 influenced the work of furniture designers for decades. (Photograph: Herman Miller, Inc.)

98. The 4100 Blueprint group of 1941 was designed by Gilbert Rohde to be economical and functional. It utilized storage compartments with pull-out leaves that became tables and slipped away out of sight when not in use. This approach to space-saving designs was necessary due to the cramped housing conditions of the years during and immediately following World War II. (Photograph: Herman Miller, Inc.)

99. Rohde's 4100 Blueprint group also extended into the bedroom, where its component units could be organized for a multiplicity of storage needs. (Photograph: Herman Miller, Inc.)

100. Gilbert Rohde's Paldao group (1941) heralds the biomorphic forms that were to become symbolic of the postwar period. In the right foreground is an early version of a "step" end table. (Photograph: Herman Miller, Inc.)

101. The 4200 Blueprint group by Gilbert Rohde (1942) was a fine indicator of things to come. It not only provided ample storage in modular sections that could be assembled in endless combinations to suit the user, but it proved highly influential on later postwar designers. (Photograph: Herman Miller, Inc.)

102. The Gilbert Rohde Executive Office Group (EOG) of 1942, in which he incorporated his sectional seating units of 1939. The EOG was years ahead of its time in relation to public taste. It was comprised of 15 modular units that could be grouped into over 400 different configurations and, in retrospect, can be viewed as the forerunner of the Eames/Saarinen systems that were publicly unveiled during the next decade. (Photograph: Herman Miller, Inc.)

103. This version of the desk unit in Rohde's Executive Office group (1942) shows a difference in the base-unit cabinet and height adjustment. (Photograph: Herman Miller, Inc.)

104. A Rohde grouping at home, which shows that his designs were readily adaptable to both contract and residential applications. (Photograph: Herman Miller, Inc.)

105. The Isamu Noguchi table was in production from 1947 to 1973. A special limited edition of 400 was made in 1980, but due to popular demand, the table was reintroduced by Herman Miller in 1984. (Photograph: Herman Miller, Inc.)

106. Isamu Noguchi's Rocking stool (1954) was influenced by one of his trips to Japan. (Photograph: Knoll International)

107. A grouping of Isamu Noguchi's Rocking stools, which can also double as tables. (Photograph: Knoll International)

108. Isamu Noguchi's biomorphic sofa and footrest were designed in the late 1940s but were considered too strange to be mass-produced. Yet, the sweeping lines and conical legs were freely copied well into the late 1950s and for many people continue to symbolize the postwar furniture style. (Photograph: Herman Miller, Inc.)

109. This group shot shows Noguchi's parabolic leg table, Eames's plywood screen, and Nelson's cabinet and clock. (Photograph: Herman Miller, Inc.)

110. Arne Jacobsen's three-legged 3100 Ant chair was introduced in 1952. (Photograph: Fritz Hansen)

111. Construction details are clearly visible in this photograph of Arne Jacobsen's 3100 Ant chair (1952). (Photograph: Fritz Hansen)

112. The 3137 chair is a member of Arne Jacobsen's Series 7 group. (Photograph: Fritz Hansen)

113. The 3107 chair, another member of Jacobsen's Series 7 group. (Photograph: Fritz Hansen)

114. Arne Jacobsen's 3207 armchair (1955). (Photograph: Fritz Hansen)

115. A dining group by Arne Jacobsen. (Photograph: Arne Jacobsen)

116. Scandinavian design at its best—the work of Arne Jacobsen in a setting that is typical of the "Scandinavian look" of the postwar period. (Photograph: Arne Jacobsen)

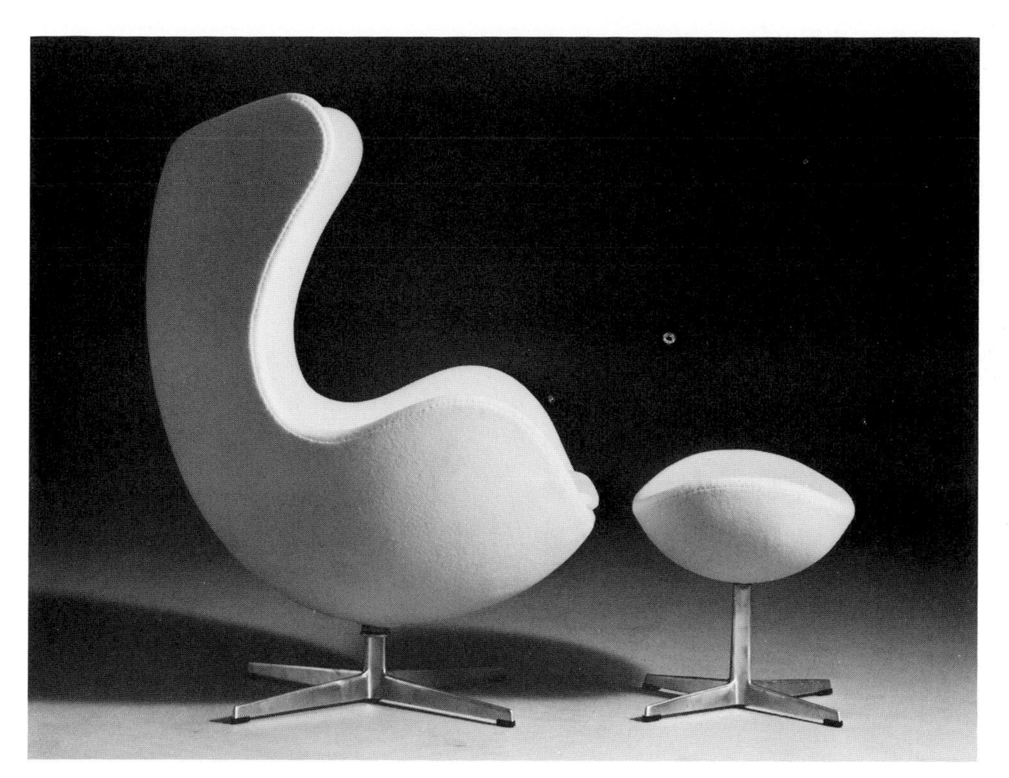

117. Arne Jacobsen's Egg chair of 1958 with its matching ottoman. This chair continues in production and is currently available in fabric, leather, or vinyl. (Photograph: Fritz Hansen)

118. The Arne Jacobsen Swan chair, designed in 1958, is still in production and is available in two versions: a low model 3320 and a high model 3322, which can be upholstered in fabric, leather, or vinyl. (Photograph: Fritz Hansen)

119. Arne Jacobsen's Oxford chair (shown here in the 3171 and 3271 armchair models). (Photograph: Fritz Hansen)

120. A high-back version of Jacobsen's Oxford chair. (Photograph: Fritz Hansen)

121. Stainless steel flatware designed by Arne Jacobsen in 1957. This highly innovative design is in the collection of the Cooper-Hewitt Museum in New York.
(Photograph: A. Michelsen, Copenhagen)
Royal Copenhagen A/S [Georg Jensen Silversmiths])

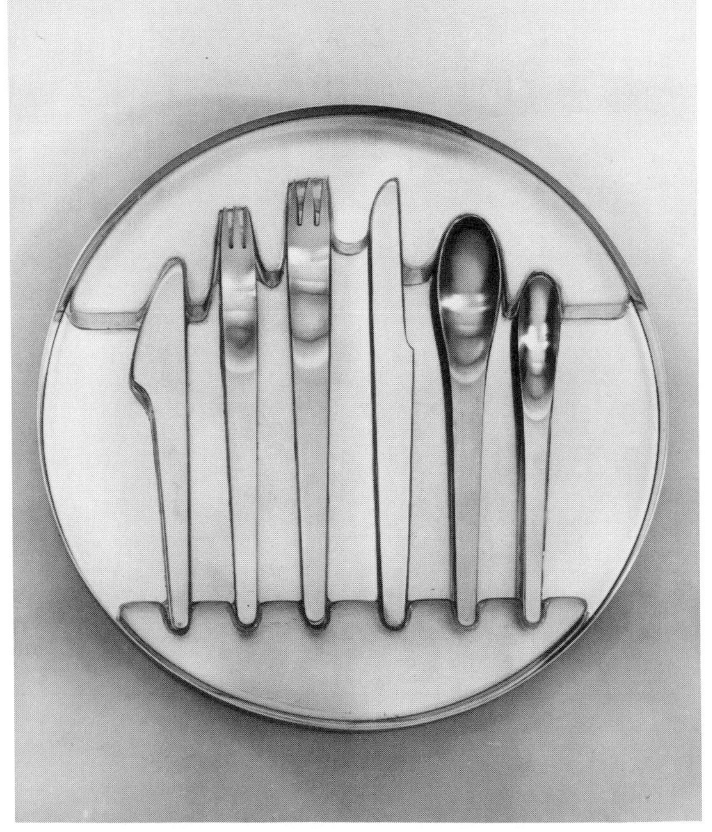

122. Jacobsen's cutlery shown nesting in a serving tray for eight place settings. This beautifully simple shape seems elemental to eating utensils. The broad handle gives an unstrained hold and control of the implements.
(Photograph: A. Michelsen, Copenhagen
Royal Copenhagen A/S [Georg Jensen Silversmiths])

123. An exterior view of the Boligens Byggeskabe (BB) storage system, designed by Grethe Meyer and Børge Mogensen and introduced in 1954. (Photograph: Grethe Meyer)

124. The interior of the Boligens Byggeskabe system, showing how the units could be used separately or in combination to form modular storage covering an entire wall. (Photograph: Grethe Meyer)

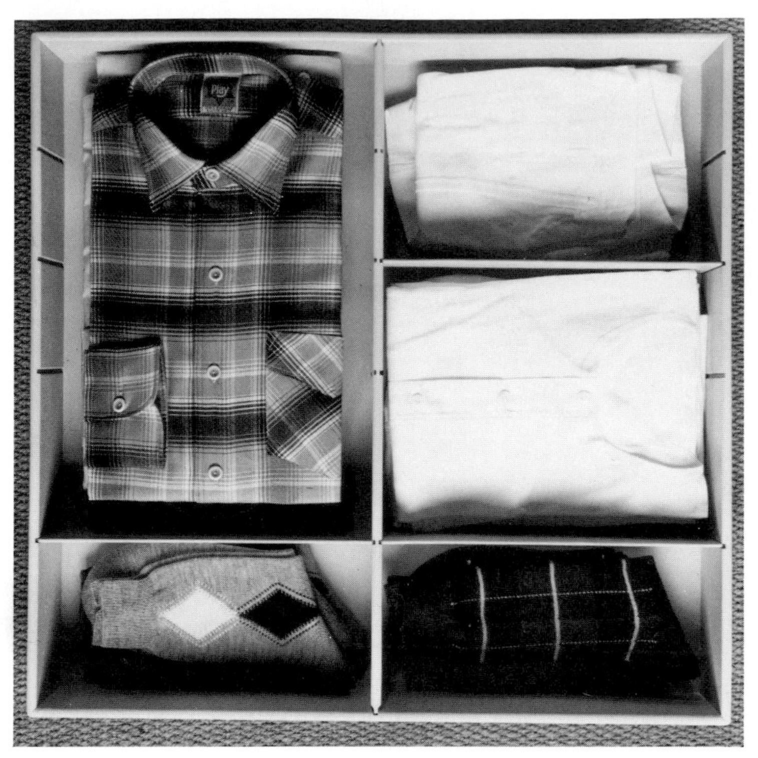

125. "A place for everything and everything in its place" must have been on Grethe Meyer's and Børge Mogensen's minds when they designed the Boligens Byggeskabe system. The interiors of drawers were easily adaptable to store any articles neatly. (Photograph: Grethe Meyer)

126. The BB system was readily adaptable to the storage of books, phonograph equipment, and objets d'art, making a functional architectural statement. Also pictured here is Børge Mogensen's sofa. (Photo: Grethe Meyer)

127. Hans J. Wegner's Chinese chair of 1944 paid homage to the simplicity of line and form found in Oriental furniture designs. (Photograph: Hans J. Wegner)

128. Hans J. Wegner's Peacock chair (1947). (Photograph: Hans J. Wegner)

129. The Chair, the Classic chair, or the Round chair, as it is variously known, was designed by Hans J. Wegner in 1949. (Photograph: Hans J. Wegner)

130. This version of Hans J. Wegner's Classic chair (1949) is of solid teak with a woven cane seat. (Photograph: Hans J. Wegner)

131. Hans J. Wegner's 1949 Folding chair. (Photograph: Hans J. Wegner)

132. Hans J. Wegner's Three-legged chair (1951). (Photograph: Hans J. Wegner)

133. Wegner's Three-legged chair showing its stacking feature. (Photograph: Hans J. Wegner)

134. Hans J. Wegner designed the three-legged version of his Valet chair in 1951. A four-legged model followed in 1953. (Photograph: Hans J. Wegner)

135. Wegner's Valet chair in use. (Photograph: Hans J. Wegner)

136. An early example of Russel Wright's furniture, this piece from his Modern Living furniture line was designed in 1935 but sold well into the '40s and '50s. (Photograph: Fifty/50, New York)

137. Carlo Mollino's 1949 side chair is typical of his fanciful, freeform approach to furniture design. (Photograph: Fifty/50, New York)

138. The Carlo Mollino room from the "Italy at Work" exhibit at the Brooklyn Museum (November 30, 1950 to January 31, 1951). Mollino's sculptured organic-form chairs and innovative upholstered pieces followed his philosophy that "everything is permissible as long as it is fantastic." (Photograph: The Brooklyn Museum)

139. A Carlo Mollino table (1950) of maple plywood and glass, manufactured by F. Apelli and L. Varesio. This is Mollino at his fanciful best, epitomizing the free-spirited aspect of Italian design. (Photograph: The Brooklyn Museum)

140. Gio Ponti's side chair of 1949. (Photograph: Fifty/50, New York)

141. An unusual table by Gio Ponti using a jack form as a base. In this piece he shows the Italian flair for showmanship in design and some of the whimsy of Carlo Mollino. (Photograph: Boomerang Gallery, Chicago, Illinois)

142. Italian designer Marco Zanuso's Lady armchair (1951) for Arflex incorporated the new synthetic materials of Nastrocord and Pirelli Sapsa. After the war, the Pirelli company was trying to find applications for its new foam rubber and presented architect Zanuso with the challenge; the Lady armchair was his solution. (Photograph: Fifty/50, New York)

143. This Robert Mango Basket chair of 1954 is typical of the ingenuity of Italian postwar design. (Photograph: Fifty/50, New York)

144. Alexander Girard's Cut-Out pattern on white batiste dates from 1954. (Photograph: Herman Miller, Inc.)

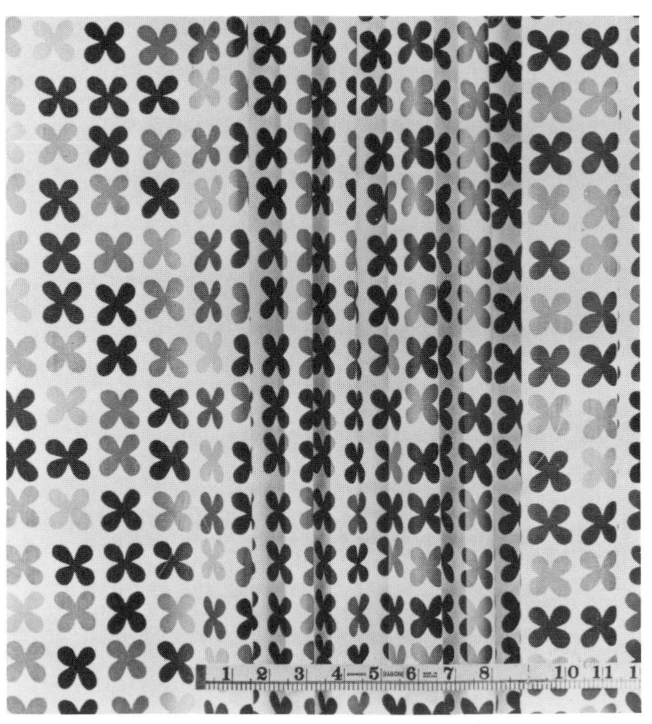

145. Alexander Girard's textile Quatrefoil on chintz dates from 1954. It was available in five colors. (Photograph: Herman Miller, Inc.)

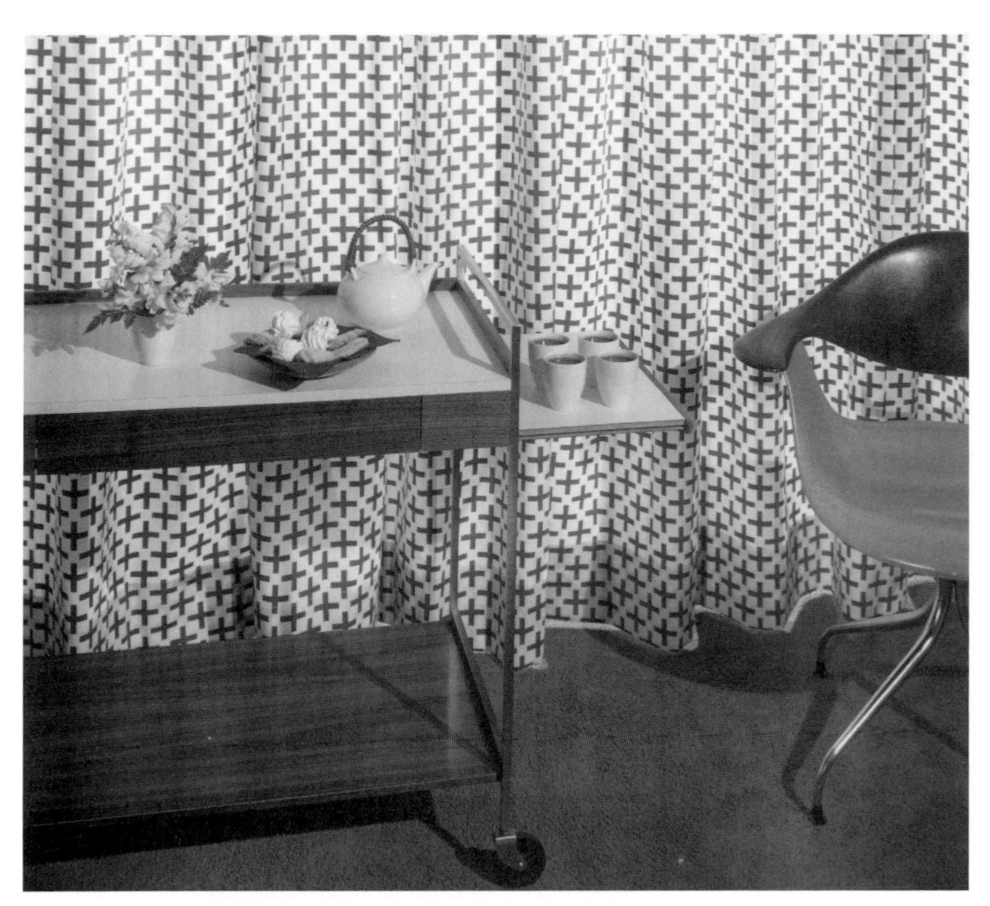

146. Girard's Plusses pattern of 1959 in combination with a George Nelson teacart and Nelson's DAF chair. (Photograph: Herman Miller, Inc.)

147. These Alexander Girard textiles—Millozenge, Millchek, Millcheklet, and Millmosaic—show the transition into sixties op-art. They date from 1960–61. (Photograph: Herman Miller, Inc.)

148. A Girard textile drapery of 1960. (Photograph: Herman Miller, Inc.)

149. This experimental model of an early '40s molded wood chair by Poul Kjaerholm bears a striking resemblance to some of Charles Eames's designs. (Photograph: Hanne Kjaerholm)

150. This is a very rare example of an early chair by Poul Kjaerholm in which he experimented with the materials (string and metal) and style that were to become his trademark. (Photograph: Hanne Kjaerholm)

151. This early '50s string and steel design by Poul Kjaerholm illustrates his attention to detail in the padding of the steel rails and the seat edge to provide greater comfort. (Photograph: Fritz Hansen)

152. An early (1952) chair design by Poul Kjaerholm, that experiments with the boomerang shape in the armrests. (Photograph: Fritz Hansen)

153. Two versions of a Poul Kjaerholm design, one in woven cane, the other in leather. The leather version (1956) won the Grand Prize at the Milan Triennale of 1957. (Photograph: Fritz Hansen)

154. This easy chair was designed by Poul Kjaerholm in the late '50s but was not produced until 1968. The base is of chrome-plated steel, with an oxhide cover. (Photograph: Herman Miller, Inc.)

155. Designed by Poul Kjaerholm in 1956, this chair has a chrome-plated tubular steel frame and woven cane back and seat. (Photograph: Fritz Hansen)

156. A grouping showing Poul Kjaerholm's high and low easy chairs. Kjaerholm products were introduced in Denmark in the period 1955–65 and in the United States by Herman Miller from 1973–77. (Photograph: Herman Miller, Inc.)

157. A Poul Kjaerholm chair and table showing his preference for steel combined with wood and canvas. (Photograph: Fritz Hansen)

158. A steel and glass table by Poul Kjaerholm, dating from the mid-50s. (Photograph: Fritz Hansen)

160. This 1947 table light was designed by Ebsen Klint, the son of Kaare Klint. Both father and son designed lighting for the firm of Le Klint that still continues to be in production. (Photograph: Le Klint)

159. This Danish-designed lampshade was manufactured by Le Klint. Since the turn of the century, the Klint family had been pleating paper into lampshades as a hobby. Tage Klint turned the hobby into a business, producing designs by Kaare Klint, Ebsen Klint (to whom he was not related), and other Danish designers. During the postwar period, Le Klint lampshades were exported worldwide and continue to be so today. (Photograph: Le Klint)

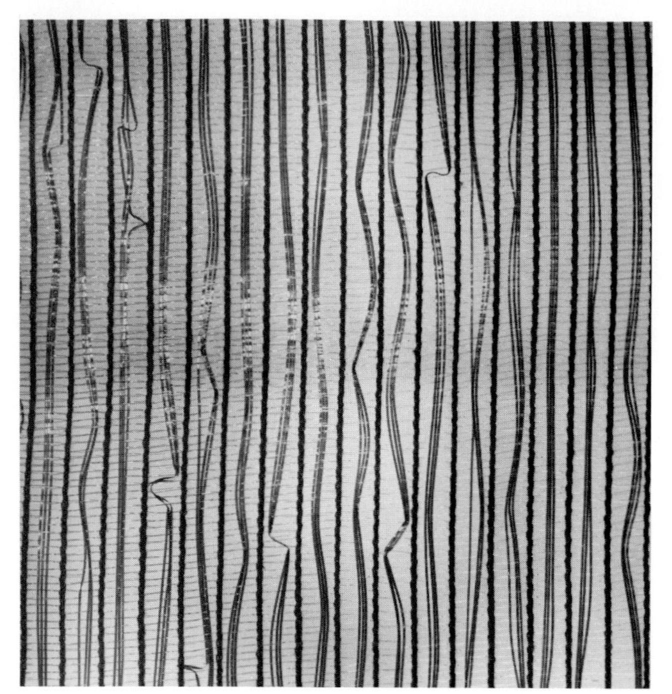

161. Limelight is a 1953 textile design by Jack Lenor Larsen. It is a knit casement in which Larsen continues his preoccupation with extruded monofilament yarns. The lightning silhouette is produced through a tension differential. No two patterns are exactly the same across the width. Limelight is fade-resistant, washable, snag-proof, soil-resistant and flame-retardant. It is available in Smoked Pearl, Jet, and Porcelain. (Photograph: Jack Lenor Larsen, Inc.)

162. Bouquet Garni, a Larsen Design sheer print, was introduced in 1955 in the Spice Garden Collection. Designed by Don Wight and printed in Germany of 60 percent polyester and 40 percent rayon, Bouquet Garni is approximately 60 inches wide with an approximate pattern repeat of 45 inches. (Photograph: Jack Lenor Larsen, Inc.)

163. Spice Garden, a Larsen Design linen print, designed by June Groff and Larsen Design Studio, was introduced in the Spice Garden Collection in 1956. Spice Garden is a handscreen printed on Eidelweiss linen in four colors: saffron, paprika, rosemary, and spice fire. (Photograph: Jack Lenor Larsen, Inc.)

164. Primavera, designed by Don Wight in 1959 and introduced in the Art Nouveau collection, was a cotton velvet print with a 48-inch width and a 36-inch pattern repeat. It was available in neutrals, nasturtium, red, deep blue, bitter green, slate, apricot, and copper luster. (Photograph: Jack Lenor Larsen, Inc.)

165. The Shape 2000 was reintroduced in 1984 at the Frankfurt International Autumn Fair as a tribute to the American pioneers of design, Raymond Loewy and Richard Latham, who designed the original for Rosenthal in 1954. (Photograph: Rosenthal)

166. This Paul McCobb side chair dates from 1954. (Photograph: Fifty/50, New York)

167. Verner Panton's Heart chair dates from 1959. (Photograph: Fifty/50, New York)

168. Alvar Aalto's armchair of 1934 (right) clearly shows its influence on the bentwood frame and upholstery armchair of the postwar period (left). The string-based coffee table by Cenedese, also a postwar design, incorporates early Scandinavian influences in its use of materials—string and wood. (Photograph: Boomerang Gallery, Chicago, Illinois)

169. This low, cork-topped table was designed by Paul Frankl and manufactured by the Johnson Furniture Company in 1949. It is typical of Frankl's unusual use of materials. Another version of the same table was available with mahogany legs and a lacquered pine top. Dimensions: 15 inches high; 41½ inches long; 35½ inches deep.

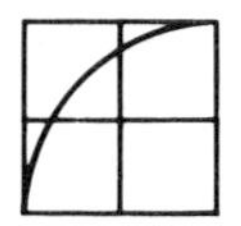

Appendix A: Resources

The sources of the postwar designs presented here are many and varied. Some postwar furniture designs are still in production and are available through manufacturers and distributors. Period pieces can be obtained through private sellers, at used furniture outlets, or at specialized retail outlets.

One of the best-known retail outlets specializing in postwar design is Fifty/50 gallery in New York. It is considered one of the most important showcases of mid-twentieth-century decorative arts and design in the world. The 4,500-square-foot tri-level exhibition space features furniture, lighting, ceramics, glass, and jewelry by internationally renowned architects and designers such as Eames, Mollino, Ponti, Noguchi, and Frank Lloyd Wright, among others. Partners Mark Isaacson, Mark McDonald, and Ralph Cutler have recently organized exhibitions of Italian art glass of the postwar period, American modernist jewelry, furniture designs of Charles and Ray Eames, and the work of Frank Lloyd Wright, all of which has focused the attention of serious collectors and museums as well as bringing the postwar period to public attention as an exciting new area of collecting. Additional information can be obtained by contacting Fifty/50 gallery directly at 793 Broadway, New York, NY 10003.

Another excellent source of twentieth-century furniture and accessories is Boomerang of Chicago, Illinois. Owners Randy Nixon and David Pinson opened Boomerang in 1983 as a result of their passion for collecting dynamic furnishings of the postwar period. Their collection began in 1978 with their discovery of an Alvar Aalto chair. Since then, both as collectors and as owner/operators of Boomerang, their focus has been on the finest designs of the period.

Boomerang now provides the Midwest with an alternate design source for its large number of architectural and interior design firms as well as for the discerning collector. In addition to furniture, the gallery stocks a good selection of postwar art and accessories including sculpture, textiles, pottery, glass, lighting, and carpets. For further information, contact Boomerang at 3352 N. Halsted, Chicago, IL 60657.

A listing of additional sources of postwar furnishings follows. Sources for some of the prewar furnishings discussed in Part 1 are included as well.

THE MANUFACTURERS AND DISTRIBUTORS

Abitare
212 East 57th Street
New York, NY 10022
(Italian Design)

Artek
Keskuskatu 3
00100 Helsinki 10
Finland
(Alvar Aalto)

U.S. Distributor:
Scandinavian Design
127 East 59th Street
New York, NY 10022

AB Karn Andersson & Soner
Mobelfabrik
Husdvarna, Sweden
(Børge Mogensen)

Artemide
Via Burghiera
2000 Pregnanna Milanese
Milan, Italy
(Italian Design)

U.S. Distributor:
Artemide
150 East 58th Street
New York, NY 10155

Cassina
Via Luigi Busnelli 1
20036 Meda
Milan, Italy
(Le Corbusier, Gio Ponti, Gianfranco Frattini, Luisa and Ico Parisi)

U.S. Distributor:
Atelier International Ltd.
595 Madison Avenue
New York, NY 10022

Ecart International
6 rue Pavee
75004 Paris
France
(Eileen Gray)

U.S. Distributor:
Furniture of the Twentieth Century
154 West 18th Street
New York, NY 10155

Fritz Hansen
DK-3450, Allerød
Denmark
(Arne Jacobsen, Poul Kjaerholm)

U.S. Distributor:
ICF (U.S.)
305 East 63rd Street
New York, NY 10021

Herman Miller Inc.
3500 Byron Road
Zeeland, Michigan 49464
(Charles Eames, George Nelson, Isamu Noguchi, Poul Kjaerholm, Gilbert Rohde)

Iittala Glassworks
14500 Iittala
Finland
(Alvar Aalto)

U.S. Distributor:
Ahlstrom Trading, Inc.
Iittala U.S.A.
175 Clearbrook Road
Elmsford, NY 10523

Images/Kaleidos
San Marco 3159
30124 Venice, Italy
(Eileen Gray)

U.S. Distributor:
Images of America
329 Blair Street
Thomasville, NC 27630

Johannes Hansen
311 Gladsakevej
DK-1860
Soeborg, Denmark
(Hans J. Wegner)

Vladimir Kagan Designs Inc.
232 East 59th Street
New York, NY 10022
(Vladimir Kagan)

Knoll International
The Knoll Building
655 Madison Avenue
New York, NY 10021
(Eero Saarinen, Florence Knoll, Harry Bertoia, Isamu Noguchi, Hardoy chair, Marcel Breuer, Ludwig Mies van der Rohe)

Jack Lenor Larsen
232 East 59th Street
New York, NY 10022
(Jack Lenor Larsen)

Laverne International
RFD 1480
Syosset, NY 11791
(Katavolos, Littell, Kelley; Laverne Originals)

Le Klint
Egestrubben 13–15
DK-5270 Odesne N.
Denmark
(Kaare Klint, Ebsen Klint)

A. Michelsen
Ragnade 7
DK-2100 Copenhagen
Denmark
(Arne Jacobsen)

Louis Poulsen
A/S Nyhavn 11
DK-1004 Copenhagen
Denmark
(Scandinavian design)

U.S. Distributor:
Scan Furniture
Greenbelt Consumer Services, Inc.
Greenwood Place
Savage, MD 20863

Rosenthal Aktiengesellschaft
Postfach 1520
8672, Selb/Bayern
West Germany
(Walter Gropius, Raymond Loewy)

Ivan Schlechter
Soegaardsvej 30
DK-3250 Gilleleje
Denmark
(Finn Juhl)

Stilnovo
Via F. Ferruccio 8
20145, Milan
Italy
(Italian design)

Tecta Mobel
Sohnreystrasse 18
3471 Lauenforde
West Germany
(Walter Gropius)

Tecno s.p.a.
Via Bigli 22
1–20121, Milan
Italy
(Oswaldo Borsani)

Thonet
491 East Prince Street
P.O. Box 1587
York, PA 17405
(Thonet, Mies van der Rohe)

RETAIL OUTLETS

Atomic Age Furnishings
225 Gough Street
San Francisco, CA 94102
(415) 861-6558

Beige Gallery
119 Wooster Street
New York, NY 10012
(212) 691-5488

Boomerang
3352 N. Halsted
Chicago, IL 60657
(312) 348-7755

City Barn
360 Atlantic Avenue
Brooklyn, NY 12217
(718) 855-8566

Decorative Antiques
190 Tenth Avenue
New York, NY 10011
(212) 206-0780

Fifty/50
793 Broadway
New York, NY 10003
(212) 777-3208

Furniture of the Twentieth Century
154 W. 18th St.
New York, NY 10011
(212) 929-6023

Metropolis
100 Wooster Street
New York, NY 10012
(212) 226-6117

Modern Age Galleries
795 Broadway
New York, NY 10003
(212) 674-5603

Modernism
984 Madison Avenue
New York, NY 10021
(212) 744-9040

Alan Moss
88 Wooster Street
New York, NY 10012
(212) 219-1663

Retro-Modern Studio
30 E. 10th Street
New York, NY 10003
(212) 674-0530

Second Hand Rose
573 Hudson Street
New York, NY 10011
(212) 989-9776

Skank World
7205 Beverly Boulevard
Los Angeles, CA 90036
(213) 939-7858

30s/40s/50s
320 Atlantic Avenue
Brooklyn, NY 11217
(718) 875-4181

20th Century Furnishings
220 Eighth
San Francisco, CA 94102
(415) 626-0542

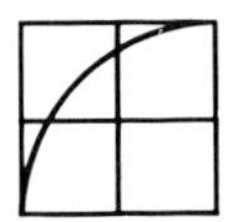

Appendix B: Supplemental Charts

CONTEMPORARY DESIGN MOVEMENTS

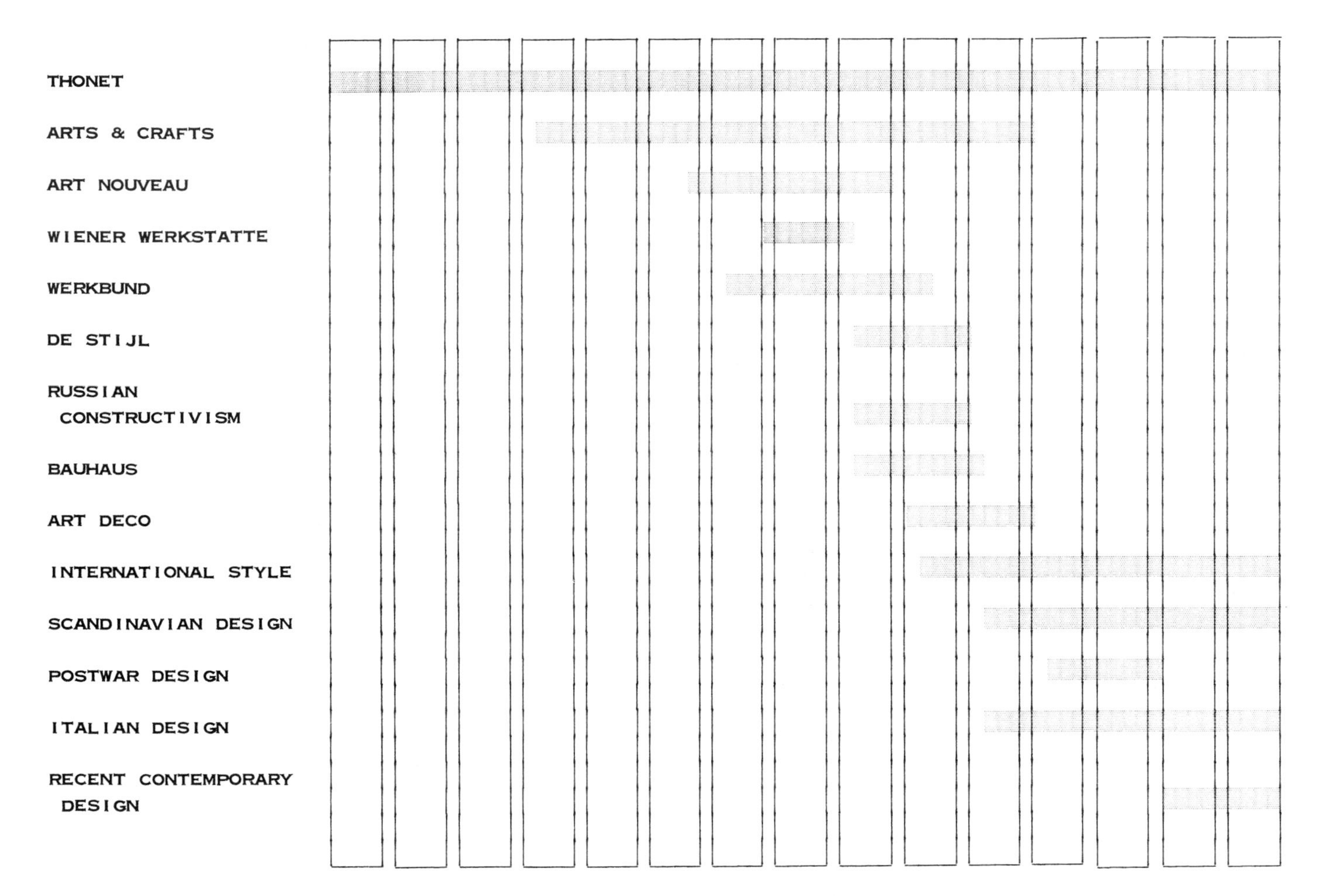

INFLUENCES OF CONTEMPORARY DESIGN MOVEMENTS

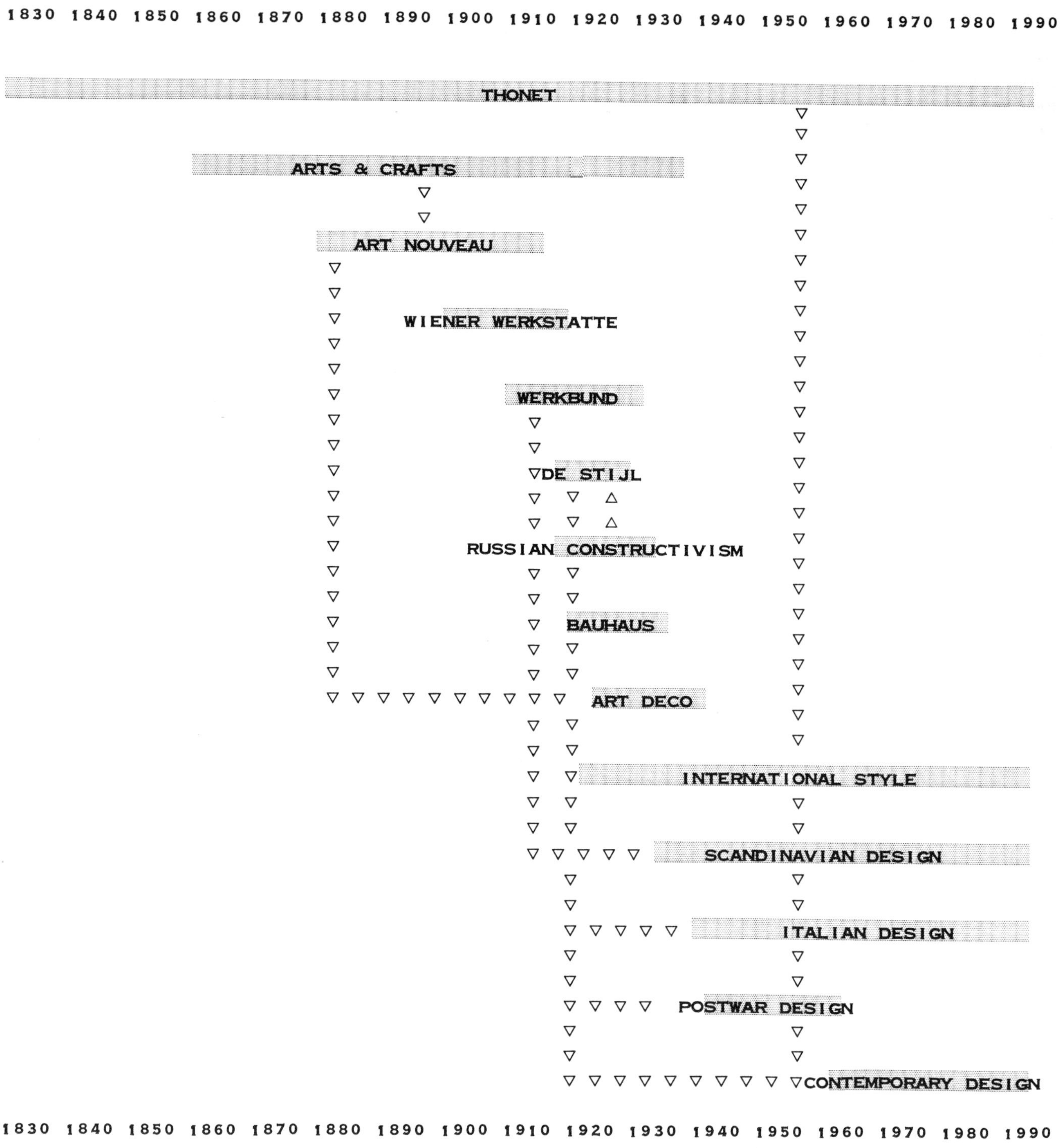

1830 1840 1850 1860 1870 1880 1890 1900 1910 1920 1930 1940 1950 1960 1970 1980 1990

THONET

ARTS & CRAFTS

ART NOUVEAU

WIENER WERKSTATTE

WERKBUND

DE STIJL

RUSSIAN CONSTRUCTIVISM

BAUHAUS

ART DECO

INTERNATIONAL STYLE

SCANDINAVIAN DESIGN

ITALIAN DESIGN

POSTWAR DESIGN

CONTEMPORARY DESIGN

1830 1840 1850 1860 1870 1880 1890 1900 1910 1920 1930 1940 1950 1960 1970 1980 1990

INTRODUCTION OF MAJOR FURNITURE DESIGNS OF THE POSTWAR PERIOD

	19-- (40 41 42 43 44 45 46 47 48 49 50 51 52 53 54 55 56 57 58 59 60)
EAMES LCM CHAIR	45
EAMES DAR SHELL CHAIR	49
EAMES UPHOLSTERED DAR CHAIR	50
EAMES WIRE DKR CHAIR	53
EAMES LOUNGE CHAIR/OTTOMAN	56
EAMES ALUMINUM GROUP	58
SAARINEN NO. 71 CHAIR	51
SAARINEN WOMB CHAIR	45
SAARINEN PEDESTAL GROUP	57
NELSON STORAGEWALL	45
NELSON CSS SYSTEM	59
NELSON MARSHMALLOW SOFA	46
NELSON COCONUT CHAIR	46
NELSON KANGAROO CHAIR	46
NELSON DAF CHAIR	58
BERTOIA DIAMOND CHAIR	52
KNOLL STACKING STOOL	48
ROHDE 4100 SERIES	41
ROHDE BLUEPRINT GROUP	42
ROHDE PALDAO GROUP	41
NOGUCHI TABLE	47
NOGUCHI AKARI LAMP	48
JACOBSEN 3100 ANT CHAIR	52
JACOBSEN EGG CHAIR	58
JACOBSEN SWAN CHAIR	58
JACOBSEN SERIES 7 GROUP	57
MOGENSEN/MEYER BB SYSTEM	54
MOGENSEN ØRESUND SYSTEM	55
WEGNER CHINESE CHAIR	44
WEGNER PEACOCK CHAIR	47
WEGNER FOLDING CHAIR	49
WEGNER CLASSIC CHAIR	49
WEGNER 3-LEGGED VALET CHAIR	51
WEGNER 4-LEGGED VALET CHAIR	53
WEGNER CHAIR 24	52
WRIGHT EASIER LIVING GROUP	50
KJAERHOLM LEATHER/STEEL CHAIR	56
MC COBB PLANNER GROUP	50
MØLGAARD-NIELSEN AX SERIES	50
PANTON CONE CHAIR	59
RACE BA CHAIR	46
RACE ANTELOPE CHAIR	52

Notes

INTRODUCTION

1. Eliot F. Noyes, *Organic Design in Home Furnishings* (exhibit catalog) (New York: Museum of Modern Art, 1941).

PART 1

1. Karl Mang, *History of Modern Furniture* (New York: Harry N. Abrams, Inc., 1979), p. 108.
2. *1972–1982 Bericht einer Deutschen Unternehmung* (Berlin: Alexander Verlag, 1983), p. 14.
3. Edward Lucie Smith, *Furniture: A Concise History* (London: Thames and Hudson Ltd., 1979), p. 177.
4. Ibid.
5. *1972–1982 Bericht einer Deutschen Unternehmung,* p. 27.
6. Ibid., p. 26.
7. Adolf Loose, "Ornament und Verbrechen," 1908.
8. H.L.C. Jaffe, *De Stijl, 1917–1931: Der Niederlandische Beitrag zur Modernen Kunst* (Berlin: Ullstein, 1965).
9. Ibid.
10. Henry-Russell Hitchcock and Philip Johnson, *The International Style: Architecture Since 1922* (New York: W.W. Norton, 1932).
11. Aino and Alvar Aalto, *Alvar Aalto* (Aurich: Verlag für Architectur, 1963).

PART 2

CHARLES EAMES

1. Arthur Drexler, *Charles Eames Furniture from the Design Collection* (New York: Museum of Modern Art, 1973), p. 3.
2. Ralph Caplan, *The Design of Herman Miller* (New York: Whitney Library of Design, 1976).
3. Ibid., p. 44.
4. Ibid., p. 32.
5. Ibid.
6. Ibid., p. 46

EERO SAARINEN

1. Albert Christ-Janer, *Eliel Saarinen* (Chicago: University of Chicago Press, 1948 and 1979), p. 20.
2. Ibid., p. 80.
3. Marian Page, *Furniture Designed by Architects* (New York: Whitney Library of Design, 1980), p. 208.
4. Ibid., p. 209.
5. Charles D. Gandy and Susan Zimmermann-Stidham, *Contemporary Classics* (New York: McGraw-Hill, Inc., 1981), p. 152.
6. Jay Doblin, *One Hundred Great Product Designs* (New York: Van Nostrand Reinhold Company, 1970), p. 109.
7. Page, *Furniture Designed by Architects,* p. 209.
8. Ibid., p. 206.
9. Ibid.
10. Ibid.
11. *Architectural Digest,* August, 1957.
12. Page, *Furniture Designed by Architects,* p. 209.

GEORGE NELSON

1. George Nelson, *Problems of Design* (New York: Whitney Library of Design, 1957), p. ix.
2. Ibid., p. ix.
3. Ralph Caplan, *The Design of Herman Miller* (New York: Whitney Library of Design, 1976), p. 30.
4. Ibid., p. 31.
5. Herman Miller Catalog, 1948.
6. Ibid.
7. Nelson, *Problems of Design,* p. 56.
8. Ibid.
9. Ibid.
10. Ibid., p. 65.
11. Ibid., p. 67.
12. Ibid., p. 63.
13. Ibid., p. 67.
14. Ibid., p. 74.
15. Ibid., p. 168.
16. Ibid., p. 174.
17. Ibid., p. 180.
18. Ibid., p. 182.
19. Ibid., p. 183.
20. Ibid.
21. Ibid., p. 193.

HARRY BERTOIA

1. Robert Judson Clark, et al., Detroit Institute of Arts/Metropolitan Museum of Art, *Design in America: The Cranbrook Vision 1925–1950* (New York: Harry N. Abrams, Inc., 1983), p. 167.
2. Eric Larrabee and Massimo Vignelli, *Knoll Design* (New York: Harry N. Abrams, Inc., 1981), p. 68.
3. Ibid., p. 69.
4. Ibid.
5. *History of Furniture* (New York: William Morrow & Company, Inc., 1976), p. 302.
6. Clark, et al., *Design in America,* p. 256.
7. Larrabee and Vignelli, *Knoll Design,* p. 71.

HANS AND FLORENCE KNOLL

1. Eric Larrabee and Massimo Vignelli, *Knoll Design* (New York: Harry N. Abrams, Inc., 1981), p. 77.
2. Ibid., p. 22.
3. Ibid., p. 16.
4. Ibid., p. 22.
5. Ibid., p. 77.
6. Ibid.
7. Ibid.
8. Ibid.
9. Ibid., p. 80.
10. Ibid.
11. Ibid.
12. Ibid., p. 93.
13. Ibid.
14. Ibid., p. 128.

GILBERT ROHDE

1. Ralph Caplan, *The Design of Herman Miller* (New York: Whitney Library of Design, 1976), p. 27.

2. Ibid., p. 24.
3. Ibid., p. 27.
4. Archives, Herman Miller Furniture Company.

ISAMU NOGUCHI

1. Isamu Noguchi, *A Sculptor's World* (New York: Harper & Row, 1968), p. 13.
2. Ibid., p. 11.
3. Ibid., p. 14.
4. Ibid., p. 15.
5. Ibid.
6. Herman Miller Inc., *Reference Points*, 1984.
7. Noguchi, *A Sculptor's World*, p. 27.
8. Ibid., p. 21.
9. Ibid.
10. Ibid., p. 125.
11. Ibid., p. 23.
12. Ibid., p. 24.
13. Ibid., p. 25.
14. Ibid., p. 26.
15. Ibid., p. 27.
16. Ibid.
17. Noguchi, *A Sculptor's World*, p. 40.

ARNE JACOBSEN

1. Tobias Faber, *Arne Jacobsen* (Stuttgart: Verlag Gerd Hatje, 1964), p. xxii.

HANS J. WEGNER

1. Charles D. Gandy and Susan Zimmermann-Stidham, *Contemporary Classics* (New York: McGraw-Hill, Inc., 1981), p. 115.
2. Philadelphia Museum of Art, *Design Since 1945* (New York: Rizzoli, 1983), p. 235.

RUSSEL WRIGHT

1. William J. Hennessey, *Russel Wright, American Designer* (Cambridge: The MIT Press, 1983), p. 48.
2. Mary and Russel Wright, *Guide to Easier Living* (New York: Simon and Schuster, 1950), p. 42.
3. Ibid.

THE ITALIANS

1. Andrea Branzi, *The Hot House: New Wave Design* (Cambridge: The MIT Press, 1984), p. 39.
2. *Italy: The New Domestic Landscape* (New York: Museum of Modern Art, 1972), p. 383.
3. Philadelphia Museum of Art, *Design Since 1945* (New York: Rizzoli, 1983), p. 223.
4. *Italy: The New Domestic Landscape*, p. 12.
5. Ibid., p. 383.
6. *Metropolitan Home*, February 1985, p. 16.

SUPPLEMENTAL DESIGNERS

1. Philadelphia Museum of Art, *Design Since 1945* (New York: Rizzoli, 1983).
2. Ibid.
3. Edgar Kaufmann, Jr., *Prize Designs for Modern Furniture from the International Competition for Low-cost Furniture Design* (New York: Museum of Modern Art, 1948).
4. Ralph Caplan, *The Design of Herman Miller* (New York: Whitney Library of Design, 1976), p. 46.
5. *Modern Chairs: 1918–1970* (London: The Whitechapel Art Gallery, 1970).
6. Kaufmann, *Prize Designs for Modern Furniture*, p. 42.

PART 3

CONSTRUCTION MATERIALS AND METHODS

1. Eric Larrabee and Massimo Vignelli, *Knoll Design* (New York: Harry N. Abrams, Inc., 1981), pp. 56, 57.
2. Edgar Kaufmann, Jr., *What Is Interior Design?* (New York: The Museum of Modern Art, 1953).
3. Larrabee and Vignelli, p. 57.
4. Edgar Kaufmann, Jr., *Prize Designs for Modern Furniture* (New York: Museum of Modern Art, 1948), p. 8.

DESIGNERS AND THEIR DESIGNS

1. Ralph Caplan, *The Design of Herman Miller* (New York: Whitney Library of Design, 1976), p. 56.
2. Ibid., p. 57.
3. Eric Larrabee and Massimo Vignelli, *Knoll Design* (New York: Harry N. Abrams, Inc., 1981), p. 56.
4. Ibid.
5. Ibid.
6. *Modern Chairs: 1918–1970* (London: The Whitechapel Art Gallery, 1970), p. 101.
7. George Nelson and Henry Wright, *Tomorrow's House* (New York: Simon and Schuster, 1945), p. 116.
8. Archives, Herman Miller Furniture Company.
9. David Hanks, *Innovative Furniture in America from 1800 to the Present* (New York: Horizon Press, 1981), p. 115.
10. Larrabee and Vignelli, *Knoll Design*, p. 80.
11. Ibid.
12. Isamu Noguchi, *A Sculptor's World* (New York: Harper & Row, 1968), p. 28.
13. William J. Hennessey, *Russel Wright, American Design* (Cambridge: The MIT Press, 1983), p. 23.
14. Reyner Banham, "The Chair as Art," *New Society*, April 20, 1967.

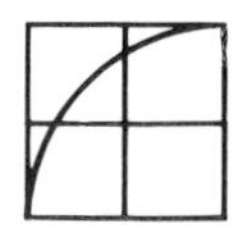

Bibliography

Aloi, Roberto. *L'Arredamento Moderno.* Milan, 1955.

Arne Jacobsen, McLellan Galleries, Glasgow, 1968.

Baroni, Daniele. *The Furniture of Gerrit Thomas Rietveld.* Woodbury: Barron's, 1978.

Branzi, Andrea. *The Hot House.* Cambridge: The MIT Press, 1984.

Caplan, Ralph. *The Design of Herman Miller.* New York: Whitney Library of Design, 1976.

Christ-Janer, Albert. *Eliel Saarinen.* Chicago: University of Chicago Press, 1979.

Dal Fabbro, Mario. *Furniture for Modern Interiors.* New York: Reinhold Publishing Corporation, 1954.

Ditzel, Nanna and Jørgen. *Danske Stole.* Høst & Søns, 1954.

Doblin, Jay. *One Hundred Great Product Designs.* New York: Van Nostrand Reinhold Company, 1970.

Drexler, Arthur. *Charles Eames Furniture from the Design Collection.* New York: Museum of Modern Art, 1973.

Emery, Marc. *Furniture by Architects.* New York: Harry N. Abrams, Inc., 1983.

Faber, Tobias. *Arne Jacobsen.* London: Alec Tiranti Ltd., 1964.

Fusco, Renato De. *Le Corbusier, Designer Furniture, 1929.* Woodbury: Barron's, 1977.

Gandy, Charles D. and Zimmermann-Stidham, Susan. *Contemporary Classics: Furniture of the Masters.* New York: McGraw-Hill Inc., 1981.

Garner, Philippe. *Twentieth Century Furniture.* New York: Van Nostrand Reinhold, 1980.

———. *Contemporary Decorative Arts.* New York: Facts on File, 1980.

Glaeser, Ludwig. *Ludwig Mies van der Rohe Furniture and Furniture Drawings.* New York: The Museum of Modern Art, 1977.

Greenberg, Cara. *Mid-Century Modern.* New York: Harmony Books, 1984.

Grow, Lawrence. *The Catalogue of Contemporary Design.* New York: Collier Books, 1983.

Hanks, David A. *The Decorative Designs of Frank Lloyd Wright.* New York: E. P. Dutton, 1979.

———. *Innovative Furniture in America from 1980 to the Present.* New York: Horizon Press, 1981.

Hard af Segerstad, Ulf. *Modern Finnish Design.* London: Weidenfeld and Nicholson Ltd., 1969.

———. *Modern Scandinavian Furniture.* Totowa: The Bedminster Press, 1963.

Hennessey, William J. *Russel Wright, American Designer.* Cambridge: The MIT Press, 1983.

Hiesinger, Kathryn B. and Marcus, George H., eds. *Design Since 1945.* Philadelphia Museum of Art, Rizzoli, New York, 1983, 249 pp.

The History of Furniture. New York: William Morrow & Company, 1976.

Italian Re-evolution: Design in Italian Society in the Eighties. La Jolla Museum of Contemporary Art.

Italy: The New Domestic Landscape. New York: Museum of Modern Art, New York Graphic Society Ltd., 1972.

Karlsen, Arne. *Mobler tegnet af Børge Mogensen.* Arkitektens Forlag, 1968.

Ketchum, William C. *Furniture 2: Neoclassic to the Present.* New York: Cooper-Hewitt Museum, 1981.

Larrabee, Eric and Vignelli, Massimo. *Knoll Design.* New York: Harry N. Abrams, Inc., 1981.

Lucie-Smith, Edward. *Furniture: A Concise History.* New York: Oxford University Press, 1979.

Mang, Karl. *History of Modern Furniture.* New York: Harry N. Abrams, Inc., 1978.

Modern Chairs: 1918–1970. London: The Whitechapel Art Gallery, 1970.

Nelson, George and Wright, Henry. *Tomorrow's House.* New York: Simon and Schuster, 1945.

Noguchi, Isamu. *A Sculptor's World.* New York: Harper & Row, 1968.

Noyes, Eliot F. "Modern Furniture." *Consumer Reports,* September 1947, pp. 363–65.

———. *Organic Design in Home Furnishings.* New York: The Museum of Modern Art, 1941.

Oates, Phyllis Bennett. *The Story of Western Furniture.* New York: Harper & Row, 1981.

"Organic Design." *Magazine of Art,* November 1941, pp. 482–83.

Page, Marian. *Furniture Designed by Architects.* New York: Whitney Library of Design, 1980.

Pile, John F. *Modern Furniture.* New York: John Wiley & Sons, 1979.

Russell, Frank, ed. *A Century of Chair Design.* New York: Rizzoli, 1980.

Spade, Rupert and Futagawa, Yukio. *Eero Saarinen.* London: Thames and Hudson, 1971.

Temko, Allan. *Eero Saarinen.* New York: George Brazille.

Index

Aalto, Alvar, 6, 8, 9–10, 44, *128, 129, 186*
Ahlmann, Lis, 58, 76
Aicher, Otl, 77
Akari light sculptures, 50, 106
Albers, Anni, 76
Albini, Franco, 37, 72, 73, 76
Albinson, Don, 20
Aluminum
  furniture, 20–21, 100
  tableware, 67, 89
Aluminum group (Eames), *135*
American design, 8, 10
American Modern dinnerware (R. Wright), 65–66
American Way furnishings (R. Wright), 66–67
Anderson, Winslow, 76
Ant chair (Jacobsen), 106, *166*
Appelli, F., 177
The Architect's Collective, *115*
Architecture, 6
  C. Eames on, 17–18
  G. Nelson and, 30–31
  relationship to interior design, 24, 38–39, 52, 58, 71
Armour Institute, 38, 39
Art deco style, 7
Asimow, Morris, 20
Atom clock (Nelson), 104, *142, 165*
Ax chair (Molgaard-Nielsen), 82

Bäckström, Olof, 76
Banham, Reyner, 112
Barcelona chair (Mies van der Rohe), 4, 39–40, *116*
Basic Storage Components (BSC) system (Nelson), *138*, 139
Basket chair (Mango), *178*
Bassett, Florence. *See* Knoll, Florence
Bassett, Harry, 40
Bauhaus, 3–5
  "new," 77, 79
Baumann, Hans Theo, 76–77
Bedroom furniture, *146, 158*
Bellman, Hans, 37
Bentsen, Ivar, 52
Bernadotte, Sigvard, 77
Bertoia, Harry, 17, 24, 34–36, 40, *147*
  construction materials/methods of, 104
Bibendum chair (Gray), *126*
Bill, Max, 77,79
Bishop, Frances, 20
Bjørn, Acton, 77
Blueprint group, 4100/4200 (Rohde), *160, 161*
Boelter, L.M.K., 20
Boligens Byggeskabe (BB) storage system (Meyer/Mogensen), 59, 108–9, *171*
Bonet, Antonio, 37, 148
Booth, George G., 23
Borglum, Gutzon, 46
Bouquet Garni textile design (Wight), *184*
Branzi, Andrea, 71
Braun, Artur, 77
Breuer, Marcel, 4–5, 6, 38, 40, 89, *117, 118*
Brunori, Bubi, 111
Butler, Lewis, 41
Butterfly chair, 37, *148, 149*

Cabinetmakers' Guild, Danish, 57, 58, 59, 61
Caccia-Cominioni, 72
Casiers Standard storage system (Le Corbusier), *120, 121*, 134
Castiglioni, Achille, 77–78
Castiglioni brothers, 72, 74
Castiglioni, Livio, 77
Castiglioni, Piergiacomo, 77
Cesca chair (Breuer), *118*
Chairs, 111–12, *115, 116, 122, 128, 129, 132, 135, 138, 139, 141, 175, 177, 179, 180, 181, 182, 185, 186*
  Ant, 106, *166*
  Ax, 82
  Barcelona, 4, 39–40, *116*
  Bibendum, *126*
  Butterfly, 37, *148, 149*
  Cesca, *118*
  Chinese, 61, 109
  Classic, 62–63, 109
  Coconut, 29, 103, *142*
  Cube, *122*
  Diamond, 35, 40, 104, *147*
  Eames, 17–18, 34–35, 93–100, *130, 132*
  Egg, 54, 106, *169*
  Extended Lounge, *123*
  Folding, 63, 109, *174*
  Grand Confort, *122*
  Grasshopper, *136*
  Hardoy, 37, *148, 149*
  Heart, *185*
  Kangaroo, 29, 103, *142*, 143
  Lady, *178*
  Mogensen school, 59–60
  No. 71/72, 101, *136, 137*
  Oxford, 107–8, *170*
  Peacock, 61–62, 109
  Red and Blue, 6
  Rohde side-, 44
  Series 7, 107
  Swagged-leg, 103, *143, 145*
  Swan, 8, 54, 106, *169*
  3100, 54, *166*
  3107, *166*
  3137, *166*
  3207, *167*
  Three-legged, *174*
  Tugendhat, *117*
  Valet, 63, 109, *175*
  Wassily, 4, 89–90, *117*
  Womb, 24–25, 100, *136*
Cheti, Fede, 78
Chicago World Exhibition (1893), 8
Chinese chair (Wegner), 61, 109
Clarke, Arundell, 40
Classic chair (Wegner), 62–63, 109
Classic chair (Wegner), 62–63, 109
Coconut chair (Nelson), 29, 103, *142*
Cogan, Marshall S., 40–41
Color, 36
  R. Wright's use of, 65–66, 68
Compasso d'Oro Award, 72, 74
Comprehensive Storage System (Nelson), 102, 138, *144, 145*
Connor, James, 20
Construction methods and materials, 87–92. *See also* specific materials
  aluminum, 20–21, 89
  bentwood, 9
  engineering, 91–92
  foam, 10, 91
  plywood, 10, 18, 87–88
  wire, 4
  wood, 87–89
Contemporary American Industrial Art Show (1931), 67
Cranbrook Academy of Art, 17, 23–24, 34, 37
Crate furniture (Rietveld), 6
Cube chair (Le Corbusier/Perriand), *122*
Curry, John, 67
Cut-Out textile pattern (Girard), *178*

Danish Cooperative Wholesale Society, 57
Day, Lucienne, 78
Day, Robin, 78
De Pree, D.J., 18, 28, 43
Design for Living exhibition, 42
Design Laboratory, 42
Design philosophy
  A. Aalto's, 9
  at the Bauhaus, 3, 4
  C. Eames's, 19
  G. Nelson's, 30–31
  G. Rohde, 44
  E. Saarinen, 87

Design philosophy *(continued)*
De Stijl's, 6
H. Wegner, 62
R. Wright, 67–68
Desks, *140*
De Stijl design, 6
Diamond chair (Bertoia), 35, 40, 104, *147*
Diamond, Freda, 43, 78–79
Dinnerware, 65–66, 67–68, *170*
Dominioni, Luigi Caccia, 78
Dragon Rock, New York, 110–11
Drexler, Arthur, 28, 32
Dutch design. *See* De Stijl design

Eames chair, 17–18, 34–35, 93–100, *130, 132*
Eames, Charles, 8, 17–22, 30, 34, *130, 131, 132, 133, 134, 135, 141, 165,* 180
construction methods/materials of, 93–100
Eames Contract storage system, 21
Eames, Ray, 17, 18, 20
Easier Living furniture (R. Wright), 68, 110
Eger, Jeffrey, 36
Egg chair (Jacobsen), 54, 107, *169*
Ehrman, Marli, 94
Eichler, Fritz, 77
Electric House, 71
Entenze, John, 18
Eppinger, Jimmy, 42
Executive Office group (Nelson), *140*
Executive Office group (Rohde), 43, 44, 105, *162*
Extended Lounge chair (Le Corbusier), *123*

Fenby, Joseph, 37, 148
Figini, Luigi, 71
Fiskars scissors, 76
Fisker, Kay, 52
Folding cnair (Wegner), 63, 109, *174*
Form, and function, 5, 9, 32, 57, 62
Fornaroli, Antonio, 73
Frank, Jean Michel, 49
Frank, Josef, 5
Frankl, Paul, 79, *186*
Frette, Guido, 71
Fritz, Hansen manufacturer, 9, 54
Fuller, Buckminster, 28, 47
Function, and form, 5, 9, 32, 57, 62
Furniture
and architecture, 24, 38–39, 52, 58
art deco, 7
construction. *See* Construction methods and materials
effect of war on, 3, 8, 44
engineering of, 91–92
hardware in, 18, 19
knockdown, 82, 102
modular, interchangeable, 43–44
outdoor, 44
and technology, 8
X-shaped, 63

General Motors Technical Center, 35
Gibblings, Robsjohn, 49
Gil, Gio Accolti, 111
Girard, Alexander, 79, *178, 179*
Glassware, 78, 82
Goodyear table (Noguchi), 49
Gorky, Arshile, 49
Gottlob, Kay, 52
Graham, Martha, 47, 48
Grand Confort chair (Le Corbusier/Perriand), *122*
Grasshopper chair (Eero Saarinen), *136*
Grass-on-Main-Street concept, 31, 102
Gray, Eileen, 7, 11–12, 117, *126, 127*
Groff, June, *184*
Gropius, Walter, 3–4, 6, 12, 38, *115*
Group 7, 71
Gugelot, Hans, 77, 79

Hamby, William, 28
Hansen, Johannes, 61
Haraszty, Eszter, 40, 79–80
Hardoy chair, 37, *148, 149*
Hardoy, Jorge Ferrari, 148
Harrison, Wallace, 38
Heart chair (Panton), *185*
Herman Miller Company
C. Eames for, 18, 20
G. Nelson for, 28–30
I. Noguchi for, 47, 50
G. Rohde for, 42
textiles at, 79
Heywood-Wakefield Company, 44, 66, 94
Hill, Evelyn, 40, 79
Hirokawa, Masami, 47
Hitchcock, Henry-Russell, 6
Hjejle, Thorkel, 52
Hoffman, Hans, 17
Hoffman, Joseph, 9
Holistic design, 17. *See also* Organic design
Huguenin, Suzanne, 40
Human anatomy and design, 24, 57, 59–60, 62
Humanistic design, 4
Hvidt, Peter, 82

Ideal Toy Company, 68
Interior design. *See also* Design philosophy
and architecture, 24, 38–39, 52, 58, 71
International Competition for Low-cost Furniture Design, 19–20, 62, 78, 90
International style, 6–10
Italian design, 8, 71–75, 111

Jacobsen, Arne, 8, 9, 52–56, 61, 82, *166, 167, 168, 169, 170*
construction methods/materials of, 106–8
Jacobsen, Jonna, 53
Jakobsen, Robert, 20
Japanese design, 6, 7, 8, 9, 110
Jeanneret, Charles Edouard. *See* Le Corbusier
Jean T table (Gray), *127*
Jenneret, Pierre, 37, *120, 122, 123*
Jewelry, 34
Johnson, Philip, 6, 116
Juhl, Finn, 9, 80

Kaiser, Ray. *See* Eames, Ray
Kandinsky, Wassily, 117
Kangaroo chair (Nelson), 29, 103, *142,* 143
Karl Andersson & Soner, 57
Kartell, 73, 78
Katavolos, William, 80
Kaufmann, Edgar, Jr., 67, 88, 90
Kelley, Douglas, 80
Kjaerholm, Poul, 80, *180, 181,* 182
Klint, Ebsen, 59, 80, *183*
Klint, Kaare, 8, 9, 12, 57, 183
Klint, Tage, 183
Knoll Associates, 20, 24, 37–41, 49
Knoll, Florence, 17, 34, 35, 37–41, 100, *149–50, 151–53, 154, 155,* 156, *157*
construction materials/methods of, 104–5
Knoll, Hans, 25, 34, 35, 37–41, 148, 149, 156
Knoll Nylon Homespun, 40
Knoll Planning Unit, 38–39, *156*
Knoll, Walter C., 37
Knorr, Don R., 20, 111
Komai, Ray, 80
Kratka, Charles, 20
Kurchar, Juan, 37, 148

Lacquering, 7
Lady armchair (Zanuso), *178*
Laminated wood furniture, 9, 10, 18, 19, 62, 87–88
Larco, Sebastiano, 71
Larsen, Jack Lenor, 81, *184*
Lassen, Flemming, 52
Laszlo, Paul, 30
Latham, Richard, 185
Latimer, Clive, 78

Le Corbusier, 6–7, 12–13, 117, *119, 120, 121, 122, 123,* 134
Le Klint, 183, *183*
Leowald, George, 20
Libera, Adalberto, 71
Lighting designs, 77
A. Aalto's, *129*
E. Gray's, *127*
E. Klint's, *183*
I. Noguchi's, 47, 49, 50, 106
Limelight textile design (Larsen), *184*
Lindberg, Stig, 79
Littell, Ross, 80
Loewy, Raymond, 42, 67, 81, 185
Longwell, Bob, 39, 105
Loos, Adolf, 5–6, 7, 13

McCobb, Paul, 81–82, *185*
McMillen, Louis A., *115*
Malmsten, Carl, 8, 9
Mango, Robert, 111, *178*
Markelius, Sven, 79
Marks, Edwin, 67
Marshmallow sofa (Nelson), 29, 103, *141*
Marx, Enid, 81
Mathsson, Bruno, 9
Meladur dinnerware (R. Wright), 67
Memphis Group, 74, 75
Mendelssohn, Eric, 28
Metal furniture, 3, 4, 5, 29, 89–90
Metal working, 34
Metropolitan Museum of Art, 42, 44, 67
Meyer, Grethe, 82, 108, *171*
Meyers, Howard, 38
Mies van der Rohe, Ludwig, 4, 6, 13, 38, 39, 53, *116, 117,* 118, 139, *154, 155*
Millcheck textile pattern (Girard), *179*
Millcheklet textile pattern (Girard), *179*
Millmosaic textile pattern (Girard), *179*
Millozenge textile pattern (Girard), *179*
Minoletti, Giulio, 72
Modernism, 7
in Italian design, 72
Modern Living furniture (R. Wright), *175*
Mogensen, Børge, 57–60, 80, *171*
construction methods/materials of, 108–9
Molded Fiberglass group (Eames), 133
Molded Plywood group (Eames), *130, 132*
Molgaard-Nielsen, O., 61, 82
Møller, Erik, 61
Mollino, Carlo, 72, 111, *175, 176, 177*
Mondrian, Piet, 6
Monotti, Francesco, 71
Monza Biennale/Triennale, 71, 72
Mormile, Alfonso, 111
Morris, William, 9, 87, 112
Munkegards school, 53
Museum of Modern Art, 28
acquisitions criteria, 17
awards, 40, 68, 79, 81, 83
exhibits, 17, 19, 24, 62, 83, 88, 111

Nakashima, George, 38
Nelson, George, 28–33, 74, *138, 139, 140, 141, 142, 143, 144, 145, 146, 165, 179*
construction methods/materials of, 102–4
New Designs for Italian Furniture (Milan, 1960), 74
Noguchi, Isamu, 30, 46–51, *147, 163, 164, 165*
construction methods/materials of, 105–6
Noguchi table, 46, 47, 106
Noyes, Eliot, 17
No. 71/72 chairs (Saarinen), 101, *136, 137*

Office design, 29, 39, 57, *154, 155, 156, 157*
Oresund storage units, 59, 108
Organic design, 17, 24, 26, 30
Organic Design in Home Furnishings Exhibit (New York, 1940), 17, 24, 94, 111
Orr, Wesley L., 20
Oxford chair (Jacobsen), 107–8, *170*

Paldao group (Rohde), *161*
Pannaggi, Ivo, 72
Panton, Verner, 82, *185*
Paris World Exhibition, 52
Peacock chair (Wegner), 61–62, 109
Pedestal group (Saarinen), 24, 25, 101–2
PEL (Practical Equipment Limited), 3
Perriand, Charlotte, *122, 123*
Pettit, Don, 25
Planner Group designs, 82
Plastic, 90–91
dinnerware, 67, 68
furniture, 20, 80, 93, 95, 98
Pluses textile pattern (Girard), *179*
Plywood group (Eames), *131*
Pollini, Gino, 71
Ponti, Gio, 71, 72–73, 177, *177*
Pratt, Davis J., 20, 111
Primavera textile design (Wight), *184*

Quatrefoil textile pattern (Girard), *178*

Race, Ernest, 83
Radio Nurse (Noguchi), 49
Rams, Dieter, 77, 79
Rapson, Ralph, 17, 24, 37, 38
Rasmussen, Steen Eiler, 57, 108
Rationalist design, 72
Rava, Carlo Enrico, 71
Ravegnati, Mario, 111
Red and Blue chair (Rietveld), 6
Reichardt, Grete, 4
Resnikoff, Misha, 49
Richards, Irving, 66
Rietveld, Gerrit Thomas, 6, 13–14
Risom, Jens, 37, 38
Rocking stool (Noguchi), 106, *163*
Rogers, Ernesto N., 111
Rohde, Gilbert, 28, 42–45, 67, *158, 159, 160, 161, 162*
construction methods/materials of, 105
Room dividers, 28
Root, John, 67
Rosenkjaer, Niels, 52
Rosenthal Shape 2000 china, *185*
Rosselli, Alberto, 73
Rothenberg, Murray, 38, 39
Rothenborg, Max, 52
Rudolf Rasmussen, Cabinetmaker, 55
Ruhlmann, Emile-Jacques, 7
Rumley, Edward A., 46
Russell, Gordon, 8

Saarinen, Eero, 8, 17, 23–27, 35, 38, 87, 93, *136, 137, 154, 155*
construction methods/materials of, 100–102
Saarinen, Eliel, 23
Sampe, Astrid, 79
Sapsa, Pirelli, 111
Sardella, Bruno, 111
Savoy vase (Aalto), *128*
Scandinavian design, 5, 8–10, *168*
Schools
A. Jacobsen's designs for, 53
B. Mogensen's designs for, 59
R. Wright's designs for, 68
Schultz, Richard (Dick), 38, 105
Schust, Florence. *See* Knoll, Florence
Schwadron, Ernest, 37
Screens, 19, 35, *131, 132, 141, 165*
Sculpture
H. Bertoia, 35–36
I. Noguchi, 46–50
Sequoia table (Mogensen), 58
Series 7 chairs (Jacobsen), 107
Shopping malls, 31, 102
Sling sofa (Nelson), *143*
Snorrason, Eigil, 59, 80
Sofas, 20, 29, 43, 66, 103, *123, 141, 143, 158, 159, 164*
Sorenson, Abel, 38
Sottsass, Ettore, Jr., 74, 111
Sound sculptures, 35–36

Space, 6, 7
  and colors, 36
  G. Nelson on interior, 31–32
  planning, 6, 39
Spice Garden textile design (Groff), *184*
Stam, Mart, 5, 14, *118*
Statton Furniture Co., 68
Steubenville Pottery Company, 65
Stone, Edward, 67
Storage systems, 111
  Eames/Saarinen, 18, 21, *134*
  Le Corbusier, *120, 121,* 134
  B. Mogensen, 57, 59, 108, *171*
  G. Nelson, 28, 102, *138,* 139, *144, 145*
  G. Rohde, 43
Strengell, Marianne, 40, 79
Sullivan, Louis, 5, 7
Svenska Tenn Company, 5
Swagged-leg chair (Nelson), 103, *143, 145*
Swan chair (Jacobsen), 8, 54, *169*
Swid, Stephen, C., 40–41

Tables, 7
  Breuer, *117, 118*
  Cenedese, *186*
  Eames, *132*
  Frankl, *186*
  Goodyear, 49–50
  Gray, *126, 127*
  Kjaerholm, *182, 183*
  Le Corbusier, *119*
  Mies van der Rohe, *117*
  Mollino, *177*
  Noguchi, 46, 47, 106, *147, 163, 165*
  Ponti, *177*
  Sequoia, 58
Teague, Walter, 42, 67
Terragini, Giuseppe, 71
Testa, Angelo, 79
Textiles, 76, 78, 79, 81, *178, 179*
  A. Jacobsen's, 53
  A. Girard's, *178, 179*
  at Knoll Associates, 40
  J. Larsen's, *184*
  B. Mogensen's, 58–59
Theater set designs, 48
Thin Edge Case group (Nelson), 146
3100 chair (Jacobsen), 54, *166*
3107 chair (Jacobsen), *166*
3137 chair (Jacobsen), *166*
3207 chair (Jacobsen), 167
3323 bedroom suite (Rohde), *158*
3900 series (Rohde), *159*
Thonet, Michael, 87
Three-legged chair (Wegner), *174*
Transportation Cloth, 40
Troy Sunshade Company, 44
Tugendhat chair (Mies van der Rohe), *117*

Urban planning, 31
Usher, Frederick, Jr., 20
Utilitarianism, 67, 68
Utility furniture, 8, 81

Valet chair (Wegner), 63, 109, *175*
Vallone, Bruno, 111
Van Doesburg, Théo, 6, 11
Varesio, L., 177
Vienna School of design, 5–6, 9
Vincenzi, Antonello, 111
Vodder, Niels, 80

Wagner, Otto, 5, 14
Wassily chair (Breuer), 4, 89–90, *117*
Weese, Harry, 17, 24
Wegner, Hans, 9, 58, 61–64, 108, *155, 174, 175*
  construction methods/materials of, 109
Werkbund Exhibition (Stuttgart, 1927), 5
Wiener Werkstätte, 5, 9
Wight, Don, *184*
Windeleff, Aage, 57, 108
Winter, Carter, 80
Wire chairs, 4, 40, 98–100, *147*
Womb chair (Saarinen), 24–25, 100, *136*
Wood furniture, 87–89. *See also* Laminated wood furniture
Wood, Grant, 67
Wormley, Edward, 83
Wright, Frank Lloyd, 5, 7–8, 17, 26, 31–32, 49, 53, 89, 115
Wright, Henry, 28, 102
Wright, Russel, 28, 65–70, 89, 115, *175*
  construction methods/materials of, 109–11

X-shaped folding furniture, 63
X Triennale, 74

Zanuso, Marco, 73, 74, 111, *178*
Zenith Plastics, 93
Zenith Radio Company, 49